A. R. RADCLIFFE-BROWN

Structure and Function in Primitive Society

Essays and Addresses

With a Foreword by
E. E. EVANS-PRITCHARD *and* **FRED EGGAN**

THE FREE PRESS
A Division of Macmillan Publishing Co., Inc.
NEW YORK

Collier Macmillan Publishers
LONDON

ACKNOWLEDGMENT for permission to print the essays and addresses in this volume is hereby made to the following: The South African Association for the Advancement of Science, the *Iowa Law Review*, the Royal Anthropological Institute, the International African Institute, the Fourth Pacific Science Congress, the Syndics of the Cambridge University Press, the American Anthropological Association and The Macmillan Company, New York.

The Free Press
A Division of Macmillan Publishing Co., Inc.
866 Third Avenue, New York, New York 10022

Collier Macmillan Canada,Ltd.

printing number
10

FIRST FREE PRESS PAPERBACK EDITION 1965

FOREWORD

PROFESSOR RADCLIFFE-BROWN has never had much regard for what
he calls ' the odd things that I have written from time to time ' ;
his major interest has been in conveying ideas directly to students
and colleagues by personal contacts. In this he has been emi-
nently successful. He has taught social anthropology at Cambridge, London, Birmingham, Pretoria, Johannesburg, Cape
Town, Sydney, Yenching, Chicago, Oxford, Sao Paulo, Alexandria,
Manchester and Grahamstown, and in each of these places he is
remembered with affection and respect. The indebtedness of his
students has been shown in two collections of essays—one American
and one English—written in his honour. And there has hardly
been a book or article on social anthropology published during
the last quarter of a century which does not illustrate, directly
or indirectly, his teaching.

An examination of the essays in this volume will suggest that
his writings have been just as influential as his personal contacts.
He has not, considering that he has been engaged in teaching
and research in social anthropology for almost fifty years, written
as much as most persons of his academic eminence. What he has
written, however, has been faultless. We do not mean by this that
we necessarily accept his methods or conclusions in detail, but
rather that the point of view he expresses could not have been
better expressed. Each of the essays is perfect in conception
and in expression, and they are tied together by a consistency
and direction which is rare in modern anthropology.

We believe that the publication of these essays will be of value
for several reasons. In the first place, they show the development
of the thought of a distinguished anthropologist for the last twenty-
five years, and at the same time illustrate some of the more important changes in the orientation of social anthropology, with which
Professor Radcliffe-Brown was so intimately associated during this
period. These essays have also demonstrated their value in the
training of graduate students in our major centres for social
anthropology. The individual papers are widely spread in time
and place, and frequently difficult to consult. We feel that in
presenting this collection of essays we are not only showing our
esteem for Professor Radcliffe-Brown, but are also providing a
book which will be valuable to students of social anthropology
for a long time to come.

E. E. EVANS-PRITCHARD
FRED EGGAN

CONTENTS

INTRODUCTION

THE papers reprinted here are occasional papers in the fullest sense of the term; each of them was written for a particular occasion. They do, however, have some measure of unity as being written from a particular theoretical point of view.

What is meant by a theory is a scheme of interpretation which is applied, or is thought to be applicable, to the understanding of phenomena of a certain class. A theory consists of a set of analytical concepts, which should be clearly defined in their reference to concrete reality, and which should be logically connected. I propose, therefore, by way of introduction to these miscellaneous papers, to give definitions of certain concepts of which I make use for purposes of analysis of social phenomena. It must be remembered that there is very little agreement amongst anthropologists in the concepts and terms they use, so that this Introduction and the papers that follow are to be taken as an exposition of one particular theory, not of a commonly accepted theory.

History and Theory

The difference between the historical study of social institutions and the theoretical study can be easily seen by comparing economic history and theoretical economics, or by comparing the history of law with theoretical jurisprudence. In anthropology, however, there has been and still is a great deal of confusion which is maintained by discussions in which terms such as history' and 'science' or 'theory' are used by disputants in very different meanings. These confusions could be to a considerable extent avoided by using the recognised terms of logic and methodology and distinguishing between *idiographic* and *nomothetic* enquiries.

In an idiographic enquiry the purpose is to establish as acceptable certain particular or factual propositions or statements. A nomothetic enquiry, on the contrary, has for its purpose to arrive at acceptable general propositions. We define the nature of an enquiry by the kind of conclusions that are aimed at.

History, as usually understood, is the study of records and monuments for the purpose of providing knowledge about conditions and events of the past, including those investigations that are concerned with the quite recent past. It is clear that history consists primarily of idiographic enquiries. In the last century there was a dispute, the famous *Methodenstreit*, as to whether historians should admit theoretical considerations in their work or deal in generalisations. A great many historians have taken the view that nomothetic enquiries should not be included in historical studies, which should be confined to telling us what happened and how it happened. Theoretical or nomothetic enquiries should be left to sociology. But there are some writers who think that a historian may, or even should, include theoretical interpretations in his account of the past. Controversy on this subject, and on the relation between history and sociology, still continues after sixty years. Certainly there are writings by historians which are to be valued not solely as idiographic accounts of the facts of the past but as containing theoretical (nomothetic) interpretations of those facts. The tradition in French historical studies of Fustel de Coulanges and his followers, such as Gustave Glotz, illustrates this kind of combination. Some modern writers refer to it as sociological history or historical sociology.

In anthropology, meaning by that the study of what are called the primitive or backward peoples, the term ethnography applies to what is specifically a mode of idiographic enquiry, the aim of which is to give acceptable accounts of such peoples and their social life. Ethnography differs from history in that the ethnographer derives his knowledge, or some major part of it, from direct observation of or contact with the people about whom he writes, and not, like the historian, from written records. Prehistoric archaeology, which is another branch of anthropology, is clearly an idiographic study, aimed at giving us factual knowledge about the prehistoric past.

The theoretical study of social institutions in general is usually referred to as sociology, but as this name can be loosely used for many different kinds of writings about society we can speak more specifically of theoretical or comparative sociology. When Frazer gave his Inaugural Lecture as the first Professor of Social Anthropology in 1908 he defined social anthropology as that branch of sociology that deals with primitive societies.

Certain confusions amongst anthropologists result from the failure to distinguish between *historical explanation* of institutions and *theoretical understanding*. If we ask why it is that a certain institution exists in a particular society the appropriate answer is a historical statement as to its origin. To explain why the United States has a political constitution with a President, two Houses of Congress, a Cabinet, a Supreme Court, we refer to the history of North America. This is historical explanation in the proper sense of the term. The existence of an institution is explained by reference to a complex sequence of events forming a causal chain of which it is a result.

The acceptability of a historical explanation depends on the fullness and reliability of the historical record. In the primitive societies that are studied by social anthropology there are no historical records. We have no knowledge of the development of social institutions among the Australian aborigines for example. Anthropologists, thinking of their study as a kind of historical study, fall back on conjecture and imagination, and invent 'pseudo-historical' or 'pseudo-causal' explanations. We have had, for example, innumerable and sometimes conflicting pseudo-historical accounts of the origin and development of the totemic institutions of the Australian aborigines. In the papers of this volume mention is made of certain pseudo-historical speculations. The view taken here is that such speculations are not merely useless but are worse than useless. This does not in any way imply the rejection of historical explanation but quite the contrary.

Comparative sociology, of which social anthropology is a branch, is here conceived as a theoretical or nomothetic study of which the aim is to provide acceptable generalisations. The theoretical understanding of a particular institution is its interpretation in the light of such generalisations.

Social Process

A first question that must be asked if we are to formulate a systematic theory of comparative sociology is: What is the concrete, observable, phenomenal reality with which the theory is to be concerned? Some anthropologists would say that the reality consists of 'societies' conceived as being in some sense or other discrete real entities. Others, however, describe the reality that has to be studied as consisting of 'cultures', each of which is again conceived as some kind of discrete entity. Still others seem to think of the subject as concerned with both kinds of entities, 'societies' and 'cultures', so that the relation of these then presents a problem.

My own view is that the concrete reality with which the social anthropologist is concerned in observation, description, comparison and classification, is not any sort of entity but a process, the process of social life. The unit of investigation is the social life of some particular region of the earth during a certain period of time. The process itself consists of an immense multitude of actions and interactions of human beings, acting as individuals or in combinations or groups. Amidst the diversity of the particular events there are discoverable regularities, so that it is possible to give statements or descriptions of certain *general features* of the social life of a selected region. A statement of such significant general features of the process of social life constitutes a description of what may be called a *form of social life*. My conception of social anthropology is as the comparative theoretical study of forms of social life amongst primitive peoples.

A form of social life amongst a certain collection of human beings may remain approximately the same over a certain period. But over a sufficient length of time the form of social life itself undergoes change or modification. Therefore, while we can regard the events of social life as constituting a process, there is over and above this the process of change in the form of social life. In a *synchronic* description we give an account of a form of social life as it exists at a certain time, abstracting as far as possible from changes that may be taking place in its features. A *diachronic* account, on the other hand, is an account of such changes over a period. In comparative sociology we have to deal theoretically with the continuity of, and with changes in, forms of social life.

Culture

Anthropologists use the word 'culture' in a number of different senses. It seems to me that some of them use it as equivalent to what I call a form of social life. In its ordinary use in English 'culture', which is much the same idea as cultivation, refers to a process, and we can define it as the process by which a person acquires, from contact with other persons or from such things as books or works of art, knowledge, skill, ideas, beliefs.

tastes, sentiments. In a particular society we can discover certain processes of *cultural tradition*, using the word tradition in its literal meaning of handing on or handing down. The understanding and use of a language is passed on by a process of cultural tradition in this sense. An Englishman learns by such a process to understand and use the English language, but in some sections of the society he may also learn Latin, or Greek, or French, or Welsh. In complex modern societies there are a great number of separate cultural traditions. By one a person may learn to be a doctor or surgeon, by another he may learn to be an engineer or an architect. In the simplest forms of social life the number of separate cultural traditions may be reduced to two, one for men and the other for women.

If we treat the social reality that we are investigating as being not an entity but a process, then culture and cultural tradition are names for certain recognisable aspects of that process, but not, of course, the whole process. The terms are convenient ways of referring to certain aspects of human social life. It is by reason of the existence of culture and cultural traditions that human social life differs very markedly from the social life of other animal species. The transmission of learnt ways of thinking, feeling and acting constitutes the cultural process, which is a specific feature of human social life. It is, of course, part of that process of interaction amongst persons which is here defined as the social process thought of as the social reality. Continuity and change in the forms of social life being the subjects of investigation of comparative sociology, the continuity of cultural traditions and changes in those traditions are amongst the things that have to be taken into account.

Social System

It was Montesquieu who, in the middle of the eighteenth century, laid the foundations of comparative sociology, and in doing so formulated and used a conception that has been and can be referred to by the use of the term *social system*. His theory, which constituted what Comte later called 'the first law of social statics', was that in a particular form of social life there are relations of interconnection and interdependence, or what Comte called relations of solidarity, amongst the various features. The idea of a natural or phenomenal system is that of a set of relations amongst events, just as a logical system, such as the geometry of Euclid, is a set of relations amongst propositions, or an ethical system a set of relations amongst ethical judgments. When one speaks of the 'banking system' of Great Britain this refers to the fact that there is a considerable number of actions, interactions and transactions, such for example as payments by means of a signed cheque drawn on a bank, which are so connected that they constitute in their totality a process of which we can make an analytical description which will show how they are interconnected and thus form a system. We are dealing, of course, with a process, a complex part of the total social process of social life in Great Britain.

In these essays I have referred to 'kinship systems'. The idea is that in a given society we can isolate conceptually, if not in reality, a certain set of actions and interactions amongst persons which are determined by the relationships by kinship or marriage, and that in a particular society these are interconnected in such a way that we can give a general analytical description of them as constituting a system. The theoretical significance of this idea of systems is that our first step in an attempt to understand a regular feature of a form of social life, such as the use of cheques, or the custom by which a man has to avoid social contact with his wife's mother, is to discover its place in the system of which it is part.

The theory of Montesquieu, however, is what we may call a theory of a total social system, according to which all the features of social life are united into a coherent whole. As a student of jurisprudence Montesquieu was primarily concerned with laws, and he sought to show that the laws of a society are connected with the political constitution, the economic life, the religion, the climate, the size of the population, the manners and customs, and what he called the general spirit (*esprit général*)—what later writers have called the 'ethos' of the society. A theoretical law, such as this 'fundamental law of social statics', is not the same thing as an empirical law, but is a guide to investigation. It gives us reason to think that we can advance our understanding of human societies if we investigate systematically the interconnections amongst features of social life.

Statics and Dynamics

Comte pointed out that in sociology, as in other kinds of science, there are two sets of problems, which he called problems of statics and problems of dynamics. In statics we attempt to discover and define conditions of existence or of co-existence; in dynamics we try to discover conditions of change. The conditions of existence of molecules or of organisms are matters of statics, and similarly the conditions of existence of societies, social systems, or forms of social life are matters for social statics. Whereas the problems of social dynamics deal with the conditions of change of forms of social life.

The basis of science is systematic classification. It is the first task of social statics to make some attempt to compare forms of social life in order to arrive at classifications. But forms of social life cannot be classified into species and genera in the way we classify forms of organic life; the classification has to be not specific but typological, and this is a more complicated kind of investigation. It can only be reached by means of the establishing of typologies for features of social life or the complexes of features that are given in partial social systems. Not only is the task complex but it has been neglected in view of the idea that the method of anthropology should be a historical method.

But though the typological studies are one important part of social statics, there is another task, that of formulating generalisations about the conditions of existence of social systems, or of forms of social life. The so-called first law of social statics is a generalisation affirming that for any form of social life to persist or continue the various features must exhibit some kind and measure of coherence or consistence, but this only defines the problem of social statics, which is to investigate the nature of this coherence.

The study of social dynamics is concerned with establishing generalisations about how social systems change. It is a corollary of the hypothesis of the systematic connection of features of social life that changes in some features are likely to produce changes in other features.

Social Evolution

The theory of social evolution was formulated by Herbert Spencer as part of his formulation of the general theory of evolution. According to that theory the development of life on the earth constitutes a single process to which Spencer applied the term 'evolution'. The theory of organic and super-organic (social) evolution can be reduced to two essential propositions: (1) That both in the development of forms of organic life and in the development of forms of human social life there has been a process of diversification by which many different forms of organic life or of social life have been developed out of a very much smaller number of original forms. (2) That there has been a general trend of development by which more complex forms of structure and organisation (organic or social) have arisen from simpler forms. The acceptance of the theory of evolution only requires the acceptance of these propositions as giving us a scheme of interpretation to apply to the study of organic and social life. But it must be remembered that some anthropologists reject the hypothesis of evolution. We can give provisional acceptance to Spencer's fundamental theory, while rejecting the various pseudo-historical speculations which he added to it, and that acceptance gives us certain concepts which may be useful as analytical tools.

Adaptation

This is a key concept of the theory of evolution. It is, or can be, applied both to the study of the forms of organic life and to the forms of social life amongst human beings. A living organism exists and continues in existence only if it is both internally and externally adapted. The internal adaptation depends on the adjustment of the various organs and their activities, so that the various physiological processes constitute a continuing functioning system by which the life of the organism is maintained. The external adaptation is that of the organism to the environment within which it lives. The distinction of external and internal adaptation is merely a way of distinguishing two aspects of the *adaptational system* which is the same for organisms of a single species.

When we come to the social life of animals another feature of adaptation makes its appearance. The existence of a colony of bees depends on a combination of the activities of the in-dividual worker bees in the collection of honey and pollen, the manufacture of wax, the building of the cells, the tending of eggs and larvae and the feeding of the latter, the protection of the store of honey from robbers, the ventilation of the hive by fanning with their wings, the maintenance of temperature in the winter by clustering together. Spencer uses the term 'co-operation' to refer to this feature of social life. Social life and social adaptation therefore involve the adjustment of the behaviour of individual organisms to the requirements of the process by which the social life continues.

When we examine a form of social life amongst human beings as an adaptational system it is useful to distinguish three aspects of the total system. There is the way in which the social life is adjusted to the physical environment, and we can, if we wish, speak of this as the œcological adaptation. Secondly, there are the institutional arrangements by which an orderly social life is maintained, so that what Spencer calls co-operation is provided for and conflict is restrained or regulated. This we might call, if we wished, the institutional aspect of social adaptation. Thirdly, there is the social process by which an individual acquires habits and mental characteristics that fit him for a place in the social life and enable him to participate in its activities. This, if we wish, could be called cultural adaptation, in accordance with the earlier definition of cultural tradition as process. What must be emphasised is that these modes of adaptation are only different aspects from which the total adaptational system can be looked at for convenience of analysis and comparison.

The theory of social evolution therefore makes it a part of our scheme of interpretation of social systems to examine any given system as an adaptational system. The stability of the system, and therefore its continuance over a certain period, depends on the effectiveness of the adaptation.

Social Structure

The theory of evolution is one of a trend of development by which more complex types of structure come into existence by derivation from less complex ones. An address on Social Structure is included in this volume, but it was delivered in war time and was printed in abbreviated form, so that it is not as clear as it might be. When we use the term structure we are referring to some sort of ordered arrangement of parts or components. A musical composition has a structure, and so does a sentence. A building has a structure, so does a molecule or an animal. The components or units of social structure are *persons*, and a person is a human being considered not as an organism but as occupying position in a social structure.

One of the fundamental theoretical problems of sociology is that of the nature of social continuity. Continuity in forms of social life depends on structural continuity, that is, some sort of continuity in the arrangements of persons in relation to one another. At the present day there is an arrangement of persons into nations, and the fact that for seventy years I have belonged to the English nation, although I have lived much of my life in other countries, is a fact of social structure. A nation, a tribe, a clan, a body such as the French Academy, or such as the Roman Church, can continue in existence as an arrangement of persons though the personnel, the units of which each is composed, changes from time to time. There is continuity of the structure, just as a human body, of which the components are molecules, preserves a continuity of structure though the actual molecules, of which the body consists, are continually changing. In the political structure of the United States there must always be a President; at one time it is Herbert Hoover, at another time Franklin Roosevelt, but the structure as an arrangement remains continuous.

The social relationships, of which the continuing network constitute social structure, are not haphazard conjunctions of individuals, but are determined by the social process, and any relationship is one in which the conduct of persons in their interactions with each other is controlled by norms, rules or patterns. So that in any relationship within a social structure a person knows that he is expected to behave according to these norms and is justified in expecting that other persons should do the same. The established norms of conduct of a particular form of social life it is usual to refer to as *institutions*. An institution is an established norm of conduct recognised as such by a distinguishable social group or class of which therefore it is an institution. The institutions refer to a distinguishable type or class of social relationships and interactions. Thus in a given locally defined society we find that there are accepted rules for the way a man is expected to behave towards his wife and children. The relation of institutions to social structure is therefore twofold. On the one side there is the social structure, such as the family in this instance, for the constituent relationships of which the institutions provide the norms; on the other there is the group, the local society in this instance, in which the norm is established by the general recognition of it as defining proper behaviour. Institutions, if that term is used to refer to the ordering by society of the interactions of persons in social relationships, have this double connection with structure, with a group or class of which it can be said to be an institution, and with those relationships within the structural system to which the norms apply. In a social system there may be institutions which set up norms of behaviour for a king, for judges in the fulfilment of the duties of their office, for policemen, for fathers of families, and so on, and also norms of behaviour relating to persons who come into casual contact within the social life.

A brief mention may be made of the term *organisation*. The concept is clearly closely related to the concept of social structure, but it is desirable not to treat the two terms as synonymous. A convenient use, which does not depart from common usage in English, is to define social structure as an arrangement of persons in institutionally controlled or defined relationships, such as the relationship of king and subject, or that of husband and wife, and to use organisation as referring to an arrangement of activities. The organisation of a factory is the arrangement of the various activities of manager, foremen, workmen within the total activity of the factory. The structure of a family household of parents, children and servants is institutionally controlled. The activities of the various members of the persons of the household will probably be subject to some regular arrangement, and the organisation of the life of the household in this sense may be different in different families in the same society. The structure of a modern army consists, in the first place, of an arrangement into groups—regiments, divisions, army corps, etc., and in the second place an arrangement into ranks—generals, colonels, majors, corporals, etc. The organisation of the army consists of the arrangement of the activities of its personnel whether in time of peace or in time of war. Within an organisation each person may be said to have a *role*. Thus we may say that when we are dealing with a structural system we are concerned with a system of social *positions*, while in an organisation we deal with a system of *roles*.

Social Function

The term function has a very great number of different meanings in different contexts. In mathematics the word, as introduced by Euler in the eighteenth century, refers to an expression or symbol which can be written on paper, such as 'log. x', and has no relation whatever to the same word as used in such a science as physiology. In physiology the concept of function is of fundamental importance as enabling us to deal with the continuing relation of structure and process in organic life. A complex organism, such as a human body, has a structure as an arrangement of organs and tissues and fluids. Even an organism that consists of a single cell has a structure as an arrangement of molecules. An organism also has a life, and by this we refer to a process. The concept of organic function is one that is used to refer to the connection between the structure of an organism and the life process of that organism. The processes that go on within a human body while it is living are dependent on the organic structure. It is the function of the heart to pump blood through the body. The organic structure, as a living structure, depends for its continued existence on the processes that make up the total life processes. If the heart ceases to perform its function the life process comes to an end and the structure as a living structure also comes to an end. Thus process is dependent on structure and continuity of structure is dependent on process.

In reference to social systems and their theoretical understanding one way of using the concept of function is the same as its scientific use in physiology. It can be used to refer to the interconnection between the social structure and the process of social life. It is this use of the word function that seems to me to make it a useful term in comparative sociology. The three concepts of process, structure and function are thus components of a single theory as a scheme of interpretation of human social systems. The three concepts are logically interconnected, since 'function' is used to refer to the relations of process and structure. The theory is one that we can apply to the study both of continuity in forms of social life and also to processes of change in those forms.

If we consider such a feature of social life as the punishment of crime, or in other words the application, by some organised procedure, of penal sanctions for certain kinds of behaviour, and ask what is its social function, we have a fundamental problem of comparative sociology towards which a first contribution was made by Durkheim in his *Division du Travail Social*. A very wide general problem is posed when we ask what is the social function of religion. As it has been pointed out in one of the papers in this volume, the study of this problem requires the consideration of a large number of more limited problems, such as that of the social function of ancestor worship in those societies in which it is found. But in these more limited investigations, if the theory here outlined is accepted, the procedure has to be the examination of the connection between the structural features of the social life and the corresponding social process as both involved in a continuing system.

The first paper in this collection may serve to illustrate these theoretical ideas. It deals with an institution by which a sister's son is allowed privileged familiarity in his conduct towards his mother's brother. The custom is known in tribes of North America such as the Winnebago and others, in peoples of Oceania, such as the inhabitants of Fiji and Tonga, and in some tribes of Africa. My own observations on this institution were made in Tonga and Fiji, but as the paper was addressed to a South African audience it seemed preferable to refer to a single South African example, since a wider comparative discussion would have called for a much longer essay. The usual way of dealing with this institution, both in Oceania and in Africa, was to offer a pseudo-historical explanation to the effect that it was a survival in a patrilineal society from a former condition of mother-right.

The alternative method of dealing with the institution is to look for a theoretical understanding of it as a part of a kinship system of a certain type, within which it has a discoverable function. We do not yet have a systematic general typology of kinship systems, for the construction of such is a laborious undertaking. I have indicated some partial and provisional results of such an attempt to determine types in a recent publication in the form of an Introduction to a book on African Systems of Kinship and Marriage. Amongst the great diversity of kinship systems we can, I think, recognise a type of what we may call father-right, and another of mother-right. In both these types the kinship structure is based on lineages with maximum emphasis on lineage relationships. In mother-right the lineage is matrilineal, a child belonging to the lineage of the mother. Practically all the jural relations of a man are those with his matrilineal lineage and its members, and therefore he is largely dependent on his mother's brothers, who exercise authority and control over him and to whom he looks for protection and for inheritance of property. In a system of father-right, on the other hand, a man is largely dependent on his patrilineal lineage and therefore on his father and father's brothers, who exercise authority and control over him, while it is to them that he has to look for protection and for inheritance. Father-right is represented by the sysyem of *patria potestas* of ancient Rome, and there are systems that approximate more or less closely to the type to. be found in Africa and elsewhere. We may regard the BaThonga as so approximating. Mother-right is represented by the systems of the Nayar of Malabar and the Menangkubau Malays, and again there are systems elsewhere that approximate to the type.

The point of the paper on the mother's brother may be said to be to contrast with the explanation by pseudo-history the interpretation of the institution to which it refers as having a function in a kinship system with a certain type of structure. If I were to rewrite the paper after thirty years I should certainly modify and expand it. But it has been suggested to me that the paper may have a certain minor historical interest in relation to the development of thought in anthropology and it is therefore reprinted almost as it was written with only minor alterations.

Any interest this volume may have will probably be as an exposition of a theory, in the sense in which the word theory is here used as a scheme of interpretation thought to be applicable to the understanding of a class of phenomena. The theory can be stated by means of the three fundamental and connected concepts of 'process', 'structure' and 'function'. It is derived from such earlier writers as Montesquieu, Comte, Spencer, Durkheim and thus belongs to a cultural tradition of two hundred years.   This introduction contains a reformulation in which certain terms are used differently from the way they were used in the early papers here reprinted.   For example, in the earliest papers written twenty or more years ago the word 'culture' is used in the accepted meaning of that time as a general term for the way of life, including the way of thought, of a particular locally defined social group.

CHAPTER I

THE MOTHER'S BROTHER IN SOUTH AFRICA [1]

AMONGST primitive peoples in many parts of the world a good deal of importance is attached to the relationship of mother's brother and sister's son. In some instances, the sister's son has certain special rights over the property of his mother's brother. At one time it was usual to regard these customs as being connected with matriarchal institutions, and it was held that their presence in a patrilineal people could be regarded as evidence that that people had at some time in the past been matri- lineal. This view is still held by a few anthropologists and has been adopted by Mr. Junod in his book on the BaThonga people of Portuguese East Africa. Referring to the customs relating to the behaviour of the mother's brother and the sister's son to one another, he says: 'Now, having enquired with special care into this most curious feature of the Thonga system, I come to the con- clusion that the only possible explanation is that, in former and very remote times, our tribe has passed through the matriarchal stage.' (Junod, *The Life of a South African Tribe*, 1913, Vol. I, p. 253.)

It is with this theory that I wish to deal in this paper; but I do not propose to repeat or add to the objections that have been raised against it by various critics in recent years. Purely negative criticism does not advance a science. The only satisfactory way of getting rid of an unsatisfactory hypothesis is to find a better one. I propose, therefore, to put before you an alternative hypo- thesis, and if I am successful, not in proving my hypo- thesis, but in showing that it does give a possible explanation of the facts, I shall at least have refuted the view of Mr. Junod that the explanation he accepts is the 'only possible' one.

For many African tribes we have almost no information about customs of this kind. Not that the customs do not exist, or are not important to the natives themselves, but because the

[1] A paper read before the South African Association for the Advancement of Science, 9 July 1924, and printed in *South African Journal of Science*, Vol. XXI, pp. 542–55.

systematic and scientific study of the natives of this country has as yet hardly begun. I shall, therefore, have to refer chiefly to the customs of the BaThonga as recorded by Mr. Junod. These are to be found in the first volume of the work quoted above (pp. 225 *et seq.*, and pp. 253 *et seq.*). Some of the more important of them may be summarised as follows:

1. The uterine nephew all through his career is the object of special care on the part of his uncle.
2. When the nephew is sick the mother's brother sacrifices on his behalf.
3. The nephew is permitted to take many liberties with his mother's brother; for example, he may go to his uncle's home and eat up the food that has been prepared for the latter's meal.
4. The nephew claims some of the property of his mother's brother when the latter dies, and may sometimes claim one of the widows.
5. When the mother's brother offers a sacrifice to his ancestors the sister's son steals and consumes the portion of meat or beer offered to the gods.

It must not be supposed that these customs are peculiar to the BaThonga. There is evidence that similar customs may be found amongst other African tribes, and we know of the existence of similar customs amongst other peoples in various parts of the world. In South Africa itself customs of this kind have been found by Mrs. Hoernle amongst the Nama Hottentots. The sister's son may behave with great freedom towards his mother's brother, and may take any particularly fine beast from his herd of cattle, or any particularly fine object that he may possess. On the contrary, the mother's brother may take from his nephew's herd any beast that is deformed or decrepit, and may take any old and worn-out object he may possess.

What is particularly interesting to me is that in the part of Polynesia that I know best, that is, in the Friendly Islands (Tonga) and in Fiji, we find customs that show a very close resemblance to those of the BaThonga. There, also, the sister's son is permitted to take many liberties with his mother's brother, and to take any of his uncle's possessions that he may desire. And there also we find the custom that, when the uncle makes a sacrifice, the sister's son takes away the portion offered to the gods, and may eat it. I shall, therefore, make occasional references to the Tongan customs in the course of this paper.

These three peoples, the BaThonga, the Nama, and the Tongans, have patrilineal or patriarchal institutions; that is, the children belong to the social group of the father, not to that of the mother; and property is inherited in the male line, passing normally from a father to his son. The view that I am opposing is that the customs relating to the mother's brother can only be explained by supposing that, at some past time, these peoples had matrilineal institutions, such as are found today amongst other primitive peoples, with whom the children belong to the social group of the mother, and property is inherited in the female line, passing from a man to his brother and to his sister's sons.

It is a mistake to suppose that we can understand the institutions of society by studying them in isolation without regard to other institutions with which they coexist and with which they may be correlated, and I wish to call attention to a correlation that seems to exist between customs relating to the mother's brother and customs relating to the father's sister. So far as present information goes, where we find the mother's brother important we also find that the father's sister is equally important, though in a different way. The custom of allowing the sister's son to take liberties with his mother's brother seems to be generally accompanied with an obligation of particular respect and obedience to the father's sister. Mr. Junod says little about the father's sister amongst the BaThonga. Speaking of a man's behaviour to this relative (his *rarana*) he says simply: 'He shows her great respect. However, she is not in any way a mother (*mamana*)' (op. cit., p. 223). About the Nama Hottentots we have better information, and there the father's sister is the object of the very greatest respect on the part of her brother's child. In Tonga this custom is very clearly defined. A man's father's sister is the one relative above all others whom he must respect and obey. If she selects a wife for him he must marry her without even venturing to demur or to voice any objection; and so throughout his life. His father's sister is sacred to him; her word is his law; and one of the greatest offences of which he could be guilty would be to show himself lacking in respect to her.

Now this correlation (which is not confined, of course, to the three instances I have mentioned, but seems, as I have said, to be general) must be taken into account in any explanation of the customs relating to the mother's brother, for the correlated customs are, if I am right, not independent institutions, but part of one system; and no explanation of one part of the system is satisfactory unless it fits in with an analysis of the system as a whole.

In most primitive societies the social relations of individuals are very largely regulated on the basis of kinship. This is brought about by the formation of fixed and more or less definite patterns of behaviour for each of the recognised kinds of relationship. There is a special pattern of behaviour, for example, for a son towards his father, and another for a younger brother towards his elder brother. The particular patterns vary from one society to another; but there are certain fundamental principles or tendencies which appear in all societies, or in all those of a certain type. It is these general tendencies that it is the special task of social anthropology to discover and explain.

Once we start tracing out relationship to any considerable distance the number of different kinds of relatives that it is logically possible to distinguish is very large. This difficulty is avoided in primitive society by a system of classification, by which relatives of what might logically be held to be of different kinds are classified into a limited number of kinds. The principle of classification that is most commonly adopted in primitive society may be stated as that of the equivalence of brothers. In other words if I stand in a particular relation to one man I regard myself as standing in the same general kind of relation to his brother; and similarly with a woman and her sister. In this way the father's brother comes to be regarded as a sort of father, and his sons are, therefore, relatives of the same kind as brothers. Similarly, the mother's sister is regarded as another mother, and her children are therefore brothers and sisters. The system is the one to be found amongst the Bantu tribes of South Africa, and amongst the Nama Hottentots, and also in the Friendly Islands. By means of this principle primitive societies are able to arrive at definite patterns of behaviour towards uncles and aunts and cousins of certain kinds. A man's behaviour towards his father's brother must be of the same general kind as his behaviour towards his own father and he must behave to his mother's sister according to the same pattern as towards his mother. The children of his father's brother or of the mother's sister must be treated in very much the same way as brothers and sisters.

This principle, however, does not give us immediately any pattern for either the mother's brother or the father's sister. It would be possible, of course, to treat the former as being like a father and the latter as similar to a mother, and this course does seem to have been adopted in a few societies. A tendency in this direction is found in some parts of Africa and in some parts of Polynesia. But it is characteristic of societies in which the classificatory system of kinship is either not fully developed or has been partly effaced.

Where the classificatory system of kinship reaches a high degree of development or elaboration another tendency makes its appearance: the tendency to develop patterns for the mother's brother and the father's sister by regarding the former as a sort of male mother and the latter as a sort of female father. This tendency sometimes makes its appearance in language. Thus, in South Africa the common term for the mother's brother is *malume* or *umalume*, which is a compound formed from the stem for 'mother'—*ma*—and a suffix meaning 'male'. Amongst the BaThonga the father's sister is called *rarana*, a term which Mr. Junod explains as meaning 'female father'. In some South African languages there is no special term for the father's sister; thus in Xosa, she is denoted by a descriptive term *udade bo bawo*, literally 'father's sister'. In Zulu she may be referred to by a similar descriptive term or she may be spoken of simply as *ubaba*, 'father', just like the father's brothers. In the Friendly Islands the mother's brother may be denoted by a special term *tuasina*, or he may be called *fa'e tangata*, literally 'male mother'. This similarity between South Africa and Polynesia cannot, I think, be regarded as accidental; yet there is no possible connection between the Polynesian languages and the Bantu languages, and I find it very difficult to conceive that the two regions have adopted the custom of calling the mother's brother by a term meaning 'male mother' either from one another or from one common source.

Now let us see if we can deduce what ought to be the patterns of behaviour towards the mother's brother and the father's sister in a patrilineal society on the basis of the principle or tendency which I have suggested is present. To do this we must first know the patterns for the father and the mother respectively, and I think that it will, perhaps, be more reassuring if I go for the definition of these to Mr. Junod's work, as his observations will certainly not have been influenced by the hypothesis that I am trying to prove.

The relationship of father, he says, 'implies respect and even fear. The father, though he does not take much trouble with his children, is, however, their instructor, the one who scolds and punishes. So do also the father's brothers' (op. cit., p. 222). Of a man's own mother he says: 'She is his true *mamana*, and this relation is very deep and tender, combining respect with love. Love, however, generally exceeds respect' (op. cit., p. 224). Of the mother's relation to her children we read that 'She is generally weak with them and is often accused by the father of spoiling them.'

There is some danger in condensed formulæ, but I think we shall not be far wrong in saying that in a strongly patriarchal society, such as we find in South Africa, the father is the one who must be respected and obeyed, and the mother is the one from whom may be expected tenderness and indulgence. I could show you, if it were necessary, that the same thing is true of the family life of the Friendly Islanders.

If, now, we apply the principle that I have suggested is at work in these peoples it will follow that the father's sister is one who must be obeyed and treated with respect, while from the mother's brother indulgence and care may be looked for. But the matter is complicated by another factor. If we consider the relation of a nephew to his uncle and aunt, the question of sex comes in. In primitive societies there is a marked difference in the behaviour of a man towards other men and that towards women. Risking once more a formula, we may say that any considerable degree of familiarity is generally only permitted· in such a society as the BaThonga between persons of the same sex. A man must treat his female relatives with greater respect than his male relatives. Consequently the nephew must treat his father's sister with even greater respect than he does his own father. (In just the same way, owing to the principle of respect for age or seniority, a man must treat his father's elder brother with more respect than his own father.) Inversely, a man may treat his mother's brother, who is of his own sex, with a degree of familiarity that would not be possible with any woman, even his own mother. The influence of sex on the behaviour of kindred is best seen in the relations of brother and sister. In the Friendly Islands and amongst the Nama a man must pay great respect to his sister, particularly his eldest sister, and may never indulge in any familiarities with her. The same thing is true, I believe, of the South African Bantu. In many primitive societies the father's sister and the elder sisters are the objects of the same general kind of behaviour, and in some of these the two kinds of relatives are classified together and denoted by the same name.

We have deduced from our assumed principle a certain pattern of behaviour for the father's sister and for the mother's brother. Now these patterns are exactly what we find amongst the BaThonga, amongst the Hottentots, and in the Friendly Islands. The father's sister is above all relatives the one to be respected and obeyed. The mother's brother is the one relative above all from whom we may expect indulgence, with whom we may be familiar and take liberties. Here, then, is an alternative 'possible explanation' of the customs relating to the mother's brother, and it has this advantage over Mr. Junod's theory that it also explains the correlated customs relating to the father's sister. This brings us, however, not to the end but to the beginning of our enquiry. It is easy enough to invent hypotheses. The important and difficult work begins when we set out to verify them. It will be impossible for me, in the short time available, to make any attempt to verify the hypothesis I have put before you. All I can do is to point out certain lines of study which will, I believe, provide that verification.

The first and most obvious thing to do is to study in detail the behaviour of the sister's son and the mother's brother to one another in matriarchal societies. Unfortunately, there is practically no information on this subject relating to Africa, and very little for any other part of the world. Moreover, there are certain false ideas connected with this distinction of societies into matriarchal and patriarchal that it is necessary to remove before we attempt to go further.

In all societies, primitive or advanced, kinship is necessarily bilateral. The individual is related to certain persons through his father and to others through his mother, and the kinship system of the society lays down what shall be the character of his dealings with his paternal relatives and his maternal relatives respectively. But society tends to divide into segments (local groups, lineages, clans, etc.), and when the hereditary principle is accepted, as it most frequently is, as the means of determining the membership of a segment, then it is necessary to choose between maternal or paternal descent. When a society is divided into groups with a rule that the children belong to the group of the father we have patrilineal descent, while if the children always belong to the group of the mother the descent is matrilineal.

There is, unfortunately, a great deal of looseness in the use of the terms matriarchal and patriarchal, and for that reason many anthropologists refuse to use them. If we are to use them at all, we must first give exact definitions. A society may be called patriarchal when descent is patrilineal (i.e. the children belong to the group of the father), marriage is patrilocal (i.e. the wife removes to the local group of the husband), inheritance (of property) and succession (to rank) are in the male line, and the family is patripotestal (i.e. the authority over the members of the family is in the hands of the father or his relatives). On the other hand, a society can be called matriarchal when descent, inheritance and succession are in the female line, marriage is matrilocal (the husband removing to the home of his wife), and when the authority over the children is wielded by the mother's relatives.

If this definition of these opposing terms is accepted, it is at once obvious that a great number of primitive societies are neither matriarchal nor patriarchal, though some may incline more to the one side, and others more to the other. Thus, if we examine the tribes of Eastern Australia, which are sometimes spoken of as matriarchal, we find that marriage is patrilocal, so that membership of the local group is inherited in the male line, the authority over the children is chiefly in the hands of the father and his brothers, property (what there is of it) is mostly inherited in the male line, while, as rank is not recognised, there is no question of succession. The only matrilineal institution is the descent of the totemic group, which is through the mother, so that these tribes, so far from being matriarchal, incline rather to the patriarchal side. Kinship amongst them is thoroughly bilateral, but for most purposes kinship through the father is of more importance than kinship through the mother. There is some evidence, for example, that the obligation to avenge a death falls upon the relatives in the male line rather than upon those in the female line.

We find an interesting instance of this bilateralism, if it may be so called, in South Africa, in the OvaHerero tribe. The facts are not quite certain, but it would seem that this tribe is sub-divided into two sets of segments crossing one another. For one set (the *omaanda*) descent is matrilineal, while for the other (*otuzo*) it is patrilineal. A child belongs to the *eanda* of its mother and inherits cattle from its mother's brothers, but belongs to the *oruzo* of its father and inherits his ancestral spirits. Authority over the children would seem to be in the hands of the father and his brothers and sisters.

It is now clear, I hope, that the distinction between matriarchal and patriarchal societies is not an absolute but a relative one. Even in the most strongly patriarchal society some social importance is attached to kinship through the mother; and similarly in the most strongly matriarchal society the father and his kindred are always of some importance in the life of the individual.

In Africa we have in the south-east a group of tribes that incline strongly to patriarchy, so much so, in fact, that we may perhaps justifiably speak of them as patriarchal. Descent of the social group, inheritance of property, succession to chieftain-ship, are all in the male line; marriage is patrilocal, and authority in the family is strongly patripotestal. In the north of Africa, in Kenya and the surrounding countries, there is another group of strongly patriarchal peoples, some of them Bantu-speaking, while others are Nilotic or Hamitic. Between these two patriarchal regions there is a band of peoples stretching apparently right across Africa from east to west, on the level of Nyasaland and Northern Rhodesia, in which the tendency is towards matriarchal institutions. Descent of the social group, inheritance of property, and succession to the kingship or chieftainship are in the female line. In some of the tribes marriage seems to be matrilocal, at any rate temporarily if not permanently, i.e. a man on marriage has to go and live with his wife's people.

It is about these people and their customs that we urgently need information if we are to understand such matters as the subject of this paper. Of one tribe of this region we have a fairly full description in the work of Smith and Dale (*The Ila-speaking People of Northern Rhodesia*, 1920). Unfortunately, on the very points with which I am now dealing the information is scanty and certainly very incomplete. There are, however, two points I wish to bring out. The first concerns the behaviour of the mother's brother to his sister's son. We are told that 'the mother's brother is a personage of vast importance; having the power even of life and death over his nephews and nieces, which no other relations, not even the parents, have; he is to be held in honour even above the father. This is *avunculi potestas*, which among the BaIla is greater than *patria potestas*. In speaking of the mother's brother, it is customary to use an honorific title given to people who are respected very highly' (op. cit., Vol. I, p. 230). This kind of relation between the mother's brother and the sister's son is obviously what we might expect in a strongly matriarchal society. But how then, on Mr. Junod's theory, can we explain the change which must have taken place from this sort of relation to that which now exists among the BaThonga?

This brings me to another point which it will not be possible to discuss in detail but which has an important bearing on the argument. We have been considering the relation of the sister's son to his mother's brother; but if we are to reach a really final explanation, we must study also the behaviour of a man to his other relatives on the mother's side, and to his mother's group as a whole. Now in the Friendly Islands the peculiar relation between a sister's son and a mother's brother exists also between a daughter's son and his mother's father. The daughter's son must be honoured by his grandfather. He is 'a chief' to him. He may take his grandfather's property, and he may take away the offering that his grandfather makes to the gods at a kava ceremony. The mother's father and the mother's brother are the objects of very similar behaviour patterns, of which the outstanding feature is the indulgence on the one side and the liberty permitted on the other. Now there is evidence of the same thing amongst the BaThonga, but again we lack the full information that we need. Mr. Junod writes that a grandfather 'is more lenient to his grandson by his daughter than his grandson by his son' (op cit. p. 227). In this connection the custom of calling the mother's brother *kokwana* (grandfather) is significant.

Now here is something that it seems impossible to explain on Mr. Junod's theory. In a strongly matriarchal society the mother's father does not belong to the same group as his grandchild and is not a person from whom property can be inherited or who can exercise authority. Any explanation of the liberties permitted towards the mother's brother cannot be satisfactory unless it also explains the similar liberties towards the mother's father which are found in Polynesia, and apparently to some extent in South Africa. This Mr. Junod's theory clearly does not do, and cannot do.

But on the hypothesis that I have put forward the matter is fairly simple. In primitive society there is a strongly marked tendency to merge the individual in the group to which he or she belongs. The result of this in relation to kinship is a tendency to extend to all the members of a group a certain type of behaviour which has its origin in a relationship to one particular member of the group. Thus the tendency in the BaThonga tribe would seem to be to extend to all the members of the mother's group (family or lineage) a certain pattern of behaviour which is derived from the special pattern that appears in the behaviour of a son towards his mother. Since it is from his mother that he expects care and indulgence he looks for the same sort of treatment from the people of his mother's group, i.e. from all his maternal kin. On the other hand it is to his paternal kin that he owes obedience and respect. The patterns that thus arise in relation to the father and the mother are generalised and extended to the kindred on the one side and on the other. If I had time I think I could show you quite conclusively that this is really the principle that governs the relations between an individual and his mother's kindred in the patriarchal tribes of South Africa. I must leave the demonstration, however, to another occasion. I can do no more now than illustrate my statement.

The custom, often miscalled bride-purchase and generally known in South Africa as *lobola*, is, as Mr. Junod has well shown, a payment made in compensation to a girl's family for her loss when she is taken away in marriage. Now, since in the patriarchal tribes of South Africa a woman belongs to her father's people, the compensation has to be paid to them. But you will find that in many of the tribes a certain portion of the 'marriage payment' is handed over to the mother's brother of the girl for whom it is paid. Thus, amongst the BaPedi, out of the *lenyalo* cattle one head (called *hloho*) is handed to the mother's brother of the girl. Amongst the BaSotho a portion of the cattle received for a girl on her marriage may sometimes be taken by her mother's brother, this being known as *ditsoa*. Now the natives state that the *ditsoa* cattle received by the mother's brother are really held by him on behalf of his sister's children. If one of his sister's sons or daughters is ill he may be required to offer a sacrifice to his ancestral spirits, and he then takes a beast from the *ditsoa* herd. Also, when the sister's son wishes to obtain a wife, he may go to his mother's brother to help him to find the necessary cattle and his uncle may give him some of the *ditsoa* cattle received at the marriage of his sister, or may even give him cattle from his own herd, trusting to being repaid from the *ditsoa* cattle to be received in the future from the marriage of a niece. I believe that the Native Appeal Court has decided that the payment of *ditsoa* to the mother's brother is a voluntary matter and cannot be regarded as a legal obligation, and with that judgment I am in agreement. I quote this custom because it illustrates the sort of interest that the mother's brother is expected to take in his sister's son, in helping him and looking after his welfare. It brings us back to the question as to why the mother's brother may be asked to offer sacrifices when his nephew is sick.

In south-east Africa ancestor worship is patrilineal, i.e. a man worships and takes part in sacrifices to the spirits of his deceased relatives in the male line. Mr. Junod's statements about the BaThonga are not entirely clear. In one place he says that each family has two sets of gods, those on the father's side and those on the mother's; they are equal in dignity and both can be invoked (op. cit., II, p. 349, and I, p. 256, note). But in another place it is stated that if an offering has to be made to the gods of the mother's family this must be through the maternal relatives, the *malume* (op. cit., II, p. 367). Other passages confirm this and show us that ancestral spirits can only be directly approached in any ritual by their descendants in the male line.

The natives of the Transkei are very definite in their statements to me that a person's maternal gods, the patrilineal ancestors of his mother, will never inflict supernatural punishment upon him by making him sick. (I am not quite so sure about the Sotho tribes, but I think that they probably have similar views.) On the other hand a married woman can receive protection from the ancestral spirits of her patrilineal lineage, and so can her young children as long as they are attached to her. For children are only fully incorporated in their father's lineage when they reach adolescence. So in the Transkei a woman, when she marries, should be given a cow, the *ubulunga* cow, by her father, from the herd of her lineage, which she can take to her new home. Since she may not drink the milk from her husband's herd during the early period of her married life she can be provided with milk from this beast that comes from her lineage. This cow constitutes a link between herself and her lineage, its cattle, and its gods, for cattle are the material link between the living members of the lineage and the ancestral spirits. So if she is sick she can make for herself a necklace of hairs from the tail of this cow and so put herself under the protection of her lineage gods. Moreover, if one of her infant children is sick, she can make a similar necklace which is thought to give protection to the child. When her son is grown up he should receive an *ubulunga* bull from his father's herd, and thereafter it is from the tail of this beast that he will make a protective amulet; similarly the daughter, when she marries, is detached from her mother, and may receive an *ubulunga* cow from her father.

But though, according to the statements made to me, the maternal ancestors will not punish their descendant with sickness, they can be appealed to for help. When, therefore, a child is sick the parents may go to the mother's brother of the child, or to the mother's father if he is still living, and ask that a sacrifice shall be offered, and an appeal for help made to the child's maternal ancestors. This, at any rate, is stated as a practice in the Sotho tribes, and one of the purposes of the *ditsoa* cattle that go from the marriage payment to the mother's brother of the bride is said to be to make provision for such sacrifices if they should be needed.

This brings us to the final extension of the principle that I have suggested as the basis of the customs relating to the mother's brother. The pattern of behaviour towards the mother, which is developed in the family by reason of the nature of the family group and its social life, is extended with suitable modifications to the mother's sister and to the mother's brother, then to the group of maternal kindred as a whole, and finally to the maternal gods, the ancestors of the mother's group. In the same way the pattern of behaviour towards the father is extended to the father's brothers and sisters, and to the whole of the father's group (or rather to all the older members of it, the principle of age making important modifications necessary), and finally to the paternal gods.

The father and his relatives must be obeyed and respected (even worshipped, in the original sense of the word), and so therefore also must be the paternal ancestors. The father punishes his children, and so may the ancestors on the father's side. On the other hand, the mother is tender and indulgent to her child, and her relatives are expected to be the same, and so also the maternal spirits.

A very important principle, which I have tried to demonstrate elsewhere (*The Andaman Islanders*, Chapter V), is that the social values current in a primitive society are maintained by being expressed in ceremonial or ritual customs. The set of values that we here meet with in the relations of an individual to his kindred on the two sides must, therefore, also have their proper ritual expression. The subject is too vast to deal with at all adequately here, but I wish to discuss one point. Amongst the BaThonga, and also in Western Polynesia (Fiji and Tonga), the sister's son (or in Tonga also the daughter's son) intervenes in the sacrificial ritual. Mr. Junod describes a ceremony of crushing down the hut of a dead man in which the *batukulu* (sister's children) play an important part. They kill and distribute the sacrificial victims and when the officiating priest makes his prayer to the spirit of the dead man it is the sister's sons who, after a time, interrupt or 'cut' the prayer and bring it to an end. They then, among the BaThonga clans, seize the portions of the sacrifice that have been dedicated to the spirit of the dead man and run away with them, 'stealing' them (op. cit., I, p. 162).

I would suggest that the meaning of this is that it gives a ritual expression to the special relation that exists between the sister's son and the mother's brother. When the uncle is alive the nephews have the right to go to his village and take his food. Now that he is dead they come and do this again, as part of the funeral ritual, and as it were for the last time, i.e. they come and steal portions of meat and beer that are put aside as the portion of the deceased man.

The same sort of explanation will be found to hold, I think, of the part played in sacrificial and other ritual by the sister's son both amongst the Bantu of South Africa and also in Tonga and Fiji. As a man fears his father, so he fears and reverences his paternal ancestors, but he has no fear of his mother's brother, and so may act irreverently to his maternal ancestors; he is, indeed, required by custom so to act on certain occasions, thus giving ritual expression to the special social relations between a man and his maternal relatives in accordance with the general function of ritual, as I understand it.

It will, perhaps, be of help if I give you a final brief statement of the hypothesis I am advancing, with the assumptions involved in it and some of its important implications.

1. The characteristic of most of these societies that we call primitive is that the conduct of individuals to one another is very largely regulated on the basis of kinship, this being brought about by the formation of fixed patterns of behaviour for each recognised kind of kinship relation.

2. This is sometimes associated with a segmentary organisation of society, i.e. a condition in which the whole society is divided into a number of segments (lineages, clans).

3. While kinship is always and necessarily bilateral, or cognatic, the segmentary organisation requires the adoption of the unilineal principle, and a choice has to be made between patrilineal and matrilineal institutions.

4. In patrilineal societies of a certain type, the special pattern of behaviour between a sister's son and the mother's brother is derived from the pattern of behaviour between the child and the mother, which is itself the product of the social life within the family in the narrow sense.

5. This same kind of behaviour tends to be extended to all the maternal relatives, i.e. to the whole family or group to which the mother's brother belongs.[1]

---

[1] This extension from the mother's brother to the other maternal relatives is shown in the BaThonga tribe in the kinship terminology. The term *malume*, primarily applied to the mother's brother, is extended to the sons of those men, who are also *malume*. If my mother's brothers are dead it is their sons who will have to sacrifice on my behalf to my maternal ancestors. In the northern part of the tribe the term *malume* has gone out of use, and the mother's father, the mother's brother, and the sons of the mother's brother are all called *kokwana* (grandfather). However absurd it may seem to us to call a mother's brother's son, who may be actually younger than the speaker, by a word meaning 'grandfather', the argument of this paper will enable us to see some meaning in it. The person who must sacrifice on my behalf to my maternal

6. In societies with patrilineal ancestor worship (such as the BaThonga and the Friendly Islanders) the same type of behaviour may also be extended to the gods of the mother's family.

7. The special kind of behaviour to the maternal relatives (living and dead) or to the maternal group and its gods and sacra, is expressed in definite ritual customs, the function of ritual here, as elsewhere, being to fix and make permanent certain types of behaviour, with the obligations and sentiments involved therein.

In conclusion, may I point out that I have selected the subject of my contribution to this meeting because it is one not only of theoretical but also of practical interest. For instance, there is the question as to whether the Native Appeal Court was really right in its judgment that the payment of the *ditsoa* cattle to the mother's brother of a bride is not a legal but only a moral obligation. So far as I have been able to form an opinion, I should say that the judgment was right.

The whole subject of the payments at marriage (*lobola*) is one of considerable practical importance at the present time to missionaries and magistrates, and to the natives themselves. Now the study of the exact position in which a person stands to his maternal relatives is one without which it is impossible to arrive at a completely accurate understanding of the customs of *lobola*. One of the chief functions of *lobola* is to fix the social position of the children of a marriage. If the proper payment is made by a family, then the children of the woman who comes to them in exchange for the cattle belong to that family, and its gods are their gods. The natives consider that the strongest of all social bonds is that between a child and its mother, and therefore by the extension that inevitably takes place there is a very strong bond between the child and its mother's family. The function of the *lobola* payment is not to destroy but to modify this bond, and to place the children definitely in the father's family and group for all matters concerning not only the social but also the religious

ancestors is first my mother's father, then, if he is dead, my mother's brother, and after the decease of the latter, his son, who may be younger than I am. There is a similarity of function for these three relationships, a single general pattern of behaviour for me towards them all and this is again similar in general to that for grandfathers. The nomenclature is, therefore, appropriate.

life of the tribe. If no *lobola* is paid the child inevitably belongs to the mother's family, though its position is then irregular. But the woman for whom the *lobola* is paid does not become a member of the husband's family; their gods are not her gods; and that is the final test. I have said enough, I hope, to show that the proper understanding of customs relating to the mother's brother is a necessary preliminary to any final theory of *lobola*.

CHAPTER II

PATRILINEAL AND MATRILINEAL SUCCESSION [1]

IF we are to understand aright the laws and customs of non-European peoples we must be careful not to interpret them in terms of our own legal conceptions, which, simple and obvious as some of them may seem to us, are the product of a long and complex historical development and are special to our own culture. If, for instance, we attempt to apply to the customs of the simpler peoples our own precise distinctions between the law relating to persons and the law relating to things we shall produce nothing but confusion in the result.

With us one of the most important aspects of succession is the transmission of property by inheritance. Yet in some of the simplest societies this is a matter of almost no significance at all. In an Australian tribe, for example, a man possesses a few weapons, tools, utensils and personal ornaments, things of little value or permanence. On his death some of them may be destroyed, others may be distributed among his relatives and friends. But their disposal is of so little importance, unless in relation to ritual, that it is often difficult to find any rules of customary procedure. But even in such simple societies, where inheritance of private property may be said not to exist or to be of minimal importance, there are problems of succession in the widest sense of the term.

The term 'succession' will here be taken as referring to the transmission of rights in general. A right exists in, and is definable in terms of, recognised social usage. A right may be that of an individual or a collection of individuals. It may be defined as a measure of control that a person, or a collection of persons, has over the acts of some person or persons, said to be thereby made liable to the performance of a duty. Rights may be classified as of three main kinds:

(a) Rights over a person imposing some duty or duties upon that person. This is the *jus in personam* of Roman law. A father may exercise such rights over his son, or a nation over its citizens.

[1] Reprinted from *The Iowa Law Review*, Vol. XX, No. 2, January 1935.

(b) Rights over a person 'as against the world', i.e. imposing duties on all other persons in respect of that particular person. This is the *jus in rem* of Roman law in relation to persons.

(c) Rights over a thing, i.e. some object other than a person, as against the world, imposing duties on other persons in relation to that thing.

The rights classified under (b) and (c) are fundamentally of the same kind, distinguished only as they relate to persons or to things, and are of a different kind from those classified under (a).

We may consider a few examples from such a simple society as an Australian tribe. A man has certain rights over his wife. Some of them are rights *in personam* whereby he may require from her the performance of certain duties. Others are rights *in rem*. If anyone should kill the wife he commits an injury against the husband. If anyone should have sexual intercourse with the wife without the consent of the husband he commits an injury against the latter. In some tribes a man may lend his wife to another; this is an exercise by the husband both of his rights *in personam* and of his rights *in rem*.

In a great number of Australian tribes the custom of the levirate holds sway. By this, when a man dies all his rights over his wife (and over his immature children) are transferred to his younger brother, or failing such, to an agnatic cousin. This is a simple instance of fraternal succession. What is transferred is certain rights *in personam* and *in rem* over certain persons (the wife and children) and with these rights there go, of course, certain obligations or duties.

Let us next consider, in such a tribe as the Kariera of Western Australia, the nature of the group that I shall call a 'horde'. This is a body of persons who jointly possess, occupy and exploit a certain defined area of country. The rights of the horde over its territory can be briefly indicated by saying that no person who is not a member of the horde has the right to any animal, vegetable or mineral product from the territory except by invitation or consent of members of the horde. Acts of trespass against this exclusive right of a horde to its territory seem to have been very rare in the social life of the aborigines but it appears to have been generally held that anyone committing such a trespass could justifiably be killed.[1] This exclusive use of its territory by a horde is modified by obligations of hospitality whereby, when there is an abundance of some kind of food at a certain time, members of friendly neighbouring hordes are invited to come in and share it. The son of any woman born in the horde and married elsewhere is always entitled to visit his mother's horde and hunt in its territory.

It is convenient to speak of such a group as the Kariera horde as a 'corporation' having an 'estate'. This is an extension of the terms 'corporation' and 'estate' as they are commonly used in law, but I think this extension is justifiable, and hope that at any rate it will be admitted for the purposes of the present exposition. By an estate is here meant a collection of rights (whether over persons or things) with the implied duties, the unity of which is constituted either by the fact that they are the rights of a single person and can be transmitted, as a whole, or in division, to some other person or persons, or that they are the rights of a defined group (the corporation) which maintains a continuity of possession. A personal estate thus corresponds to that *universitas juris* which is what, in Roman law, was transmitted by inheritance.[2] . . .

The corporate estate of a Kariera horde includes in the first place its rights over its territory. The continuity of the horde is maintained by the continuity of possession of the territory, which remains constant, not subject to division or increase, for the Australian aborigines have no conception of the possibility of territorial conquest by armed force. The relation of a horde to its territory does not correspond exactly to what we regard as 'ownership' in modern law. It has some of the qualities of corporate ownership, but also partakes of the nature of the relation of a modern state to its territory, which we may speak of as the exercise of 'dominion'. Rights of ownership over land and rights of dominion have seemingly both had their origin by development and differentiation from such a simple relation as that exemplified in the Australian horde.

---

[1] We have records from a part of South Australia of occasional deliberate acts of trespass with armed force, a body of men invading a territory in which red ochre was found for the purpose of obtaining a supply. This was actually an act of war and as the invaders took care to come in force the horde whose rights were thus invaded had no effective remedy.

[2] *Hereditas est successio in universum jus quod defunctus habuit:* an inheritance is a succession to the entire legal position of a deceased man.

The estate of a horde includes not only its rights over a territory, but also its rights, *in personam* and *in rem*, over its members. The adult male members of the horde owe certain duties to it so that it has rights *in personam* over them. It also has rights *in rem*, for if one of them is killed, by violence or by sorcery, the horde as a whole conceives itself to have been injured and takes steps to obtain satisfaction. Women and children are not members of the horde in the same sense as adult males. If a man's wife is 'stolen' it is he as an individual who seeks satisfaction though he will have the backing of the other members of the horde. But indirectly she also belongs to the horde so that when her husband dies she should by custom pass into the possession of some other member of the horde and not to some person outside.

Since the Kariera horde is exogamous every female child passes by marriage out of the possession of her parents and out of the possession of the horde into the possession of her husband in another horde. By Australian custom this transfer of possession, i.e. of rights, *in personam* and *in rem*, over a person, should normally involve compensation or indemnification, which, in many tribes, is provided by the man who receives a wife giving his sister in exchange to be the wife of his brother-in-law. Male children may be said to pass out of the possession of the parents and into direct possession of the horde at initiation. This is, in some tribes, symbolically expressed in the initiation ritual.

The Kariera horde affords an example of perpetual corporate succession. It will be obvious, I think, that it contains the germs of the state and of sovereignty as we know them in more complex developments. Thus, as the terms have been used above, the United States of America is a 'corporation' having as its constituent 'estate' possession of, or dominion over, a certain territory (subject, unlike that of an Australian horde, to increase by conquest or purchase) and certain specific rights, *in personam* and *in rem*, over the persons of its citizens.

The continuity of a corporation such as the Australian horde is dependent on the continuity of its estate. In the first place there is continuity of possession of the territory. Secondly, there is a continuity which transcends the space of a human life by the fact that as the group loses some members by death it acquires new members by the birth of children and the initiation of boys into the status of men.

If now we turn from considering the horde as a whole to consider the individual male members we find here also a process of customary transmission of rights. Children 'belong', we may say, primarily to the father, i.e. it is he who exercises over them rights *in personam* and *in rem*. As the father in turn belongs to the horde this horde has some rights over his children. When a girl reaches puberty the rights over her are transferred (perhaps not in entirety but in great part) from her father and his horde to her husband. When the boy reaches puberty he is transferred from his position of dependence on his father to that of an adult member of the horde. Now a member of the horde has certain rights over other members and over the territory of the horde. These rights are part of his personal estate or status. Thus there is a process of 'patrilineal succession' whereby the sons of male members of the horde become in their turn members, thus acquiring rights and having a share in the estate.

We are thus brought, after necessary and it is hoped not too tedious preliminary considerations, to the problem with which this paper is to deal, that of the nature and function of the unilineal transmission of rights. In the patrilineal succession of the Australian horde the most considerable part of the body of rights of a male person, his status, his personal estate as a sharer or co-parcener in the estate of a horde, are derived by him through his father to the exclusion of his mother and are transmitted in turn to his sons to the exclusion of his daughters. It is important, however, to recognise that in this instance, and, so far as we know, in all instances of patrilineal succession, some rights are also transmitted through the mother. Thus in the Kariera tribe a man has certain quite important rights over his mother's horde, over its individual members, and over its territory.

In matrilineal succession the greater part of the body of rights of an individual, over things, over persons, or as a member of a corporation, are derived by him through his mother and cannot be transmitted to his children but devolve upon his sister's children.

As an example of a very thorough system of matrilineal succession we may consider the *taravad* of the Nayar caste of Malabar. A *taravad* is an incorporated matrilineal lineage. It includes all living descendants in the female line of an original ancestress. It has therefore both male and female members, all of whom are children of female members of the group. It is constituted as a corporation (a joint-family in the terminology of Indian lawyers) by the possession of an estate which includes in the first instance possession of a house or houses and land, and in the second place rights over the persons of its members. The control of the estate is in the hands of a 'manager' who is normally the oldest male member of the group. In order that the group may retain complete and exclusive possession of the children born to its female members the Nayars have established a system which denies all legal rights to a male parent. A Nayar girl is 'married' while still very young to a suitable bridegroom by the Hindu religious ceremony of the tying of a jewel. (It is probable that in former times the 'bridegroom' ceremoniously deflowered the virgin 'bride'.) On the third day the newly-wedded pair are divorced by the Hindu ceremony of dividing a piece of cloth. Thereafter the divorced bridegroom has no rights over the person, the estate or the children of his bride. At a later period the girl takes a lover. In former times, amongst some of the Nayar, if not generally, a woman was permitted by custom to have two or more lovers at the same time. As the lover is not married to the woman he also has no legal claims over her person or estate or over any children that may be born of the union.

The Nayar system is the most thoroughgoing example of perpetual matrilineal succession. The lineage group maintains its continuity and its unity by not admitting any outside person to any share in its estate. It retains possession of its own women and claims exclusive rights over the children born to them.

The status[1] of an individual at a given moment of time may be defined as the totality of all his rights and duties as recognised in the social usages (laws and customs) of the society to which he belongs. The rights constituting a status, and similarly the duties, are of many different kinds, some relating to 'the world at large', to the society as a whole, others relating to some definite social group of which the individual is a member (e.g. a man's rights over and duties towards his own clan), or to some group of which he is not a member but to which he stands in a special relation (e.g. a man's relation to his mother's clan in a patrilineal clan system, or to his father's clan in a matrilineal system), and

---

[1] It is well always to remember that *status, estate, state*, and the French *état* are all different forms of one and the same word, the late Latin *estatus*.

yet others concern his special relations as an individual with other individuals.

Everywhere in human society the status of an individual is very largely determined by birth as the child of a particular father and particular mother. Behind the question of succession, therefore, lies the question of what elements of status, i.e. what rights and duties, are transmitted to the child by the father on the one hand and by the mother on the other. Every society has to establish its system of rules in this matter and there is an immense diversity of systems to be found in surviving and historic communities. The almost universal rule is that an individual derives some elements of his status from or through his father, and others from or through his mother.

It has to be remembered that in all societies there is a general difference between the status of a man and that of a woman, and in some societies these differences are very marked and very important. Thus when a son 'succeeds' his father he may attain a status very similar to that of his father, but a daughter cannot do so to the same extent. The reverse holds true in the instance of a mother and her daughter on the one hand and her son on the other. Thus in African kingdoms where succession is matrilineal a king is succeeded by his younger brother and then by his sister's son. The heir therefore acquires, through his mother, important elements of the status of his mother's brother. The king's sister, who holds a very important position, is, of course, succeeded by her daughter.

One solution of the problem of the determination of status would be to let the sons derive from the father and daughters from the mother. This principle is only known to be adopted in a few tribes, about which we know very little, in East Africa and in New Britain. As a working arrangement it has weighty objections which cannot be gone into here.

It is possible to have a system in which a child, by birth, acquires the same rights, of the same kind and to an equal degree, over the persons to whom he is related through his father and those to whom he is related through his mother. An instance of this is that where a person has an equal expectation of testamentary or intestate succession to the estate of the brothers and sisters of his father and those of his mother. A further instance is provided by the customs relating to *wergild* amongst the Teutonic peoples.

By birth a man acquired rights over a number of persons who constituted his *sib*.[1] This included all his relatives through his father and through his mother, counting either through males or through females, within a certain range. This range varied in different Teutonic communities and perhaps in the same community at different times. Amongst some of the Anglo-Saxons it extended as far as fifth cousins. If a man were killed all the members of his sib could claim a share in the indemnity (*wergild*) paid by the killer, proportionate to the degree of the relationship. Inversely, if a man killed another all members of his sib were under obligation to contribute to the blood-money he had to pay, each contributing in the same proportion as he would receive if the man himself had been killed. The members of a man's sib had specific rights *in rem* in relation to him and specific duties *in personam* towards him.

The solution adopted by the great majority of human societies of the problem relating to the determination of status has been one by which a child derives certain rights and duties through the father and others of a different kind through the mother. Where the rights and duties derived through the father preponderate in social importance over those derived through the mother we have what it is usual to call a patrilineal system. Inversely a matrilineal system is one in which the rights and duties derived through the mother preponderate over those derived through the father.

There are, however, some societies in which there is a fairly even balance between the elements of status derived through the father and those through the mother. An example is provided by the OvaHerero of south-west Africa. Through his mother a child derives membership in an *eanda*, a matrilineal clan; through his father he becomes a member of an *oruzo*, a patrilineal clan. There is thus a double system of clans crossing one another. As both kinds of clans are exogamous a man cannot belong to the *eanda* of his father or to the *oruzo* of his mother. Through his mother and as a member of her *eanda* he has certain rights over, and duties towards, that group and particularly his mother's

---

[1] Professor Lowie and some American writers use the term 'sib' as equivalent to what is here, in accordance with European usage, called a 'clan'. It seems desirable to retain the word 'sib' for the bilateral group of kindred to which it was originally applied.

brothers and his sister's children. Secular property is inherited only within the *eanda* so that a man inherits such property from his mother's brother and transmits it to his sister's son. On the other hand through his father and as a member of his *oruzo* he has rights and duties of other kinds in relation to that group. Certain sacred cattle may only be inherited within the *oruzo* and are therefore transmitted from father to son.

There are to be found in Africa and in Oceania other instances of systems in which patrilineal and matrilineal succession are combined and more or less balanced against one another. In a considerable part of Africa this is rationalised by a conception that every human being is compounded of two principles, one, called the 'blood' in Ashanti, derived from the mother, the other, the 'spirit', derived from the father.

Probably the most important factor in determining the nature of succession in the simpler societies is the need of defining rights *in rem* over persons. When a child is born there is the question, 'To whom does the child belong?' It may, of course, be regarded as belonging jointly to the two parents. Both have an interest in it, both have rights *in personam* and *in rem* in relation to it. But there are other persons who have rights, *in personam* and *in rem* over the father (his parents, and brothers and sisters) and others who similarly have rights over the mother. In any society in which kinship is of fundamental importance in the total social structure, as it is in the majority of non-European societies, it is essential for social stability and continuity that the rights of different individuals over a given individual should be defined in such a way as to avoid as far as possible conflicts of rights. We have seen how the ancient Teutonic system gives similar, and in some instances equal, rights *in rem* to the father's kin and to the mother's kin of a given individual so that if he is killed all members of his sib (i.e. his kindred on both sides) are entitled to compensation. Let us now consider examples of the solution of this problem in matrilineal and patrilineal systems.

For a matrilineal system we may return to the Nayar as affording an extreme, and therefore crucial instance. In that system the *taravad*, or joint-family, maintains intact and absolute its rights *in rem* over all its members. Marriage normally gives the husband certain rights *in rem* over his wife and over the children. The Nayars may be said either to have eliminated marriage or to have eliminated this aspect of marriage. It is true that the union of a Nayar woman and her *sambandham* lover is often a life-long union of great affection and that the lover has a great attachment to the children. But legally he has no rights over his 'wife', if we call her such, or over the children. In turn the group has no rights *in rem* over him for these remain with his own *taravad*. The *taravad* as a corporation retains undivided and undisputed possession of its own estate.

As an instance of a definitely patrilineal solution of the problem of the distribution of rights *in rem* we may take the Zulu-Kaffir tribes of South Africa. In these tribes marriage requires the payment of an indemnity in the form of a number of cattle, called the *Ikazi*, the act of transfer of these being known as *uku-lobola*. An unmarried girl belongs to her father, or to her guardian (father's brother or brother) if her father be dead, and to her agnatic kindred. They have over her certain rights *in personam* and *in rem*. An offence committed against her, as rape, seduction, maiming or homicide, is an injury to her kin and they have the right to be indemnified. A father may bring before the chief an action for compensation for an offence committed against his daughter. By the act of marriage the father and the agnatic kindred surrender a great part of these rights over the daughter to her husband and to his agnatic kindred. The payment of cattle is an indemnification for this surrender of rights. For these people the great value of a woman is as the mother of children. (For this reason there is no more unhappy, unwanted person among them than a barren woman.) The act of *lobola* is therefore primarily a procedure whereby those paying the cattle acquire undivided and indisputable rights over all children born to the woman. This is readily demonstrated by an analysis that would be out of place here. The natives state the principle in two ways: 'Cattle beget children'; 'The children are where the cattle are not.' In case of divorce either the wife and her children return to her father and any cattle paid are returned, or if (as is usual) the husband retains the children he must abandon claim to the cattle he has paid or to some portion thereof. On the death of a wife who has borne children (a barren wife may be repudiated and the re-payment of the cattle or the substitution of a sister may be claimed) if all the cattle have been paid, the children remain with the father and the mother's kin have no rights *in rem* over them. The system here outlined is a simple legal procedure for giving the father and his agnatic kindred indisputable and undivided rights *in rem* over his children.

Thus the system of patrilineal or matrilineal succession centres largely around the system of marriage. In an extreme matrilineal society a man has no rights *in rem* over his children, though he does usually have certain rights *in personam*. The rights remain with the mother and her relatives. The result is to emphasise and maintain a close bond between brother and sister at the expense of the bond between husband and wife. Consequently the rights of the husband over his wife are limited. In an extreme patrilineal society we have exactly the opposite. Rights *in rem* over the children are exclusively exercised by the father and his relatives. The bond between husband and wife is strengthened at the expense of the bond between brother and sister. The rights of the husband over his wife are considerable; she is *in manu*, under his *potestas*.

Extreme patrilineal systems are comparatively rare, and extreme matrilineal systems perhaps even rarer. Generally there is some modification by which, while the kindred on the one side have a preponderant right, some rights are recognised on the other side also. Thus in the Cherokee tribe of North American Indians, while a man belonged to his mother's clan, so that if he were killed they and they alone would demand satisfaction, yet he stood in a very special relation to his father and to his father's clan.

Little has been said so far about the inheritance of property. This is because in the simpler societies the transmission of property is generally dependent upon the transmission of status. Thus amongst the Nayar the important property (land, houses, etc.) is the undivided or joint possession of a corporation constituted by a matrilineal lineage. Amongst the Zulu-Kaffir tribes the sons succeed to a share of the father's estate to the exclusion of daughters and their descendants. In general, though there are a few exceptions, it may be said that the transmission of property follows the same line as does the transmission of status.

With regard to the institutions of patrilineal and matrilineal succession the question is frequently asked as to what is their origin. The term 'origin' is ambiguous. In one sense we may talk of the 'historical origin'. The historical origin of the Nayar system, or that of the Zulu-Kaffirs, or of any other system, is a series of unique events extending often over a long period of gradual growth. The determination of the origin in this sense of any social system is the task of a historian. For the simpler peoples these histories are unknown and are the subject only of pure speculation, to my mind largely unprofitable. But the term 'origin' may be used in another sense, and very frequently it is used ambiguously with a confusion of the two meanings.

Any social system, to survive, must conform to certain conditions. If we can define adequately one of these universal conditions, i.e. one to which all human societies must conform, we have a sociological law. Thereupon if it can be shown that a particular institution in a particular society is the means by which that society conforms to the law, i.e. to the necessary condition, we may speak of this as the ' sociological origin' of the institution. Thus an institution may be said to have its general *raison d'être* (sociological origin) and its particular *raison d'être* (historical origin). The first is for the sociologist or social anthropologist to discover by the comparative method. The second is for the historian to discover by examination of records or for the ethnologist, in the absence of records, to speculate about.

One such law, or necessary condition of continued existence, is that of a certain degree of functional consistency amongst the constituent parts of the social system. Functional consistency is not the same thing as logical consistency; the latter is one special form of the former. Functional inconsistency exists whenever two aspects of the social system produce a conflict which can only be resolved by some change in the system itself. It is always a question of the functioning, i.e. the working of the system as a whole. Consistency is a relative matter. No social system ever attains to a perfect consistency, and it is for this reason that every system is constantly undergoing change. Any insufficiency in this respect in a social system tends to induce change, sometimes, though by no means always, through the conscious recognition of the insufficiency by members of the society and the conscious seeking of a remedy. To this law of the necessity of a certain degree of functional consistency we may add a second, which is a special instance of the first. Any human social life requires the establishment of a social structure consisting of a network of relations between individuals and groups of individuals. These relations all involve certain rights and duties which need to be defined in such a way that conflicts of rights can be resolved without destroying the structure. It is this need that is met by the establishment of systems of justice and legal institutions.

Every system of rights necessarily involves the existence of common, joint or divided rights over the same person or thing. The father and the mother of a child both have rights *in personam* over their child. In an orderly family it is necessary that there should be no unresolved or unresolvable conflict between these rights. The same thing is true throughout a society as a whole in all the various relations into which persons are brought. When two persons A and B have rights over something Z or rights *in rem* over some person Z, there are three ways of adjusting these rights so as to avoid unresolvable conflicts. One is the mode of *rights in common*; A and B have similar and equal rights over Z and these are such that the rights of A will not conflict with those of B. An instance is to be found in the native tribes of South Africa in which, as the native saying is, 'grass and water are common'. Any member of a tribe has the right to graze his cattle or water them, or take water for his own use, in any part of the territory over which the tribe (represented by its chief) exercises dominion. A second is the mode of *joint rights* in which A and B (or any number of persons) exercise jointly certain rights over Z. The establishment of such joint rights immediately establishes what is here called a corporation. An infringement of the rights normally calls for a joint action on the part of the corporation, which may, of course, be carried out by its official representatives. A South African tribe has joint possession of its territory, the possession (the estate) being vested in the chief. An infringement of these rights may be adjusted by the chief or may lead to the action of war, in which, under the chief, the whole tribe seeks to maintain its rights. The third mode is that of *rights in division*. Here A has certain definite rights over Z and B has certain other definite rights; the respective rights may be defined either by custom or by a specific contract, or agreement. An example is the relation of owner and tenant of a leased land or building.

So far as rights over persons go the exercise of rights in common is necessarily very limited. In an unfamiliar region one may ask direction from any person one meets and expect to receive whatever information that person can give. In English law the king's officers can demand from any passer-by 'in the king's name' assistance in the arrest of a malefactor.[1] Rights over persons *in personam* are usually exercised either jointly or in division.

Rights over persons *in rem* can obviously never be exercised in common. We have seen, from the example of the Teutonic customs relating to *wergild*, that they can be held in division. But such a thing is rare and for the reason that it requires a complicated definition of the respective shares of various kindred in their interest in their kinsmen. One has only to glance at some of the early laws of Norway and Sweden relating to the division of the *wergild* between agnatic and cognatic kin of different degrees to realise with what difficulties such a system is confronted in its working.

It results from this that rights *in rem* over a person must as a general rule either be exclusively personal, i.e. confined to a single individual (a condition to which the rights of an owner over a slave may approximate in some instances) or must be joint. The rights of a Roman father over his children were nearly exclusive but even these, at certain periods of history certainly, were subject to the rights, exercised jointly, of the *gens* or of the state; even the *potestas* of a *pater familias* was not absolute. Thus we may say that any society that recognises rights *in rem* over persons (and all known societies do so to some extent) will normally, and with only the rarest exceptions, make some prdvision for the joint exercise of such rights. This implies the existence of corporations of some kind, since a corporation is here defined as a collection of persons who jointly exercise some right or rights.

A corporation can only form itself on the basis of a common interest. In the simplest societies the easiest, perhaps almost the only, ways in which common interests can be created are on the basis of locality, i.e. residence in the same local community or neighbourhood, or kinship. Corporations therefore tend to be established either on the one basis or the other or on both combined (the Kariera horde is an example of the latter) or else a double system of local groups and kinship groups is formed.

We must here appeal to another sociological law, the necessity not merely for stability, definiteness and consistency in the social structure, but also for continuity. To provide continuity of social

---

[1] The latter instance, however, might be interpreted as the exercise of a joint right, since the king is the representative of the nation which, as a corporation, has joint rights over the persons of its citizens.

structure is essentially a function of corporations. Thus a modern nation has its continuity as a corporation exercising joint rights over its territory and over the persons of its citizens.

We can imagine as a possibility an incorporated local community which was completely endogamous and which would therefore not have to face the issue of choosing between matrilineal and patrilineal succession, since any child born in the community would have both its parents there. But the moment there are intermarriages between two corporate local groups the question of lineal succession does arise. In such a situation it is possible that no customary rule may be established, each instance being adjusted by agreement of the persons most nearly concerned. It seems that this was the case of the hordes or local groups of the Andaman Islanders. The result is to produce a loose and indefinite structure. If any definite rule does arise it must usually take the form of one either of matrilineal or of patrilineal succession.

If any society establishes a system of corporations on the basis of kinship—clans, joint-families, incorporated lineages—it must necessarily adopt a system of unilineal reckoning of succession. It would, of course, be theoretically possible to establish some sort of rule whereby, when the parents belong to different groups, in certain definite circumstances the children belong to the father's group and in others to the mother's. This would produce complicated conditions, and in general any complicated definition of rights is likely to be functionally inefficient as compared with a simpler one.

Thus the existence of unilineal (patrilineal or matrilineal) succession in the great majority of human societies can be traced to its sociological 'cause' or 'origin' in certain fundamental social necessities. Chief amongst them, I have suggested, is the need of defining, with sufficient precision to avoid unresolvable conflicts, the rights *in rem* over persons. The need of precise definition of rights *in personam* and of rights over things would seem to be secondary but still important factors.

There are many facts which might be adduced to support this hypothesis. I will mention only one kind. In societies organised on the basis of clans one of the most important activities of the clan is to exact vengeance or indemnification when a clansman is killed. The list of known instances of this would fill many pages. The clan as a corporation has rights *in rem* over all its clansmen.

If one is killed the clan is injured and it has the right, and its members are under an obligation, to proceed to some action towards receiving satisfaction, either through vengeance or by receiving an indemnity.

Thus the cause of the decay of the clan (the *genos* or *gens*) in ancient Greece and Rome was the transfer of its rights *in rem* (and necessarily therefore of some of its rights *in personam*) to the city or state, the nature of these rights being inevitably considerably modified in the process of transference. But the decay of the *gens* in Rome still left the patriarchal family as a corporation (as Maine long ago pointed out) the basis of which, however, was not merely the exercise of rights *in rem* by the *pater familias* over his children, but also the exercise of joint rights over property and the maintenance of a religious cult of ancestor-worship.

The sociological laws, i.e. the necessary conditions of existence of a society, that have here been suggested as underlying the customs of unilineal (patrilineal or matrilineal) succession are:

1. The need for a formulation of rights over persons and things sufficiently precise in their general recognition as to avoid as far as possible unresolved conflicts.
2. The need for continuity of the social structure as a system of relations between persons, such relations being definable in terms of rights and duties.

By American ethnologists who object to the method of explanation adopted in the preceding argument it is said that any sociological laws that can be formulated must necessarily be truisms. The laws formulated above, if they be true, as I believe, even if not adequately expressed, may be truisms. But even so they would seem to need to be brought to the attention of at least some ethnologists. A recent writer on the subject of matrilineal and patrilineal succession[1] makes the following statements : 'Unilateral institutions are in themselves anomalous and artificial. Matrilineal ones are doubly so.' 'Unilateral institutions, wherever found, represent deviations from the expectable, abnormalities in the social structure.' 'Unilateral reckoning contradicts the duality of parenthood and results in an unnatural stressing of one

[1] Ronald L. Olson, 'Clan and Moiety in North America', *University of California Publications*, Vol. 33, pp. 409, 411.

side of the family to the exclusion of the other.' On the basis of these assertions he seems to conclude that unilineal determination of status must have had a single origin in some one aberrant people and to have spread from them, by a process of 'diffusion', to vast numbers of peoples in Europe, Asia, Africa, Australia, Oceania and America. (One wonders, of course, why so many societies of so many different types should have accepted and retained such 'anomalous', 'abnormal' and 'unnatural' institutions.)

I hope that the argument of this paper has shown, on the contrary, that unilineal institutions in some form, are almost, if not entirely, a necessity in any ordered social system. What is therefore unusual or rare (we need not say abnormal or anomalous and still less unnatural) is the discovery of a people such as the Teutonic peoples of Europe (apparently alone amongst Indo-European speaking peoples) maintaining for some period, until the coming of feudalism and Roman law, a system in which there is considerable, if not quite complete, avoidance of the unilineal principle, in which a person derives similar and equal rights through the father and through the mother.[1]

It might well be expected that such a paper as this would deal with the question of what general factors determine the selection by some people of the matrilineal and by others of the patrilineal principle in determining status or succession. My opinion is that our knowledge and understanding are not sufficient to permit us to deal with this problem in any satisfactory manner.

[1] There are systems of bilateral kinship with succession through both males and females in some parts of Indonesia, e.g. in the Ifugao of the Philippine Islands. The discussion of these would be complex and require space that is not available.

CHAPTER III

THE STUDY OF KINSHIP SYSTEMS[1]

FOR seventy-five years the subject of kinship has occupied a special and important position in social anthropology. I propose in this address to consider the methods that have been and are being used in that branch of our studies and the kinds of results that we may reasonably expect to arrive at by those methods. I shall consider and compare two methods which I shall speak of as that of conjectural history and that of structural or sociological analysis.

One of these methods was first applied to some social institutions by French and British (mostly Scots) writers of the eighteenth century. It was of this method that Dugald Stewart wrote in 1795: 'To this species of philosophical investigation, which has no appropriated name in our language, I shall take the liberty of giving the title of *Theoretical* or *Conjectural History*; an expression which coincides pretty nearly in its meaning with that of *Natural History*, as employed by Mr. Hume (see his *Natural History of Religion*), and with what some French writers have called *Histoire Raisonnée*.' I shall accept Dugald Stewart's suggestion and shall use the name 'conjectural history'.

The method of conjectural history is used in a number of different ways. One is to attempt to base on general considerations, on what Dugald Stewart calls 'known principles of human nature', conjectures as to first beginnings—of political society (Hobbes), of language (Adam Smith), of religion (Tylor), of the family (Westermarck), and so on. Sometimes an attempt is made to deal with the whole course of development of human society, as in the works of Morgan, Father Schmidt and Elliot Smith. Sometimes we are offered a conjectural history of the development of a particular institution, as in Robertson Smith's treatment of sacrifice. The special form of the method with which we shall be concerned in what follows is the attempt to explain a particular feature of one or more social systems by a hypothesis as to how it came into existence.

[1] Presidential Address to the Royal Anthropological Institute, 1941. Reprinted from the *Journal of the Royal Anthropological Institute*.

An early example of the method of conjectural history applied to kinship is to be found in the essay on *Primitive Marriage* published by John F. M'Lennan in 1865. You will remember the two principal theses put forward in that book: the origin of the custom of exogamy from marriage by capture, and the proposition that 'the most ancient system in which the idea of blood relationship was embodied was a system of kinship through females only'. Six years later there appeared *The Systems of Consanguinity and Affinity* of Lewis Morgan, a monument of scholarly, patient research in the collection of data, to be followed in 1877 by his *Ancient Society*, in which he offered a conjectural outline history of the whole course of social development. These works of M'Lennan and Morgan were followed by a considerable mass of literature, which has continued to be produced down to the present day, in which the method of conjectural history has been applied in different forms to various features of kinship organisation.

As I think you know, I regard the pursuit of this method as one of the chief obstacles to the development of a scientific theory of human society. But my position has often been misunderstood. My objection to conjectural history is not that it is historical, but that it is conjectural. History shows us how certain events or changes in the past have led to certain other events or conditions, and thus reveals human life in a particular region of the world as a chain of connected happenings. But it can do this only when there is direct evidence for both the preceding and succeeding events or conditions and also some actual evidence of their interconnection. In conjectural history we have direct knowledge about a state of affairs existing at a certain time and place, without any adequate knowledge of the preceding conditions and events, about which we are therefore reduced to making conjectures. To establish any probability for such conjectures we should need to have a knowledge of laws of social development which we certainly do not possess and to which I do not think we shall ever attain.

My own study of kinship began in 1904 under Rivers, when I was his first and at that time his only student in social anthropology, having for three years previously studied psychology under him. I owe a great deal to that contact with Rivers, and more rather than less because from the outset it appeared that we disagreed on the subject of method. For Rivers followed the method of conjectural history, at first under the influence of Morgan, and later in the form of what he called ethnological analysis, as exemplified in his *History of Melanesian Society* (1914*a*). But in his field work Rivers had discovered and revealed to others the importance of the investigation of the behaviour of relatives to one another as a means of understanding a system of kinship. In what follows I shall be criticising one side of Rivers' work, but the position I now hold is the one I held in my friendly discussions with him during a period of ten years, ending in an agreement to go on disagreeing. My esteem for Rivers as man, as teacher, and as scientist, is in no way diminished by the fact that I find myself obliged to criticise adversely his use of the method of conjectural history.

At the outset it is necessary to give a definition. I shall use the term 'kinship system' as short for a system of kinship and marriage or kinship and affinity. It is a pity that there is no inclusive term in English for all relationships which result from the existence of the family and marriage. It would be very tiresome to speak all the time of a system of kinship and affinity. I hope, therefore, that my use of the term will be accepted. It need not lead to ambiguity.

The unit of structure from which a kinship system is built up is the group which I call an 'elementary family', consisting of a man and his wife and their child or children, whether they are living together or not. A childless married couple does not constitute a family in this sense. Children may be acquired, and thus made members of an elementary family, by adoption as well as by birth. We must also recognise the existence of compound families. In a polygynous family there is only one husband with two or more wives and their respective children. Another form of compound family is produced in monogamous societies by a second marriage, giving rise to what we call step-relationships and such relationships as that of half-brothers. Compound families can be regarded as formed of elementary families with a common member.

The existence of the elementary family creates three special kinds of social relationship, that between parent and child, that between children of the same parents (siblings), and that between husband and wife as parents of the same child or children. A person is born or adopted into a family in which he or she is son or daughter and brother or sister. When a man marries and has children he now belongs to a second elementary family, in which he is husband and father. This interlocking of elementary families creates a network of what I shall call, for lack of any better term, genealogical relations, spreading out indefinitely.

The three relationships that exist within the elementary family constitute what I call the first order. Relationships of the second order are those which depend on the connection of two elementary families through a common member, and are such as father's father, mother's brother, wife's sister, and so on. In the third order are such as father's brother's son and mother's brother's wife. Thus we can trace, if we have genealogical information, relationships of the fourth, fifth or nth order. In any given society a certain number of these relationships are recognised for social purposes, i.e. they have attached to them certain rights and duties, or certain distinctive modes of behaviour. It is the relations that are recognised in this way that constitute what I am calling a kinship system, or, in full, a system of kinship and affinity.

A most important character of a kinship system is its range. In a narrow range system, such as the English system of the present day, only a limited number of relatives are recognised as such in any way that entails any special behaviour or any specific rights and duties. In ancient times in England the range was wider, since a fifth cousin had a claim to a share of the *wergild* when a man was killed. In systems of very wide range, such as are found in some non-European societies, a man may recognise many hundreds of relatives, towards each of whom his behaviour is qualified by the existence of the relationship.

It must be noted also that in some societies persons are regarded as being connected by relationships of the same kind although no actual genealogical tie is known. Thus the members of a clan are regarded as being kinsmen, although for some of them it may not be possible to show their descent from a common ancestor. It is this that distinguishes what will here be called a clan from a lineage.

Thus a kinship system, as I am using the term, or a system of kinship and affinity if you prefer so to call it, is in the first place a system of dyadic relations between person and person in a community, the behaviour of any two persons in any of these relations being regulated in some way, and to a greater or less extent, by social usage.

A kinship system also includes the existence of definite social groups. The first of these is the domestic family, which is a group of persons who at a particular time are living together in one dwelling, or collection of dwellings, with some sort of economic arrangement that we may call joint housekeeping. There are many varieties of the domestic family, varying in their form, their size, and the manner of their common life. A domestic family may consist of a single elementary family, or it may be a group including a hundred or more persons, such as the *zadruga* of the Southern Slavs or the *taravad* of the Nayar. Important in some societies is what may be called a local cluster of domestic families. In many kinship systems unilinear groups of kindred—lineage groups, clans and moieties—play an important part.

By a kinship system, then, I mean a network of social relations of the kind just defined, which thus constitutes part of that total network of social relations that I call social structure. The rights and duties of relatives to one another and the social usages that they observe in their social contacts, since it is by these that the relations are described, are part of the system. I regard ancestor-worship, where it exists, as in a real sense part of the kinship system, constituted as it is by the relations of living persons to their deceased kindred, and affecting as it does the relations of living persons to one another. The terms used in a society in addressing or referring to relatives are a part of the system, and so are the ideas that the people themselves have about kinship.

You will perceive that by using the word 'system' I have made an assumption, an important and far-reaching assumption; for that word implies that whatever it is applied to is a complex unity, an organised whole. My explicit hypothesis is that between the various features of a particular kinship system there is a complex relation of interdependence. The formulation of this working hypothesis leads immediately to the method of sociological analysis, by which we seek to discover the nature of kinship systems as systems, if they be really such. For this purpose we need to make a systematic comparison of a sufficient number of sufficiently diverse systems. We must compare them, not in reference to single, superficial, and therefore immediately observable characters, but as wholes, as systems, and in reference, therefore, to general characters which are only discovered in the process of comparison. Our purpose is to arrive at valid abstractions or general ideas in terms of which the phenomena can be described and classified. (Kinship)

I propose to illustrate the two methods, that of conjectural history and that of system analysis, by means of a particular example, and for this purpose I select a peculiar feature of the kinship terminology of a number of scattered tribes. When Morgan made his study of the terminology of kinship in North American tribes, he noted certain peculiarities in the terms for cousins. In the Choctaw tribe he found that a man calls his father's sister's son by the same term of relationship that he applies to his own father and his father's brother. We may say that the father's sister's son is thus treated in the terminology as though he were a younger brother of the father. Reciprocally a man calls his mother's brother's son by the term for 'son'. Consistently with this he applies one term of relationship to his father's sister and her daughter, and speaks of his mother's brother's daughter as a 'daughter'. In the Omaha tribe, on the other hand, Morgan found that a man calls his mother's brother's son 'uncle', i.e. mother's brother, and calls his mother's brother's daughter 'mother', so that reciprocally he speaks of his father's sister's son by the term that he uses for his sister's son, and a woman uses a single term for her own son, her sister's son and her father's sister's son. Figs. 1 and 2 will help to make these terminologies clear.

Terminologies similar to the Omaha are found in a number of regions: (1) in the Siouan tribes related to the Omaha, such as the Osage, Winnebago, etc.; (2) in certain Algonquian tribes, of which we may take the Fox Indians as an example; (3) in an area of California which includes the Miwok; (4) in some tribes of East Africa, both Bantu and non-Bantu, including the Nandi and the BaThonga; (5) amongst the Lhota Nagas of Assam; and (6) in some New Guinea tribes. Terminologies similar to the Choctaw are found: (1) in other south-eastern tribes of the United States, including the Cherokee; (2) in the Crow and Hidatsa tribes of the Plains area; (3) amongst the Hopi and some other Pueblo Indians; (4) in the Tlingit and Haida of the north-west coast of America; (5) in the Banks Islands in Melanesia; and (6) in one Twi-speaking community of West Africa.

There are some who would regard this kind of terminology
as 'contrary to common sense', but that means no more than that
it is not in accordance with our modern European ideas of kinship
and its terminology. It ought to be easy for any anthropologist to
recognise that what is common sense in one society may be the

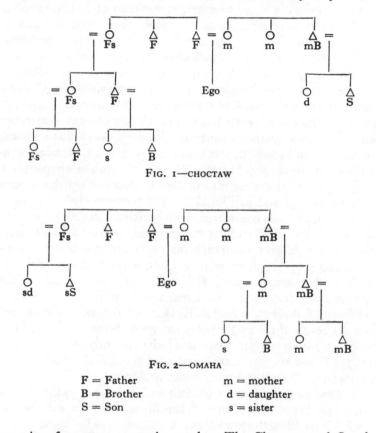

FIG. 1—CHOCTAW

FIG. 2—OMAHA

F = Father   m = mother
B = Brother   d = daughter
S = Son   s = sister

opposite of common sense in another. The Choctaw and Omaha
terminologies do call for some explanation; but so does the
English terminology, in which we use the word 'cousin' for all
children of both brothers and sisters of both mother and father—
a procedure which would probably seem to some non-Europeans
to be contrary not only to common sense but also to morals. What
I wish to attempt, therefore, is to show you that the Choctaw
and Omaha terminologies are just as reasonable and fitting in the

social systems in which they occur as our own terminology is in our own social system.

I would point out that the Choctaw system and the Omaha system exhibit a single structural principle applied in different ways, in what we may perhaps call opposite directions. We shall therefore consider them together, as varieties of a single species.

Attempts have been made to explain these terminologies by the method of conjectural history. The first was that of Kohler in 1897, in his essay 'Zur Urgeschichte der Ehe'. Kohler set out to defend Morgan's theory of group-marriage, and used the Choctaw and Omaha systems for his argument. He explained the Choctaw terminology as the result of marriage with the mother's brother's wife, and the Omaha system as the result of a custom of marriage with the wife's brother's daughter. Kohler's essay was reviewed by Durkheim (1898) in what was an important, if brief, contribution to the theory of kinship. He rejected Kohler's hypotheses, and pointed out the connection of the Choctaw and Omaha systems with matrilineal and patrilineal descent respectively.

The subject was considered again by Rivers in reference to the Banks Islands, and, without bringing in, as Kohler had done, the question of group-marriage, he explained the Banks Islands terminology as resulting from a custom of marriage with the mother's brother's widow. Gifford (1916), having found the characteristic feature of the Omaha system in the Miwok of California, followed the lead of Kohler and Rivers, and explained it as the result of the custom of marriage with the wife's brother's daughter. About the same time, and independently, Mrs. Seligman (1917) offered the same explanation of the Omaha feature as it occurs in the Nandi and other tribes of Africa.

Let me summarise the argument with reference to the Omaha type. The hypothesis is that in certain societies, mostly having a definite patrilineal organisation, a custom was for some reason adopted of permitting a man to marry his wife's brother's daughter. Referring to Fig. 3, this means that D 'would be allowed to marry f. When such a marriage occurred, then for G and h, f, who is their mother's brother's daughter, would become their step-mother, and E, their mother's brother's son, would become the brother of their step-mother. The hypothesis then assumes that the kinship terminology was so modified as to anticipate this form of marriage wherever it might occur. G and h will call f, their mother's brother's daughter and therefore their possible future step-mother, 'mother', and her brother E they will call 'mother's brother'. Reciprocally f will call G 'son' and E will call him 'sister's son'. There is an exactly parallel argument for the Choctaw system. A custom arises by which a man may occasionally marry the widow of his mother's brother. In the figure, G would marry b, the wife of his mother's brother A. Thus E and f would become his step-children. If this marriage is anticipated in the terminology, then E and f will call G 'father' and h 'father's sister'.

Let us note that in the Omaha tribe and in some others having a similar terminology it is régarded as permissible for a man to marry his wife's brother's daughter. Marriage with the mother's brother's widow does not seem to occur regularly with the Choctaw

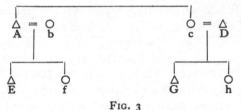

FIG. 3

Note—A and c are brother and sister

terminology, and does certainly occur without it, even in tribes with an Omaha terminology such as the BaThonga.

The basis of what we may call the Kohler hypothesis is the obvious fact that in each of the two varieties the terminology and the special form of marriage are consistent; the two things fit together in what may be called a logical way. This, I think, anyone can see by inspection of the data. But the hypothesis goes far beyond this. It supposes that there is some sort of causal connection such that the marriage custom can be said to have caused, produced, or resulted in, the special terminology. No evidence is adduced that this is actually the way in which things happened. The argument is entirely *a priori*. It is the essential weakness of conjectural history that its hypotheses cannot be verified. Thus this hypothesis cannot be considered as anything more than a speculation or conjecture as to how things might have happened.

Now it would be equally plausible to suggest that the special form of marriage is the result of the terminology. If, as in the terminology of the Omaha type, I treat my wife's brother's daughter as being the younger sister of my wife, and, by the custom of the sororate, it is considered proper for me to marry my wife's younger sister, then I might well be permitted to marry the woman who, in the terminological system, is treated as such, namely her brother's daughter. This hypothesis is, of course, equally lacking in proof. If we adopt the Kohler hypothesis the terminology is conceived to be in some sense explained, but there is no explanation of the marriage custom. By the alternative hypothesis the marriage custom is explained, but the terminology is not. I do not see how there can be any ground for a choice of one of these two hypotheses in preference to the other except purely personal predilection.

However, while we could conceive of the marriage custom as being the immediate result of the terminology in a society which already has sororal polygyny, the terminology cannot be the immediate result of the marriage custom without the concomitant action of some other undetermined factor. We have examples of societies in which a man sometimes marries the widow of his mother's brother, but only uses the terminology which this marriage makes appropriate after the marriage has taken place. Although we have no recorded instance of this procedure in marriage with the wife's brother's daughter it is at least conceivable that it might occur. What is lacking in the hypothesis we are examining is some reason why the whole terminology should be adjusted so as to fit a particular form of marriage which only occasionally occurs.

Let us now leave the hypothesis and examine the structural principles of those kinship systems in which this terminology occurs, whether in the Choctaw or the Omaha form. It is necessary, however, to say something on the subject of kinship terminologies, about which there has been a great deal of controversy. Morgan's first interest in the subject was as an ethnologist, i.e. one seeking to discover the historical relations of the peoples of the earth. He thought that by collecting a sufficient sample of terminologies and comparing them he could reveal the historical relation of the American Indians (the Ganowanian peoples as he called them) to the peoples of Asia. In the course of his work, however, he decided that these terminologies could be used to infer the former existence of forms of social organisation. He supposed that the classificatory terminology which he found in North American tribes such as the Iroquois was inconsistent with the form of social organisation with which it is actually found, and therefore could not have arisen in a society so organised, but must be a 'survival' from some different kind of social system.

This was, of course, pure assumption, but it is the kind of assumption that the method of conjectural history encourages us to make, often unconsciously or implicitly. Morgan was thus led to a hypothesis that is one of the most fantastic in a subject that is full of fantastic hypotheses. The truth is that he had quite failed to understand the nature and function of the classificatory terminology. There is nothing that so effectively prevents the perception and understanding of things as they are as hypotheses of conjectural history, or the desire to invent such hypotheses.

One of Morgan's early critics, Starcke (1889), was, I believe, the first to maintain the position which has always been my own. He held that in general a kinship nomenclature is 'the faithful reflection of the juridical relations which arise between the nearest kinsfolk in each tribe'. He condemned as unsound the attempt to use such nomenclatures to make historical reconstructions of past societies. It would be interesting to consider why it is that Starcke has had so few followers and Morgan so many, but that I cannot here undertake.

In 1909 Kroeber published in our *Journal* a paper on 'Classificatory Systems of Relationship'. To the contentions of that paper Rivers made a reply in his lectures on *Kinship and Social Organisation* (1914b), and Kroeber answered the criticisms of Rivers in his *California Kinship Systems* (1917).

I discussed Kroeber's paper with Rivers when it appeared and found myself in the position of disagreeing with both sides of the controversy. Kroeber wrote: 'Nothing is more precarious than the common method of deducing the recent existence of social or marital institutions from a designation of relationship.' This is a restatement of Starcke's contention of 1889, and with it I was, and still am, in complete agreement, thereby disagreeing with Rivers. Kroeber also wrote: 'It has been an unfortunate characteristic of the anthropology of recent years to seek in a great measure specific causes for specific events, connection between which can be established only through evidence that is subjectively selected. On wider knowledge and freedom from motive it is becoming increasingly apparent that causal explanations of detached anthropological phenomena can be but rarely found in other detached phenomena.' With this statement I am in agreement.

But both Kroeber and Rivers seemed to agree that causal explanations are necessary for the constitution of what Kroeber calls 'true science'. For Rivers anthropology is a true science because, or to the extent that, it can show causal connections; for Kroeber it is not a true science. Here I disagree with both Kroeber and Rivers, holding that a pure theoretical science (whether physical, biological or social) is not concerned with causal relations in this sense. The concept of cause and effect belongs properly to applied science, to practical life and its arts and techniques and to history.

This brings us to the crux of the Rivers-Kroeber debate. Rivers held that the characteristics of a kinship nomenclature are determined by social or sociological factors, that particular features of terminology result from particular features of social organisation. Against this Kroeber held that the features of a system of terminology 'are determined primarily by language' and 'reflect psychology not sociology'. 'Terms of relationship', he wrote, 'are determined primarily by linguistic factors and are only occasionally, and then indirectly, affected by social circumstances.' But in his later paper Kroeber explains that what he calls psychological factors 'are social or cultural phenomena as thoroughly and completely as institutions, beliefs or industries are social phenomena'. His thesis is therefore concerned with a distinction between two kinds of social phenomena. One of these he calls institutional, defined as 'practices connected with marriage, descent, personal relations, and the like'. These are what he called in his first paper 'social factors'. The other kind he speaks of as the 'psyche' of a culture, 'that is, the ways of thinking and feeling characteristic of the culture'. These constitute what he calls the psychological factors.

Thus Kroeber's thesis, on its positive side, is that similarities and differences of kinship nomenclature are to be interpreted or understood by reference to similarities and differences in the general 'manner of thought'. On its negative side, and it is with this that we are concerned, Kroeber's thesis is that there is no regular close connection between similarities and differences of kinship nomenclature and similarities and differences of 'institutions', i.e. practices connected with marriage, descent and personal relations. He admits, in 1917, the existence of 'undoubted correspondence of terminology and social practice in certain parts of Australia and Oceania', but denies that such are to be found in California. It may be pointed out that in Australia and Oceania they have been deliberately looked for, in California they have not. It may well be that in the remnants of Californian tribes it is now too late to look for them.

In opposition to Kroeber, and in a certain sense in agreement with Rivers, I hold that all over the world there are important correspondences between kinship nomenclature and social practices. Such correspondences are not to be simply assumed; they must be demonstrated by field work and comparative analysis. But their absence may not be assumed either; and Kroeber's arguments from their alleged absence in California remain, I think, entirely unconvincing.

For Kroeber the kinship nomenclature of a people represents their general manner of thought as it is applied to kinship. But the institutions of a people also represent their general manner of thought about kinship and marriage. Are we to suppose that in Californian tribes the way of thinking about kinship as it appears on the one hand in the terminology and on the other hand in social customs are not merely different but are not connected? This seems to be in effect what Kroeber is proposing.

Kroeber pointed out in 1917 that his original paper represented 'a genuine attempt to understand kinship systems as kinship systems'. But by 'kinship system' Kroeber means only a system of nomenclature. Moreover, Kroeber is an ethnologist, not a social anthropologist. His chief, if not his sole, interest in the subject is in the possibility of discovering and defining the historical relations of peoples by comparison of their systems of nomenclature.

My own conception is that the nomenclature of kinship is an intrinsic part of a kinship system, just as it is also, of course, an intrinsic part of a language. The relations between the nomenclature and the rest of the system are relations within an ordered whole. My concern, both in field work in various parts of the world and in comparative studies, has been to discover the nature of these relations.

In the actual study of a kinship system the nomenclature is of the utmost importance. It affords the best possible approach to the investigation and analysis of the kinship system as a whole. This, of course, it could not do if there were no real relations of interdependence between the terminology and the rest of the system. That there are such relations I can affirm from my own field work in more than one region. It will be borne out, I believe, by any anthropologist who has made a thorough field study of a kinship system.[1]

I have dealt with the controversy between Kroeber and Rivers because, as both the controversialists point out, the real issue is not simply one concerning kinship terms, but is a very important question of the general method of anthropological studies. It seemed to me that I could best make clear my own position by showing you how it differs from that of Rivers on the one side and that of Kroeber on the other.

Kinship systems are made and re-made by man, in the same sense that languages are made and re-made, which does not mean that they are normally constructed or changed by a process of deliberation and under control of conscious purpose. A language has to work, i.e. it has to provide a more or less adequate instrument for communication, and in order that it may work it has to conform to certain general necessary conditions. A morphological comparison of languages shows us the different ways in which these conditions have been complied with by using different morphological principles such as inflection, agglutination, word order, internal modification or the use of tone or stress. A kinship system also has to work if it is to exist or persist. It has to provide an orderly and workable system of social relations defined by social usage. A comparison of different systems shows us how workable kinship systems have been created by utilising certain structural principles and certain mechanisms.

One common feature of kinship systems is the recognition of certain categories or kinds into which the various relatives of a

---

[1] My position has been misunderstood and consequently misrepresented by Dr. Opler (1937*b*) in his paper on ' Apache Data concerning the Relation of Kinship Terminology to Social Classification'; but the first two paragraphs of another of Dr. Opler's papers (1937*a*) on 'Chiricahua Apache Social Organisation', state what was at that time his, and is also my, point of view.

single person can be grouped. The actual social relation between a person and his relative, as defined by rights and duties or socially approved attitudes and modes of behaviour, is then to a greater or less extent fixed by the category to which the relative belongs. The nomenclature of kinship is commonly used as a means of establishing and recognising these categories. A single term may be used to refer to a category of relatives and different categories will be distinguished by different terms.

Let us consider a simple example from our own system. We do what is rather unusual in the general run of kinship systems: we regard the father's brother and the mother's brother as relatives of the same kind of category. We apply a single term originally denoting the mother's brother (from the Latin *avunculus*) to both of them. The legal relationship in English law, except for entailed estates and titles of nobility, is the same for a nephew and either of his uncles; for example, the nephew has the same rights of inheritance in case of intestacy over the estate of either. In what may be called the socially standardised behaviour of England it is not possible to note any regular distinction made between the maternal and the paternal uncle. Reciprocally the relation of a man to his different kinds of nephews is in general the same. By extension, no significant difference is made between the son of one's mother's brother and the son of one's father's brother.

In Montenegro, on the contrary, to take another European system, the father's brothers constitute one category and the mother's brothers another. These relatives are distinguished by different terms, and so are their respective wives, and the social relations in which a man stands to his two kinds of uncles show marked differences.

There is nothing 'natural' about the English attitude towards uncles. Indeed many peoples in many parts of the world would regard this failure to distinguish between relatives on the father's side and those on the mother's side as unnatural and even improper. But the terminology is consistent with our whole kinship system.

The kinship systems with which we shall be concerned here all have certain forms of what Morgan called the 'classificatory' terminology. What Morgan meant by this term is quite clear from his writings, but his definition is often ignored, perhaps because

people do not bother to read him. A nomenclature is classificatory
when it uses terms which primarily apply to lineal relatives, such
as 'father', to refer also to collateral relatives. Thus by Morgan's
definition the English word 'uncle' is not a classificatory term,
but the very opposite, since it is used only for collateral relatives.
Kroeber (1909) criticises Morgan and rejects his conception of
classificatory terminologies, and then proceeds to make use of the
same distinction by taking as one of the important features of
terminologies the extent to which they separate or distinguish
lineal from collateral relatives. It seems to be merely the word
'classificatory' that Kroeber does not like. Doubtless it is not the
ideal word; but it has long been in use and no better one has been
suggested, though others have been put forward.

I do not propose to deal with all systems in which the classificatory principle is applied in the terminology, but only with a
certain widespread type. In these systems the distinction between
lineal and collateral relatives is clearly recognised and is of great
importance in social life, but it is in certain respects subordinated
to another structural principle, which can be spoken of as the
principle of the solidarity of the sibling group. A group of siblings
is constituted by the sons and daughters of a man and his wife in
monogamous societies, or of a man and his wives where there
is polygyny, or of a woman and her husbands in polyandrous
communities. The bond uniting brothers and sisters together
into a social group is everywhere regarded as important, but it is
more emphasised in some societies than in others. The solidarity
of the sibling group is shown in the first instance in the social
relations between its members.

From this principle there is derived a further principle which
I shall speak of as that of the unity of the sibling group. This
refers not to the internal unity of the group as exhibited in the
behaviour of members to one another, but to its unity in relation
to a person outside it and connected with it by a specific relation
to one of its members.

A diagram may help the discussion. Fig. 4 represents a sibling
group of three brothers and two sisters, to which Ego is related
by the fact that he is the son of one of the three men. In the
kinship systems with which I am now dealing, Ego regards himself
as standing in the same general kind of relation to all the members
of the group. For him it constitutes a unity. His relation to the

brothers and sisters of his father is conceived as being of the same general kind as his relation to his father. Within the group, however, there are two principles of differentiation, sex and seniority, which have to be taken into account. In systems in which seniority is not emphasised a man treats his father's brothers, both older and younger, as being like his father. He refers to them or addresses them by the same term of kinship that he applies to his own father, and in certain important respects his behaviour towards them is similar to his behaviour towards his own father. What defines this behaviour is, of course, different in different systems. Where seniority is strongly emphasised, a man may distinguish between the senior brother and the junior brother either in behaviour alone or both in behaviour and terminology,

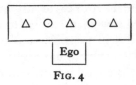

FIG. 4

but there still remains a common element in the pattern of behaviour towards all 'fathers'.

The difference of sex is more important than the difference of seniority, and in this matter there is considerable variation in the systems we are considering. But in quite a considerable number of systems, in different parts of the world, there are certain features of a man's relationship to his father's sister which can be correctly described by saying that he regards her as a sort of female father. In some of these systems he actually calls her 'female father', or some modification of the term for father. If it seems to you impossible that a man should regard his father's sister as a relative of the same kind as his own father, this is because you are thinking, not about social relationships as defined by modes of behaviour, with which we are here concerned, but about the physiological relationship, which is irrelevant.

The same kind of thing happens with the sibling group of the mother. The mother's sisters are treated as relatives of the same kind as the mother, both in terminology and in certain principles of behaviour or attitude. In a number of systems the mother's brother is also treated as a relative of the same kind as the mother.

He may be called 'male mother', as in Bantu tribes of Africa and in Tonga in the Pacific. If the principle of seniority is stressed, the mother's brothers may be distinguished according as they are older or younger than the mother.

Those of you who have never had any direct contact with systems of this kind may find it difficult to comprehend how a father's sister can be regarded as a female father or a mother's brother as a male mother. This is due to the difficulty of dissociating the terms 'father' and 'mother' from the connotations they have in our own social system. It is absolutely essential to do this if the kinship systems of other societies are ever to be understood. Perhaps it will help somewhat if I refer to another terminology which seems to us peculiar. Most of the systems with which I am now dealing have a word for 'child', or words for 'son' and 'daughter', which a man applies to his own children and his brother's children, and a woman applies to her own children and her sister's children. But in some Australian tribes there are two different words for 'child'. One is used by a man for his own child (or his brother's child) and by a woman for her brother's child; the other is used by a woman for her own or her sister's child, and by a man for his sister's child. I think you will see that this is another way of expressing in the terminology the unity that links brother and sister in relation to the child of either of them. I am called by one term by my father and his brothers and sisters; and by another term by my mother and her sisters and brothers.

The same principle, that of the unity of the sibling group, is applied to other sibling groups. Thus the father's father's brother is regarded as belonging to the same category as the father's father, with the result that his son is a somewhat more distant relative of the same kind as the father and his brothers. By means of such extension of the basic principle, a very large number of collateral relatives of different degrees of distance can be brought under a limited number of categories. A man may have many, even hundreds, of relatives whom he thus classifies as 'fathers', 'brothers', 'mother's brothers' and so on. But there are different ways in which this extension of the basic classificatory principle can be applied, so that there result systems of different types. What is common to them all is that they make some use of this structural principle which I have briefly illustrated.

What I am trying to show you is that the classificatory

terminology is a method of providing a wide-range kinship organisation, by making use of the unity of the sibling group in order to establish a few categories of relationship under which a very large number of near and distant relatives can be included. For all the relatives who are denoted by one term, there is normally some element of attitude or behaviour that is regarded as appropriate to them and not to others. But within a category there may be and always are important distinctions. There is, first, the very important distinction between one's own father and his brother. There are distinctions within the category between nearer and more distant relatives. There is sometimes an important distinction between relatives of a certain category who belong to other clans. There are other distinctions that are made in different particular systems. Thus the categories represented by the terminology never give us anything more than the skeleton of the real ordering of relatives in the social life. But in every system that I have been able to study they do give us this skeleton.

If this thesis is true, if this is what the classificatory terminology actually is in the tribes in which it exists, it is obvious that Morgan's whole theory is entirely ungrounded. The classificatory system, as thus interpreted, depends upon the recognition of the strong social ties that unite brothers and sisters of the same elementary family, and the utilisation of this tie to build up a complex orderly arrangement of social relations amongst kin. It could not come into existence except in a society based on the elementary family. Nowhere in the world are the ties between a man and his own children or between children of one father stronger than in Australian tribes, which, as you know, present an extreme example of the classificatory terminology.

The internal solidarity of the sibling group, and its unity in relation to persons connected with it, appear in a great number of different forms in different societies. I cannot make any attempt to deal with these, but for the sake of the later argument I will point out that it is in the light of this structural principle that we must interpret the customs of sororal polygyny (marriage with two or more sisters), the sororate (marriage with the deceased wife's sister), adelphic polyandry (marriage of a woman with two or more brothers, by far the commonest form of polyandry), and the levirate (marriage with the brother's widow). Sapir, using the method of conjectural history, has suggested that the classificatory terminology may be the result of the customs of the levirate and sororate. That the two things are connected is, I think, clear, but for the supposed causal connection there is no evidence whatever. Their real connection is that they are different ways of applying or using the principle of the unity of the sibling group, and they may therefore exist together or separately.

An organisation into clans or moieties is also based on the principle of the solidarity and unity of the sibling group in combination with other principles. Tylor suggested a connection between exogamous clans and the classificatory terminology. Rivers put this in terms of conjectural history, and argued that the classificatory terminology must have had its origin in the organisation of society into exogamous moieties.

II

It is necessary, for our analysis, to consider briefly another aspect of the structure of kinship systems, namely the division into generations. The distinction of generation has its basis in the elementary family, in the relation of parents and children. A certain generalising tendency is discoverable in many kinship systems in the behaviour of relatives of different generations. Thus we find very frequently that a person is expected to adopt an attitude of more or less marked respect towards all his relatives of the first ascending generation. There are restraints on behaviour which maintain a certain distance or prevent too close an intimacy. There is, in fact, a generalised relation of ascendancy and subordination between the two generations. This is usually accompanied by a relation of friendly equality between a person and his relatives of the second ascending generation. The nomenclature for grandparents and grandchildren is of significance in this connection. In some classificatory systems, such as those of Australian tribes, the grandparents on the father's side are distinguished, in terminology and in behaviour, from those on the mother's side. But in many classificatory systems the generalising tendency results in all relatives of the generation being classed together as 'grandfathers' and 'grandmothers'.

We may note in passing that in classificatory terminologies of what Morgan called the Malayan type and Rivers the Hawaiian type, this generalising process is applied to other generations, so that all relatives of the parents' generation may be called 'father' and 'mother' and all those of one's own generation may be called 'brother' and 'sister'.

There are many kinship systems in various parts of the world that exhibit a structural principle which I shall speak of as the combination of alternate generations. This means that relatives of the grandfather's generation are thought of as combined with those of one's own generation over against the relatives of the parents' generation. The extreme development of this principle is to be seen in Australian tribes. I shall refer to this later.

While some systems emphasise the distinction of generations in their terminology or in their social structure, there are also systems in which relatives of two or more generations are included in a single category. So far as I have been able to make a comparative study, the various instances of this seem to fall into four classes.

In one class of instances the term of relationship does not carry a connotation referring to any particular generation and is used to mark off a sort of marginal region between non-relatives and those close relatives towards whom specific duties and over whom specific rights are recognised. The application of the term generally only implies that since the other person is recognised as a relative he or she must be treated with a certain general attitude of friendliness and not as a stranger. A good example is provided by the terms *ol-le-sotwa* and *en-e-sotwa* in Masai. I would include the English word 'cousin' in this class.

A second class of instances includes those in which there is conflict or inconsistency between the required attitude towards a particular relative and the required general attitude towards the generation to which he belongs. Thus in some tribes in South-East Africa there is conflict between the general rule that relatives of the first ascending generation are to be treated with marked respect and the custom of privileged disrespect towards the mother's brother. This is resolved by placing the mother's brother in the second ascending generation and calling him 'grandfather'. An opposite example is found in the Masai. A man is on terms of familiarity with all his relatives of the second descending generation, who are his 'grandchildren'. But it is felt that the relation between a man and the wife of his son's son should be one not of familiarity but of marked reserve. The inconsistency is resolved by a sort of legal fiction by which she is moved out of her generation and is called 'son's wife'.

A third class of instances are those resulting from the structural principle, already mentioned, whereby alternate generations are combined. Thus the father's father may be called 'older brother' and treated as such, and the son's son may be called 'younger brother'. Or a man and his son's son may be both included in a single category of relationship. There are many illustrations of this in Australian tribes and some elsewhere. An example from the Hopi will be given later.

The fourth class of instances includes the systems of Choctaw and Omaha type and also certain others, and in these the distinction between generations is set aside in favour of another principle, that of the unity of the lineage group.

Since the word lineage is often loosely used, I must explain what I mean by it. A patrilineal or agnatic lineage consists of a man and all his descendants through males for a determinate number of generations. Thus a minimal lineage includes three generations, and we can have lineages of four, five or n generations. A matrilineal lineage consists of a woman and all her descendants through females for a determinate number of generations. A lineage group consists of all the members of a lineage who are alive at a particular time. A clan, as I shall use the term here, is a group which, though not actually or demonstrably (by genealogies) a lineage, is regarded as being in some ways similar to a lineage. It normally consists of a number of actual lineages. Lineages, both patrilineal and matrilineal, exist implicitly in any kinship system, but it is only in some systems that the solidarity of the lineage group is an important feature in the social structure.

Where lineage groups are important we can speak of the solidarity of the group, which shows itself in the first instance in the internal relations between the members. By the principle of the unity of the lineage group I mean that for a person who does not belong to the lineage but is connected with it through some important bond of kinship or by marriage, its members constitute a single category, with a distinction within the category between males and females, and possibly other distinctions also. When this principle is applied in the terminology a person connected with a lineage from outside applies to its members, of one sex, through at least three generations, the same term of relationship. In its extreme development, as applied to the clan, a person connected with a clan in a certain way applies a single term of relationship to all members of the clan. An example will be given later.

The Omaha type of terminology may be illustrated by the system of the Fox Indians, which has been carefully studied by Dr. Sol Tax (1937). The features of the system that are relevant

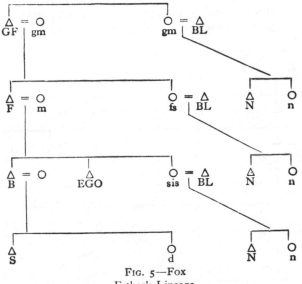

FIG. 5—FOX
Father's Lineage

to the argument are illustrated in the accompanying diagrams (Figs. 5–9).[1]

In his own patrilineal lineage a man distinguishes his relatives according to generation as 'grandfather' (GF), 'father' (F), 'older or younger brother' (B), 'son' (S), 'grandmother' (gm),

---

[1] In these diagrams △ represents a male person and ○ a female. The sign = connects a man and his wife and the lines descending from it indicate their children. The letters (capitals for males and lower case for females) stand for the kinship terms of a classificatory system, in which the same term is applied to a number of relatives. GF stands for the term used in referring to a grandfather, and similarly gm for grandmother; the others are F, father, m, mother, ms, mother's sister, fs, father's sister, MB, mother's brother, FL, father-in-law, ml, mother-in-law, B, brother, sis, sister, BL, brother-in-law, sl, sister-in-law, S, son, d, daughter, N, nephew (strictly speaking sister's son) n, niece (sister's daughter of a male) GC or gc, grandchild.

'father's sister' (fs), 'sister' (sis), and 'daughter' (d). I would draw your attention to the fact that he applies a single term, 'brother-in-law' (BL), irrespective of generation, to the husbands of the women of the lineage through three generations (his own and the two ascending generations), and that he calls the children of all these women by the same terms, 'nephew' (N) and 'niece' (n). Thus the women of Ego's own lineage of these generations constitute a sort of group, and Ego regards himself as standing in the same relationship to the children and husbands of all of them, although these persons belong to a number of different lineages.

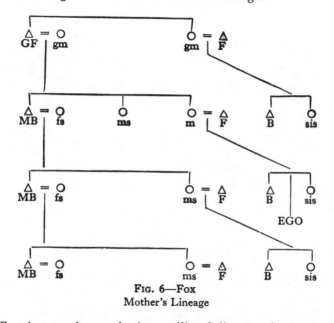

FIG. 6—Fox
Mother's Lineage

Turning to the mother's patrilineal lineage, it can be seen that a man calls his mother's father 'grandfather', but calls all the males of the lineage in the three succeeding generations 'mother's brother' (MB). Similarly he calls the women of these three generations, except his own mother, by a term translated as 'mother's sister' (ms). He applies the term 'father' (F) to the husbands of all the women of the lineage through four generations (including the husband of the mother's father's sister) and the children of all these women are his 'brothers' and 'sisters'. He is the son of one particular woman of a unified group, and the sons of the other women of the group are therefore his 'brothers'.

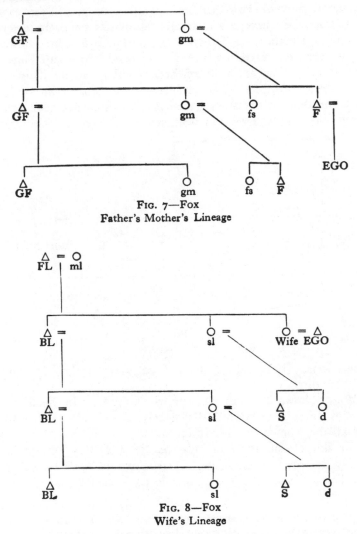

FIG. 7—Fox
Father's Mother's Lineage

FIG. 8—Fox
Wife's Lineage

In his father's mother's lineage Ego calls all the men and women throughout three generations 'grandfather' and 'grandmother'. The children of these 'grandmothers' are all his 'fathers' and 'father's sisters', irrespective of generation. In his mother's mother's lineage he also calls all the males 'grandfather' and the females 'grandmother', but I have not thought it necessary to include a figure to show this.

In his wife's lineage a man calls his wife's father by a term which we will translate 'father-in-law' (FL). It is a modification of the word for 'grandfather'.[1] The sons and brother's sons of the 'fathers-in-law' are 'brothers-in-law' (BL), and the daughters are 'sisters-in-law' (sl). The children of a 'brother-in-law' are again 'brother-in-law' and 'sister-in-law'. Thus these two terms are applied to the men and women of a lineage through three

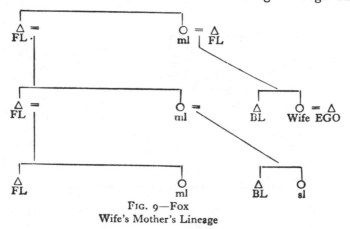

FIG. 9—Fox
Wife's Mother's Lineage

generations. The children of all these 'sisters-in-law' are 'sons' and 'daughters'.

Fig. 9 shows the lineage of the wife's mother. In this lineage, through three generations, all the men are called 'father-in-law' and all the women 'mother-in-law'.

Is the classification of relatives in the Fox terminology simply a matter of language, as some would have us believe? Dr. Tax's observations (1937) enable us to affirm that it is not. He writes:

The kinship terminology is applied to all known relatives (even in some cases where the genealogical relationship is not traceable) so that the entire tribe is divided into a small number of types of relationship

[1] The Fox terms for father-in-law and mother-in-law are modifications of the terms for grandfather and grandmother. In the Omaha tribe the terms for grandparents, without modification, are applied to the parents-in-law and to those who are called 'father-in-law' and 'mother-in-law' in the Fox tribe.

pairs. Each of these types carries with it a more or less distinct traditional pattern of behaviour. Generally speaking, the behaviour of close relatives follows the pattern in its greatest intensity, that of farther relatives in lesser degree ; but there are numerous cases where, for some reason, a pair of close relatives ' do not behave towards each other at all as they should'.

Dr. Tax goes on to define the patterns of behaviour for the various types of relationship. Thus the classification of relatives into categories, carried out by means of the nomenclature, or therein expressed, appears also in the regulation of social behaviour. There is good evidence that this is true of other systems of Omaha type, and, contrary to Kroeber's thesis, we may justifiably accept the hypothesis that it is probably true of all.

Charts similar to those given here for the Fox Indians can be made for other systems of the Omaha type. I think that a careful examination and comparison of the various systems shows that, while there are variations, there is a single structural principle underlying both the terminology and the associated social structure. A lineage of three (or sometimes more) generations is regarded as a unity. A person is related to certain lineages at particular points: in the Fox tribe to the lineages of his mother, his father's mother, his mother's mother, his wife, and his wife's mother. In each instance he regards himself as related to the succeeding generations of the lineage in the same way as he is related to the generation with which he is actually connected. Thus all the men of his mother's lineage are his 'mother's brothers', those of his 'grandmother's lineage his 'grandfathers', and those of his wife's lineage are his 'brothers-in-law'.

This structural principle of the unity of the patrilineal lineage is not a hypothetical cause of the terminology. It is a principle that is directly discoverable by comparative analysis of systems of this type; or, in other words, it is an immediate abstraction from observed facts.

Let us now examine a society in which the principle of the unity of the lineage group is applied to matrilineal lineages. For this I select the system of the Hopi Indians, which has been analysed in a masterly manner by Dr. Fred Eggan (1933) in a Ph.D. thesis which has, unfortunately, not yet been published.[1]

[1] The thesis, in a revised form, has now been published. Eggan: *Social Organisation of the Western Pueblos*. The University of Chicago Press, 1950.

The most significant features of the system are illustrated in the accompanying figures.

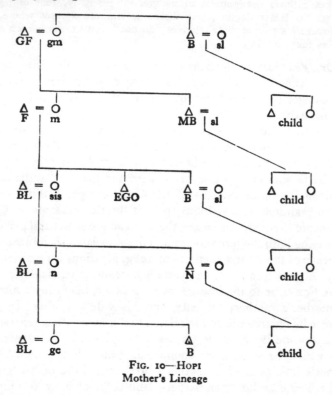

FIG. 10—HOPI
Mother's Lineage

A man's own lineage is, of course, that of his mother. He distinguishes the women of his lineage by generation as 'grandmother' (gm), 'mother' (m), 'sister' (sis), 'niece' (n), and 'grandchild' (gc). Amongst the men of his lineage he distinguishes his 'mother's brothers' (MB), 'brothers' (B) and 'nephews' (N). But he includes his mother's mother's brother and his sister's daughter's son in the same category as his brothers. The structural principle exhibited here is that already referred to as the combination of alternate generations. It should be noted that a man includes the children of all men of his own lineage, irrespective of generation, in the same category as his own children. Fig. 10 should be carefully compared with Fig. 5, for the Fox Indians, as the comparison is illuminating.

In his father's lineage a man calls all the male members through five generations 'father' and, with the exception of his father's mother (his 'grandmother'), he calls all the women 'father's sister'. The husband of any woman of the lineage is a 'grandfather', and the wife of any man of the lineage is a 'mother'.

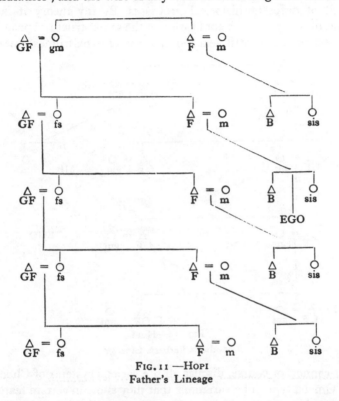

FIG. 11 —HOPI
Father's Lineage

The children of his 'fathers' are 'brothers' and 'sisters'. Fig. 11 should be carefully compared with Fig. 6.

In his mother's father's lineage a man calls all the · men and women through four generations 'grandfather' and 'grandmother'.

The Hopi do not regard a man as related to his father's father's lineage as a whole, and the principle is therefore not applied to it. He does call his own father's father 'grandfather'.

Dr. Eggan has shown that for the Hopi this classification of relatives into categories is not simply a matter of terminology or language, but is the basis of much of the regulation of social life.

What is, I think, clearly brought out by a comparison of the Fox and Hopi systems is their fundamental similarity. By the theories of conjectural history this similarity is the accidental result of different historical processes. By my theory it is the result of the systematic application of the same structural principle, in one instance to patrilineal and in the other to matrilineal lineages.

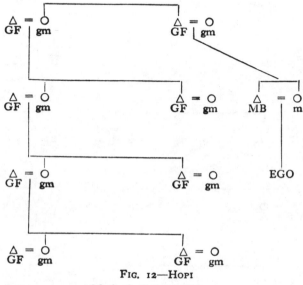

FIG. 12—HOPI
Mother's Father's Lineage

I cannot, of course, discuss all the various systems of Choctaw and Omaha type. The variations that they show in certain features are very interesting and important. If you wish to test my theory you will examine them, or some of them, for yourselves, and the easiest way to analyse any system is to reduce it to a set of lineage charts similar to those given here for the Fox and the Hopi. For any system such a set of charts will reveal the exact way in which the general principle of the unity of the lineage is applied. The manner of application varies somewhat, but the principle appears in each system of the type.

You will doubtless already have noticed that in these systems there are an extraordinary number of relatives of all ages to whom a man applies the terms 'grandfather' and 'grandmother'. There is, I believe, a good reason for this, which should be briefly indicated. It is a general rule in societies having a classificatory terminology that for all the various relatives included under a single term there is some more or less definite pattern of behaviour which is regarded as normal or appropriate. But there are important differences in this matter. In certain instances the pattern can be defined by reference to specific rights and duties, or by specific modes of behaviour. For example, in the Kariera tribe of Australia a man must practice the most careful avoidance of all women who are included in the category of 'father's sister', of whom there are very many and of whom his wife's mother is one. But in other instances all that the application of a term implies is a certain general attitude rather than any more specific relation. Within such a category there may be a specific jural or personal relation to a particular individual. In many classificatory systems the terms for grandfather and grandmother are used in this way, as implying a general attitude of friendliness, relatively free from restraint, towards all persons to whom they are applied. Grandparents and grandchildren are persons with whom one can be on free and easy terms. This is connected with an extremely widespread, indeed almost universal, way of organising the relation of alternate generations to one another.

In the Fox and Hopi systems all the members of the lineage of a grandparent are included in one category with the grandparents and the attitude that is appropriate towards a grandparent is extended to them. This does not imply any definite set of rights and duties, but only a certain general type of behaviour, of a kind that is regarded as appropriate towards relatives of the second ascending generation in a great many societies not belonging to the Choctaw and Omaha type.

I should have liked to discuss this further and to have dealt with those varieties of the Omaha type (such as the VaNdau) in which the mother's brother and the mother's brother's son are called 'grandfather'.   But I have only time to draw your attention to a special variety of the Choctaw type which is of great interest in this connection. The Cherokee were divided into seven matrilineal clans. In the father's clan a man called all the men and women of his father's and all succeeding generations 'father' and 'father's sister', and this clan and all its individual members had to be treated with great respect. A man could not marry a woman of his father's clan, and of course he could not marry into his own clan. In the clan of his father's father and that of his mother's father a man calls all the women of all generations 'grandmother'. He thus treats, not the lineage, but the whole clan as a unity, although a clan must have numbered many hundreds of persons. With any woman whom he calls 'grandmother' a man is allowed to be on free and easy terms. It was regarded as particullary appropriate that a man should marry a 'grandmother', i.e. a woman of his mother's father's or father's father's clan.

Let us now return to a brief consideration of the special customs of marriage that have been proposed as causes of the Choctaw and Omaha terminologies respectively. Marriage with the wife's brother's daughter is theoretically possible and does perhaps actually, though only occasionally, occur in some of the tribes having a system of Omaha type. Though there has been no marriage of this kind in the Fox tribe in recent times it is spoken of as a custom that formerly existed. We have seen that the marriage custom and the terminology fit consistently. The reason for this should now be easy to understand, for a little consideration will show that this particular marriage is an application of the principle of the unity of the lineage combined with the custom of the sororate or sororal polygyny. In the usual form of these customs we are concerned only with the principle of the unity of the sibling group. A man marries one woman of a particular sibling group and thereby establishes a particular relation to that group as a unity. The men are now permanently his brothers-in-law. Towards one of the women he stands in a marital relationship, and therefore towards the others he is conceived as standing in a similar relationship which may be called a quasi-marital relationship. For instance, they will regard his children as being their 'children'. Thus it is appropriate that when he takes a second wife, whether before or after the death of his first, he should marry his wife's sister.

I am quite aware that sororal polygyny can be attributed to the fact that co-wives who are sisters are less likely to quarrel seriously than two who are not so related, and that the sororate may similarly be justified by the fact that a stepmother is more likely to have proper affection for her stepchildren if they are the children of her own sister. These propositions do not conflict with my explanation but support it, for the principle of the unity of the sibling group as a structural principle is based on the solidarity of brothers and sisters within one family.

When we turn to systems of the Omaha type, we see that in place of the unity of the sibling group we now have a unity of the larger group, the lineage group of three generations. When a man marries one woman of this group he enters into a relation with the group as a unity, so that all the men are now his brothers-in-law, and he at the same time enters into what I have called a quasi-marital relationship with all the women, including not only his wife's sisters but also his wife's brother's daughters, and in some systems his wife's father's sisters. The group within which, by the principle of the sororate, he may take a second wife without entering into any new social bonds is thus extended to include his wife's brother's daughter; and the custom of marriage with this relative is simply the result of the application of the principle of the unity of the lineage in a system of patrilineal lineages. The special form of marriage and the special system of terminology, where they occur together, are directly connected by the fact that they are both applications of the one structural principle. There is no ground whatever for supposing that one is the historical cause of the other.

The matter is much more complex when we come to the custom of marriage with the mother's brother's widow. This form of marriage is found associated with terminology of the Choctaw type in the Banks Islands, in the tribes of North-West America and in the Twi-speaking Akim Abuakwa. But it is also found in many other places where that type of terminology does not exist. Nor is it correlated with matrilineal descent, for it is to be found in African societies that are markedly patrilineal in their institutions. There does not seem to be any theoretical explanation that will apply to all the known instances of this custom. There is no time on this occasion to discuss this subject by an analysis of instances.

I must briefly refer to another theory, which goes back to Durkheim's review (1898) of Kohler, and by which the Choctaw and Omaha terminologies are explained as being the direct result of emphasis on matrilineal and patrilineal descent respectively. We have, fortunately, a crucial instance to which we can refer in this connection, in the system of the Manus of the

Admiralty Islands, of which we have an excellent analysis by Dr. Margaret Mead (1934). The most important feature of the Manus system is the existence of patrilineal clans (called by Dr. Mead 'gentes') and the major emphasis is on patrilineal descent. The solidarity of the patrilineal lineage is exhibited in many features of the system, but not in the terminology. However this emphasis on patrilineal descent is to a certain extent counterbalanced by the recognition of matrilineal lineages, and this does appear in the terminology in features that make it similar to the Choctaw type. Thus a single term, *pinpapu*, is applied to the father's father's sister and to all her female descendants in the female line, and a single term, *patieye*, is applied to the father's sister and all her descendants in the female line. The unity of the matrilineal lineage is exhibited not only in the use of these terms, but also in the general social relation in which a person stands to the members of it, and is an important feature of the total complex kinship structure.

One of the strange ideas that has been, and I fear still is, current is that if a society recognises lineage at all it can only recognise either patrilineal or matrilineal lineage. I believe the origin of this absurd notion, and its persistence in the face of known facts, are the result of that early hypothesis of conjectural history that matrilineal descent is more primitive, i.e. historically earlier, than patrilineal descent. From the beginning of this century we have been acquainted with societies, such as the Herero, in which both matrilineal and patrilineal lineages are recognised; but these were dismissed as being 'transitional' forms. This is another example of the way in which attachment to the method and hypotheses of conjectural history prevents us from seeing things as they are. It was this, I think, that was responsible for Rivers' failing to discover that the Toda system recognises matrilineal lineage as well as patrilineal, and that the islands of the New Hebrides have a system of patrilineal groups in addition to their matrilineal moieties. Apart from the presuppositions of the method of conjectural history, there is no reason why a society should not build its kinship system on the basis of both patrilineal and matrilineal lineage, and we know that there are many societies that do exactly this.

In my criticism of the method of conjectural history I have insisted on the need for demonstration in anthropology. How then am I to demonstrate that my interpretation of the Choctaw-Omaha terminologies is the valid one? There are a number of possible arguments, but I have time for only one, which I hope may be considered sufficient. This is drawn from the existence of terminologies in which the unity of lineage or clan is exhibited, but which do not belong to either the Choctaw or the Omaha type; and I will mention one example, that of the Yaralde tribe of South Australia.

The Yaralde are divided into local patrilineal totemic clans. A man belongs to his father's clan, and we will consider his relation to three other clans: those of his mother, his father's mother and his mother's mother. The Yaralde, like many other Australian tribes, such as the Aranda, have four terms for grandparents, each of which is applied to both men and women. The term *maiya* is applied to the father's father and his brothers and sisters and to all members of a man's own clan of the second ascending generation. A second term, *ŋaitja*, is applied to the mother's father and his brothers and sisters, i.e. to persons of the mother's clan of the appropriate generation. The third term, *mutṣa*, is applied not only to the father's mother and her brothers and sisters, but to all persons belonging to the same clan, of all generations and of both sexes. The clan is spoken of collectively as a man's *mutṣaurui*. Similarly the term *baka* is applied to the mother's mother and her brothers and sisters and to all members of her clan of all generations, the clan being spoken of as a man's *bakaurui*. The structural principle here is that for the outside related person the clan constitutes a unity within which distinctions of generation are obliterated. Compare this with the treatment of lineages or clans of grandparents in the Fox, Hopi and Cherokee systems.

The Yaralde terminology for relatives in the mother's clan is shown in Fig. 13. It will be noted that the mother's brother's son and daughter are not called mother's brother (*wano*) and mother (*neŋko*) as in Omaha systems. But the son's son and daughter of the mother's brother are called 'mother's brother' and 'mother'. If we wish to explain this by a special form of marriage it would have to be marriage with the wife's brother's son's daughter. I am not certain that such a marriage would be prohibited by the Yaralde system, but I am quite sure that it is not a custom so regular as to be regarded as an effective cause in producing the

Yaralde terminology, and it would afford no explanation whatever
for the terminological unification of the clans of the father's
mother and the mother's mother. The structural principle involved is obviously that of the merging of alternate generations,
which is of such great importance in Australia, and which we have
also seen in the Hopi system. A system very similar to the Yaralde

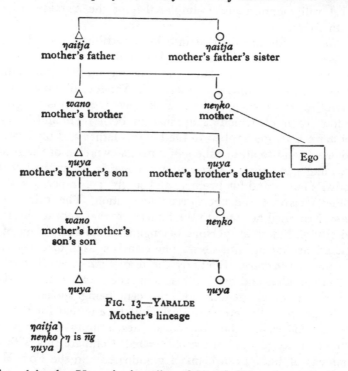

FIG. 13—YARALDE
Mother's lineage

ŋaitja
neŋko }ŋ is n̄g
ŋuya

is found in the Ungarinyin tribe of North-West Australia, but I
will not do more than refer to it.

Earlier in this address I said that I would try to show you that
the Omaha type of terminology is just as reasonable and fitting
in those social systems in which it is found as our own terminology
is in our system. I hope I have succeeded in doing this. On the
basis of the elementary family and the genealogical relationships
resulting therefrom, we English have constructed for ourselves a
certain kinship system which meets the necessities of an ordered
social life and is fairly self-consistent. The Fox or the Hopi have
on the same basis constructed a relatively self-consistent system

of a different type which provides for the needs of social cohesion in a different way and over a wider range. We understand the terminology in each instance as soon as we see it as part of an ordered system. The obvious connection of the Omaha terminology with the custom of marriage with the wife's brother's daughter is seen as a relation between two parts of a self-consistent working system, not as a relation of cause and effect.

If you ask the question, 'How is it that the Omaha (or any other of the tribes we have considered) have the system that they do?' then it is obvious that the method of structural analysis does not afford an answer. But neither does conjectural history. The proffered but purely hypothetical explanation of the Omaha terminology is that it resulted from the adoption of a certain unusual custom of marriage. This obviously gives us no explanation until we know why the Omaha and other tribes came to adopt this custom. The only possible way of answering the question why a particular society has the social system that it does have is by a detailed study of its history over a sufficient period, generally several centuries. For the tribes with which we are here concerned the materials for such a history are entirely lacking. This is, of course, very regrettable, but there is nothing that we can do about it. If you want to know how England comes to have its present system of constitutional monarchy and parliamentary government, you will go to the history books, which will give you the details of the growth of the system. If there were no records at all of this historical development, would the anthropologists think it worth while to spend their time in making conjectures as to what it might have been?

Even when there are historical records, they only enable us to discover how a particular system has grown out of a somewhat different particular system. Thus it would be possible to write a historical account of the changes of the kinship system of England during the past ten centuries. This would take us back to the Teutonic bilateral sib system, as exhibited in the institution of *wergild*. But we still should not know why the Teutonic peoples had this kind of system, while the Romans had a different system of agnatic lineages. The great value of history for a science of society is that it gives us materials for the study of how social systems change. In this respect conjectural history is absolutely worthless.

But if you ask, not how the English kinship system or the English political system came into existence, but how it works at the present time, that is a question that can be answered by research of the same kind as anthropological field-work, and historical considerations are relatively, if not absolutely, unimportant. Such knowledge of how social systems work is of great value for any understanding of human life. It often has been and still is neglected by anthropologists who consider it their principal task to write the history of peoples or institutions that have no history.

If you accept the analysis that I have given, but still wish to apply the method of conjectural history, what you have to conjecture is why all the tribes that have been enumerated elected to construct their kinship systems on the basis of the unity of the lineage.

What kind of results can we expect to obtain from the method of sociological analysis? Nothing, of course, that will be acceptable as significant by those who demand that any explanation of a social phenomenon must be a historical explanation, or by those who demand what is called psychological explanation, i.e. explanation in terms of the individual and his motives. I suggest that the results that we may reasonably expect are as follows:

1. It will enable us to make a systematic classification of kinship systems. Systematic classification is an essential in any scientific treatment of any class of phenomena, and such classification must be in terms of general properties.

2. It enables us to understand particular features of particular systems. It does this in two ways: (a) by revealing the particular feature as a part of an organised whole; (b) by showing that it is a special example of a recognisable class of phenomena. Thus I have tried to show that the Choctaw and Omaha terminologies belong to a class which also includes the Yaralde terminology, and that these are all special applications of the general principle of the solidarity and continuity of the lineage, which appears in many other forms in a great number of different societies.

3. It is the only method by which we can hope ultimately to arrive at valid generalisations about the nature of human society, i.e. about the universal characteristics of all societies, past, present, and future. It is, of course, such

generalisations that are meant when we speak of sociological laws.

In the method of conjectural history single problems are usually considered in isolation. On the other hand, the method of structural analysis aims at a general theory, and a great many different facts and problems are, therefore, considered together and in relation to one another. It is obvious that in this address, inordinately long as it has been, I have only been able to touch on a few points in the general theory of kinship structure. I have dealt briefly with one or two other points in earlier publications. That particular part of the general theory which has occupied us today may be said to be the theory of the establishment of type relationships. I have mentioned the tendency present in many societies to set up a type relationship between a person and all his relatives of the parents' generation, and the even more marked tendency to establish a type relationship, usually one of free and easy behaviour, towards the relatives of the grandparents' generation. I have not tried to deal with this except incidentally. The major part of the exposition has been concerned with two structural principles which are themselves examples of a more general structural principle or class of principles. By the principle of the unity of the sibling group a type relationship is set up between a given person and all the members of a sibling group to which he is related in a certain way. It is by reference to this principle, I hold, that we must interpret the classificatory terminology and such customs as the sororate and levirate. By the principle of the unity of the lineage group a type relationship is set up between a given person and all the members of a lineage group to which he is related in a certain way. It is by reference to this principle, I hold, that we must interpret the terminologies of the Fox, the Hopi and the Yaralde, and other similar systems in many scattered parts of the world.

If you will take the time to study two or three hundred kinship systems from all parts of the world you will be impressed, I think, by the great diversity that they exhibit. But you will also be impressed by the way in which some particular feature, such as an Omaha type of terminology, reappears in scattered and widely spread regions. To reduce this diversity to some sort of order is the task of analysis, and by its means we can, I believe, find, beneath the diversities, a limited number of general principles

Kinship analysis do one means of looking @ social structure.

applied and combined in various ways. Lineage solidarity in one form or another is found in a majority of kinship systems. There is nothing at all surprising in the fact that terminologies of the Choctaw and Omaha type, in which it finds what may be called an extreme development, should be encountered in separated regions of America, Africa, Asia and Oceania, in many different families of languages, and in association with many different types of 'culture'.

Last year I explained in general terms how I conceive the study of social structure (Radcliffe-Brown, 1940b). In this address, by means of a particular example, I have tried to show you something of the nature of a certain method of investigation. But do not think that this method can be applied only to the study of kinship. It is applicable in one way or another to all social phenomena, for it is simply the method of abstractive generalisation by the comparison of instances, which is the characteristic method of the inductive sciences.

'Why all this fuss about method?' some of you may perhaps ask. We cannot reach agreement as to the validity or the value of results unless we first reach some agreement as to objectives and the proper methods of attaining them. In the other natural sciences there is such agreement; in social anthropology there is not. Where we disagree, it should be the first purpose of discussion to define as precisely as possible the ground of difference. I have put my case before you, without, I hope, any unfairness towards those with whom I disagree. It is for you to judge which of the two methods that I have compared is most likely to provide that kind of scientific understanding of the nature of human society which it is the accepted task of the social anthropologist to provide for the guidance of mankind.

REFERENCES

Durkheim, E. (1898). 'Zur Urgeschichte der Ehe, Prof. J. Kohler', Analyses III, La Famille, *Année Sociologique*, Vol. I, pp. 306–319.

Eggan, F. (1933). 'The Kinship System and Social Organisation of the Western Pueblos with Special Reference to the Hopi', *Ph.D. thesis*, University of Chicago.

Gifford, E. W. (1916). 'Miwok Moieties', *Arch. and Ethn. Publ., Univ. California*, Vol. XII, No. 4.

Gilbert, William H., Jr. (1937). 'Eastern Cherokee Social Organisation', in *Social Anthropology of North American Tribes* (ed. Fred Eggan). Chicago University Press, pp. 283–338.

Kohler, J. (1897). 'Zur Urgeschichte der Ehe', *Zeitschrift für Vergleichende Rechtswissenschaft* (Stuttgart), Bd. 11.
Kroeber, A. L. (1909). 'Classificatory Systems of Relationship', *J. R. Anthrop. Inst.*, Vol. XXXIX, pp. 77–84.
— (1917). 'California Kinship Systems', *Arch. and Ethn. Publ. Univ. California*, Vol. XII, No. 9.
Mead, Margaret (1934). 'Kinship in the Admiralty Islands', *Anthrop. Papers Amer. Mus. Nat. History*, Vol. XXXIV, Pt. II, pp. 181–358.
M'Lennan, John F. (1865). *Primitive Marriage*. Edinburgh: Adam & Charles Black.
Morgan, Lewis H. (1871). 'The Systems of Consanguinity and Affinity', *Smithsonian Institution Contributions to Knowledge*, Vol. XVII.
— (1877). *Ancient Society or Researches in the Lines of Human Progress from Savagery to Civilisation*. London: Macmillan; New York: Henry Holt.
Opler, M. E. (1937a). 'Chiricahua Apache Social Organisation', in *Social Anthropology of North American Tribes* (ed. Fred Eggan), Chicago University Press.
— (1937b). 'Apache Data Concerning the Relation of Kinship Terminology to Social Classification', *Amer. Anthrop.*, Vol. XXXIX, pp. 201–212.
Radcliffe-Brown, A. R. (1918). 'Notes on the Social Organisation of Australian Tribes', Pt. I, *J. R. Anthrop. Inst.*, Vol. XLVIII, pp. 222–253.
— (1924). 'The Mother's Brother in South Africa', *South African J. Science*, Vol. XXI.
— (1930–31). 'The Social Organisation of Australian Tribes', Pts. I–III, *Oceania*, Vol. I, pp. 34–63, 206–246, 322–341, 426–456.
— (1935). 'Patrilineal and Matrilineal Succession', *Iowa Law Review*, Vol. XX, No. 2.
— (1940a). 'On Joking Relationships', *Africa*, Vol. XIII, No. 3, pp. 195–210.
— (1940b). 'On Social Structure', *J. R. Anthrop. Inst.*, Vol. LXX, pp. 1–12.
Rivers, W. H. R. (1907). 'On the Origin of the Classificatory System of Relationship', in *Anthropological Essays Presented to Edward Burnett Tylor*. Oxford: Clarendon Press. (Reprinted in *Social Organisation*. London: Kegan Paul, 1924, App. 1, pp. 175–192.)
— (1914a). *History of Melanesian Society*. Cambridge University Press.
— (1914b). *Kinship and Social Organisation*. London: London School of Economics.
Seligman, Brenda Z. (1917). 'The Relationship Systems of the Nandi Masai and Thonga', *Man*, Vol. XVII, 46.
Starcke, C. N. (1889). *The Primitive Family* (The International Scientific Series, Vol. LXVI). London: Kegan Paul.
Stewart, Dugald (1795). Introduction to *Essays of Adam Smith*.
Tax, Sol (1937). 'The Social Organisation of the Fox Indians', in *Social Anthropology of North American Tribes* (ed. Fred Eggan). Chicago University Press, pp. 241–282.

CHAPTER IV

ON JOKING RELATIONSHIPS[1]

THE publication of Mr. F. J. Pedler's note[2] on what are called 'joking relationships', following on two other papers on the same subject by Professor Henri Labouret[3] and Mademoiselle Denise Paulme,[4] suggests that some general theoretical discussion of the nature of these relationships may be of interest to readers of *Africa*.[5]

What is meant by the term 'joking relationship' is a relation between two persons in which one is by custom permitted, and in some instances required, to tease or make fun of the other, who in turn is required to take no offence. It is important to distinguish two main varieties. In one the relation is symmetrical; each of the two persons teases or makes fun of the other. In the other variety the relation is asymmetrical; A jokes at the expense of B and B accepts the teasing good humouredly but without retaliating; or A teases B as much as he pleases and B in return teases A only a little. There are many varieties in the form of this relationship in different societies. In some instances the joking or teasing is only verbal, in others it includes horse-play; in some the joking includes elements of obscenity, in others not.

Standardised social relationships of this kind are extremely widespread, not only in Africa but also in Asia, Oceania and North America. To arrive at a scientific understanding of the phenomenon it is necessary to make a wide comparative study. Some material for this now exists in anthropological literature, though by no means all that could be desired, since it is unfortunately still only rarely that such relationships are observed and described as exactly as they might be.

[1] Reprinted from *Africa*, Vol. XIII, No. 3, 1940, pp. 195–210.
[2] 'Joking Relationships in East Africa', *Africa*, Vol. XIII, p. 170.
[3] 'La Parenté à Plaisanteries en Afrique Occidentale', *Africa*, Vol. II, p. 244.
[4] 'Parenté à Plaisanteries et Alliance par le Sang en Afrique Occidentale', *Africa*, Vol. XII, p. 433.
[5] Professor Marcel Mauss has published a brief theoretical discussion of the subject in the *Annuaire de l'École Pratique des Hautes Études, Section des Sciences religieuses*, 1927–8. It is also dealt with by Dr. F. Eggan in *Social Anthropology of North American Tribes*, 1937, pp. 75–81.

The joking relationship is a peculiar combination of friendliness and antagonism. The behaviour is such that in any other social context it would express and arouse hostility; but it is not meant seriously and must not be taken seriously. There is a pretence of hostility and a real friendliness. To put it in another way, the relationship is one of permitted disrespect. Thus any complete theory of it must be part of, or consistent with, a theory of the place of respect in social relations and in social life generally. But this is a very wide and very important sociological problem; for it is evident that the whole maintenance of a social order depends upon the appropriate kind and degree of respect being shown towards certain persons, things and ideas or symbols.

Examples of joking relationships between relatives by marriage are very commonly found in Africa and in other parts of the world. Thus Mademoiselle Paulme[1] records that among the Dogon a man stands in a joking relationship to his wife's sisters and their daughters. Frequently the relationship holds between a man and both the brothers and sisters of his wife. But in some instances there is a distinction whereby a man is on joking terms with his wife's younger brothers and sisters but not with those who are older than she is. This joking with the wife's brothers and sisters is usually associated with a custom requiring extreme respect, often partial or complete avoidance, between a son-in-law and his wife's parents.[2]

The kind of structural situation in which the associated customs of joking and avoidance are found may be described as follows. A marriage involves a readjustment of the social structure whereby the woman's relations with her family are greatly modified and she enters into a new and very close relation with her husband. The latter is at the same time brought into a special relation with his wife's family, to which, however, he is an outsider. For the sake of brevity, though at the risk of over-simplification, we will consider only the husband's relation to his wife's family. The relation can be described as involving both attachment and separation, both social conjunction and social disjunction, if I

---

[1] *Africa*, Vol. XII, p. 438.
[2] Those who are not familiar with these widespread customs will find descriptions in Junod, *Life of a South African Tribe*, Neuchâtel, Vol. I, pp. 229–37, and in *Social Anthropology of North American Tribes*, edited by F. Eggan, Chicago, 1937, pp. 55–7.

may use the terms. The man has his own definite position in the social structure, determined for him by his birth into a certain family, lineage or clan. The great body of his rights and duties and the interests and activities that he shares with others are the result of his position. Before the marriage his wife's family are outsiders for him as he is an outsider for them. This constitutes a social disjunction which is not destroyed by the marriage. The social conjunction results from the continuance, though in altered form, of the wife's relation to her family, their continued interest in her and in her children. If the wife were really bought and paid for, as ignorant persons say that she is in Africa, there would be no place for any permanent close relation of a man with his wife's family. But though slaves can be bought, wives cannot.

Social disjunction implies divergence of interests and therefore the possibility of conflict and hostility, while conjunction requires the avoidance of strife. How can a relation which combines the two be given a stable, ordered form? There are two ways of doing this. One is to maintain between two persons so related an extreme mutual respect and a limitation of direct personal contact. This is exhibited in the very formal relations that are, in so many societies, characteristic of the behaviour of a son-in law on the one side and his wife's father and mother on the other. In its most extreme form there is complete avoidance of any social contact between a man and his mother-in-law.

This avoidance must not be mistaken for a sign of hostility. One does, of course, if one is wise, avoid having too much to do with one's enemies, but that is quite a different matter. I once asked an Australian native why he had to avoid his mother-in-law, and his reply was, 'Because she is my best friend in the world; she has given me my wife'. The mutual respect between son-in-law and parents-in-law is a mode of friendship. It prevents conflict that might arise through divergence of interest.

The alternative to this relation of extreme mutual respect and restraint is the joking relationship, one, that is, of mutual disrespect and licence. Any serious hostility is prevented by the playful antagonism of teasing, and this in its regular repetition is a constant expression or reminder of that social disjunction which is one of the essential components of the relation, while the social conjunction is maintained by the friendliness that takes no offence at insult.

The discrimination within the wife's family between those who have to be treated with extreme respect and those with whom it is a duty to be disrespectful is made on the basis of generation and sometimes of seniority within the generation. The usual respected relatives are those of the first ascending generation, the wife's mother and her sisters, the wife's father and his brothers, sometimes the wife's mother's brother. The joking relatives are those of a person's own generation; but very frequently a distinction of seniority within the generation is made; a wife's older sister or brother may be respected while those younger will be teased.

In certain societies a man may be said to have relatives by marriage long before he marries and indeed as soon as he is born into the world. This is provided by the institution of the required or preferential marriage. We will, for the sake of brevity, consider only one kind of such organisations. In many societies it is regarded as preferable that a man should marry the daughter of his mother's brother; this is a form of the custom known as cross-cousin marriage. Thus his female cousins of this kind, or all those women whom by the classificatory system he classifies as such, are potential wives for him, and their brothers are his potential brothers-in-law. Among the Ojibwa Indians of North America, the Chiga of Uganda, and in Fiji and New Caledonia, as well as elsewhere, this form of marriage is found and is accompanied by a joking relationship between a man and the sons and daughters of his mother's brother. To quote one instance of these, the following is recorded for the Ojibwa. 'When cross-cousins meet they must try to embarrass one another. They "joke" one another, making the most vulgar allegations, by their standards as well as ours. But being "kind" relations, no one can take offence. Cross-cousins who do not joke in this way are considered boorish, as not playing the social game.'[1]

The joking relationship here is of fundamentally the same kind as that already discussed. It is established before marriage and is continued, after marriage, with the brothers- and sisters-in-law.

In some parts of Africa there are joking relationships that have nothing to do with marriage. Mr. Pedler's note, mentioned above, refers to a joking relationship between two distinct tribes, the

[1] Ruth Landes in Mead, *Co-operation and Competition among Primitive Peoples*, 1937, p. 103.

Sukuma and the Zaramu, and in the evidence it was stated that there was a similar relation between the Sukuma and the Zigua and between the Ngoni and the Bemba. The woman's evidence suggests that this custom of rough teasing exists in the Sukuma tribe between persons related by marriage, as it does in so many other African tribes.[1]

While a joking relationship between two tribes is apparently rare, and certainly deserves, as Mr. Pedler suggests, to be carefully investigated, a similar relationship between clans has been observed in other parts of Africa. It is described by Professor Labouret and Mademoiselle Paulme in the articles previously mentioned, and amongst the Tallensi it has been studied by Dr. Fortes, who will deal with it in a forthcoming publication.[2]

The two clans are not, in these instances, specially connected by intermarriage. The relation between them is an alliance involving real friendliness and mutual aid combined with an appearance of hostility.

The general structural situation in these instances seems to be as follows. The individual is a member of a certain defined group, a clan, for example, within which his relations to others are defined by a complex set of rights and duties, referring to all the major aspects of social life, and supported by definite sanctions. There may be another group outside his own which is so linked with his as to be the field of extension of jural and moral relations of the same general kind. Thus, in East Africa, as we learn from Mr. Pedler's note, the Zigua and the Zaramu do not joke with one another because a yet closer bond exists between them since they are *ndugu* (brothers). But beyond the field within which social relations are thus defined there lie other groups with which, since

---

[1] Incidentally it may be said that it was hardly satisfactory for the magistrate to establish a precedent whereby the man, who was observing what was a permitted and may even have been an obligatory custom, was declared guilty of common assault, even with extenuating circumstances. It seems quite possible that the man may have committed a breach of etiquette in teasing the woman in the presence of her mother's brother, for in many parts of the world it is regarded as improper for two persons in a joking relationship to tease one another (particularly if any obscenity is involved) in the presence of certain relatives of either of them. But the breach of etiquette would still not make it an assault. A little knowledge of anthropology would have enabled the magistrate, by putting the appropriate questions to the witnesses, to have obtained a fuller understanding of the case and all that was involved in it.

[2] Fortes, M., *The Dynamics of Clanship among the Tallensi*. Oxford University Press, 1945.

they are outsiders to the individual's own group, the relation involves possible or actual hostility. In any fixed relations between the members of two such groups the separateness of the groups must be recognised. It is precisely this separateness which is not merely recognised but emphasised when a joking relationship is established. The show of hostility, the perpetual disrespect, is a continual expression of that social disjunction which is an essential part of the whole structural situation, but over which, without destroying or even weakening it, there is provided the social conjunction of friendliness and mutual aid.

The theory that is here put forward, therefore, is that both the joking relationship which constitutes an alliance between clans or tribes, and that between relatives by marriage, are modes of organising a definite and stable system of social behaviour in which conjunctive and disjunctive components, as I have called them, are maintained and combined.

To provide the full evidence for this theory by following out its implications and examining in detail its application to different instances would take a book rather than a short article. But some confirmation can perhaps be offered by a consideration of the way in which respect and disrespect appear in various kinship relations, even though nothing more can be attempted than a very brief indication of a few significant points.

In studying a kinship system it is possible to distinguish the different relatives by reference to the kind and degree of respect that is paid to them.[1] Although kinship systems vary very much in their details there are certain principles which are found to be very widespread. One of them is that by which a person is required to show a marked respect to relatives belonging to the generation immediately preceding his own. In a majority of societies the father is a relative to whom marked respect must be shown. This is so even in many so-called matrilineal societies, i.e. those which are organised into matrilineal clans or lineages. One can very frequently observe a tendency to extend this attitude of respect to all relatives of the first ascending generation and, further, to persons who are not relatives. Thus in those

[1] See, for example, the kinship systems described in *Social Anthropology of North American Tribes*, edited by Fred Eggan, University of Chicago Press, 1937; and Margaret Mead, 'Kinship in the Admiralty Islands', *Anthropological Papers of the American Museum of Natural History*, Vol. XXXIV, pp. 243–56.

tribes of East Africa that are organised into age-sets a man is required to show special respect to all men of his father's age-set and to their wives.

The social function of this is obvious. The social tradition is handed down from one generation to the next. For the tradition to be maintained it must have authority behind it. The authority is therefore normally recognised as possessed by members of the preceding generation and it is they who exercise discipline. As a result of this the relation between persons of the two generations usually contains an element of inequality, the parents and those of their generation being in a position of superiority over the children who are subordinate to them. The unequal relation between a father and his son is maintained by requiring the latter to show respect to the former. The relation is asymmetrical.

When we turn to the relation of an individual to his grandparents and their brothers and sisters we find that in the majority of human societies relatives of the second ascending generation are treated with very much less respect than those of the first ascending generation, and instead of a marked inequality there is a tendency to approximate to a friendly equality.

Considerations of space forbid any full discussion of this feature of social structure, which is one of very great importance. There are many instances in which the grandparents and their grandchildren are grouped together in the social structure in opposition to their children and parents. An important clue to the understanding of the subject is the fact that in the flow of social life through time, in which men are born, become mature and die, the grandchildren replace their grandparents.

In many societies there is an actual joking relationship, usually of a relatively mild kind, between relatives of alternate generations. Grandchildren make fun of their grandparents and of those who are called grandfather and grandmother by the classificatory system of terminology, and these reply in kind.

Grandparents and grandchildren are united by kinship; they are separated by age and by the social difference that results from the fact that as the grandchildren are in process of entering into full participation in the social life of the community the grandparents are gradually retiring from it. Important duties towards his relatives in his own and even more in his parents' generation impose upon an individual many restraints; but with those of the second ascending generation, his grandparents and collateral relatives, there can be, and usually is, established a relationship of simple friendliness relatively free from restraint. In this instance also, it is suggested, the joking relationship is a method of ordering a relation which combines social conjunction and disjunction.

This thesis could, I believe, be strongly supported if not demonstrated by considering the details of these relationships. There is space for only one illustrative point. A very common form of joke in this connection is for the grandchild to pretend that he wishes to marry the grandfather's wife, or that he intends to do so when his grandfather dies, or to treat her as already being his wife. Alternatively the grandfather may pretend that the wife of his grandchild is, or might be, his wife.[1] The point of the joke is the pretence at ignoring the difference of age between the grandparent and the grandchild.

In various parts of the world there are societies in which a sister's son teases and otherwise behaves disrespectfully towards his mother's brother. In these instances the joking relationship seems generally to be asymmetrical. For example the nephew may take his uncle's property but not vice versa; or, as amongst the Nama Hottentots, the nephew may take a fine beast from his uncle's herd and the uncle in return takes a wretched beast from that of the nephew.[2]

The kind of social structure in which this custom of privileged disrespect to the mother's brother occurs in its most marked forms, for example the Thonga of South-East Africa, Fiji and Tonga in the Pacific, and the Central Siouan tribes of North America, is characterised by emphasis on patrilineal lineage and a marked distinction between relatives through the father and relatives through the mother.

In a former publication[3] I offered an interpretation of this custom of privileged familiarity towards the mother's brother. Briefly it is as follows. For the continuance of a social system children require to be cared for and to be trained. Their care demands affectionate and unselfish devotion; their training

---

[1] For examples see Labouret, *Les Tribus du Rameau Lobi*, 1931, p. 248, and Sarat Chandra Roy, *The Oraons of Chota Nagpur*, Ranchi, 1915, pp. 352–4.

[2] A. Winifred Hoernlé, 'Social Organisation of the Nama Hottentot'; *American Anthropologist*, N.S., Vol. XXVII, 1925, pp. 1–24.

[3] 'The Mother's Brother in South Africa', *South African Journal of Science*, Vol. XXI, 1924. See Chapter I.

requires that they shall be subjected to discipline. In the societies with which we are concerned there is something of a division of function between the parents and other relatives on the two sides. The control and discipline are exercised chiefly by the father and his brothers and generally also by his sisters; these are relatives who must be respected and obeyed. It is the mother who is primarily responsible for the affectionate care; the mother and her brothers and sisters are therefore relatives who can be looked to for assistance and indulgence. The mother's brother is called 'male mother' in Tonga and in some South African tribes.

I believe that this interpretation of the special position of the mother's brother in these societies has been confirmed by further field work since I wrote the article referred to. But I was quite aware at the time it was written that the discussion and interpretation needed to be supplemented so as to bring them into line with a general theory of the social functions of respect and disrespect.

The joking relationship with the mother's brother seems to fit well with the general theory of such relationships here outlined. A person's most important duties and rights attach him to his paternal relatives, living and dead. It is to his patrilineal lineage or clan that he belongs. For the members of his mother's lineage he is an outsider, though one in whom they have a very special and tender interest. Thus here again there is a relation in which there is both attachment, or conjunction, and separation, or disjunction, between the two persons concerned.

But let us remember that in this instance the relation is asymmetrical.[1] The nephew is disrespectful and the uncle accepts the disrespect. There is inequality and the nephew is the superior. This is recognised by the natives themselves. Thus in Tonga it is said that the sister's son is a 'chief' (*eiki*) to his mother's brother, and Junod[2] quotes a Thonga native as saying 'The uterine nephew is a chief! He takes any liberty he likes with his maternal uncle'. Thus the joking relationship with the uncle does not merely annul the usual relation between the two generations, it reverses it. But while the superiority of the father and the

---

[1] There are some societies in which the relation between a mother's brother and a sister's son is approximately symmetrical, and therefore one of equality. This seems to be so in the Western Islands of Torres Straits, but we have no information as to any teasing or joking, though it is said that each of the two relatives may take the property of the other.

[2] *Life of a South African Tribe*, Vol. I, p. 255.

father's sister is exhibited in the respect that is shown to them, the nephew's superiority to his mother's brother takes the opposite form of permitted disrespect.

It has been mentioned that there is a widespread tendency to feel that a man should show respect towards, and treat as social superiors, his relatives in the generation preceding his own, and the custom of joking with, and at the expense of, the maternal uncle clearly conflicts with this tendency. This conflict between principles of behaviour helps us to understand what seems at first sight a very extraordinary feature of the kinship terminology of the Thonga tribe and the VaNdau tribe in South-East Africa. Amongst the Thonga, although there is a term *malume* (= male mother) for the mother's brother, this relative is also, and perhaps more frequently, referred to as a grandfather (*kokwana*) and he refers to his sister's son as his grandchild (*ntukulu*). In the VaNdau tribe the mother's brother and also the mother's brother's son are called 'grandfather' (*tetekulu*, literally 'great father') and their wives are called 'grandmother' (*mbiya*), while the sister's son and the father's sister's son are called 'grandchild' (*muzukulu*).

This apparently fantastic way of classifying relatives can be interpreted as a sort of legal fiction whereby the male relatives of the mother's lineage are grouped together as all standing towards an individual in the same general relation. Since this relation is one of privileged familiarity on the one side, and solicitude and indulgence on the other, it is conceived as being basically the one appropriate for a grandchild and a grandfather. This is indeed in the majority of human societies the relationship in which this pattern of behaviour most frequently occurs. By this legal fiction the mother's brother ceases to belong to the first ascending generation, of which it is felt that the members ought to be respected.

It may be worth while to justify this interpretation by considering another of the legal fictions of the VaNdau terminology. In all these south-eastern Bantu tribes both the father's sister and the sister, particularly the elder sister, are persons who must be treated with great respect. They are also both of them members of a man's own patrilineal lineage. Amongst the VaNdau the father's sister is called 'female father' (*tetadji*) and so also is the sister.[1]

---

[1] For the kinship terminology of the VaNdau see Boas, 'Das Verwandtschafts-system der Vandau', in *Zeitschrift für Ethnologie*, 1922, pp. 41–51.

Thus by the fiction of terminological classification the sister is placed in the father's generation, the one that appropriately includes persons to whom one must exhibit marked respect.

In the south-eastern Bantu tribes there is assimilation of two kinds of joking relatives, the grandfather and the mother's brother. It may help our understanding of this to consider an example in which the grandfather and the brother-in-law are similarly grouped together. The Cherokee Indians of North America, probably numbering at one time about 20,000, were divided into seven matrilineal clans.[1] A man could not marry a woman of his own clan or of his father's clan. Common membership of the same clan connects him with his brothers and his mother's brothers. Towards his father and all his relatives in his father's clan of his own or his father's generation he is required by custom to show a marked respect. He applies the kinship term for 'father' not only to his father's brothers but also to the sons of his father's sisters. Here is another example of the same kind of fiction as described above; the relatives of his own generation whom he is required to respect and who belong to his father's matrilineal lineage are spoken of as though they belonged to the generation of his parents. The body of his immediate kindred is included in these two clans, that of his mother and his father. To the other clans of the tribe he is in a sense an outsider. But with two of them he is connected, namely with the clans of his two grandfathers, his father's father and his mother's father. He speaks of all the members of these two clans, of whatever age, as 'grandfathers' and 'grandmothers'. He stands in a joking relationship with all of them. When a man marries he must respect his wife's parents but jokes with her brothers and sisters.

The interesting and critical feature is that it is regarded as particularly appropriate that a man should marry a woman whom he calls 'grandmother', i.e. a member of his father's father's clan or his mother's father's clan. If this happens his wife's brothers and sisters, whom he continues to tease, are amongst those whom he previously teased as his 'grandfathers' and 'grandmothers'. This is analogous to the widely spread organisation in which a man has a joking relationship with the children of his mother's brother and is expected to marry one of the daughters.

[1] For an account of the Cherokee see Gilbert, in *Social Anthropology of North American Tribes*, pp. 285-338.

It ought perhaps to be mentioned that the Cherokee also have a one-sided joking relationship in which a man teases his father's sister's husband. The same custom is found in Mota of the Bank Islands. In both instances we have a society organised on a matrilineal basis in which the mother's brother is respected, the father's sister's son is called 'father' (so that the father's sister's husband is the father of a 'father'), and there is a special term for the father's sister's husband. Further observation of the societies in which this custom occurs is required before we can be sure of its interpretation. I do not remember that it has been reported from any part of Africa.

What has been attempted in this paper is to define in the most general and abstract terms the kind of structural situation in which we may expect to find well-marked joking relationships. We have been dealing with societies in which the basic social structure is provided by kinship. By reason of his birth or adoption into a certain position in the social structure an individual is connected with a large number of other persons. With some of them he finds himself in a definite and specific jural relation, i.e. one which can be defined in terms of rights and duties. Who these persons will be and what will be the rights and duties depend on the form taken by the social structure. As an example of such a specific jural relation we may take that which normally exists between a father and son, or an elder brother and a younger brother. Relations of the same general type may be extended over a considerable range to all the members of a lineage or a clan or an age-set. Besides these specific jural relations which are defined not only negatively but also positively, i.e. in terms of things that must be done as well as things that must not, there are general jural relations which are expressed almost entirely in terms of prohibitions and which extend throughout the whole political society. It is forbidden to kill or wound other persons or to take or destroy their property. Besides these two classes of social relations there is another, including many very diverse varieties, which can perhaps be called relations of alliance or consociation. For example, there is a form of alliance of very great importance in many societies, in which two persons or two groups are connected by an exchange of gifts or services.[1] Another example is provided

[1] See Mauss, 'Essai sur le Don', *Année Sociologique*, Nouvelle Série, tome I, pp. 30–186.

by the institution of blood-brotherhood which is so widespread in Africa.

The argument of this paper has been intended to show that the joking relationship is one special form of alliance in this sense. An alliance by exchange of goods and services may be associated with a joking relationship, as in the instance recorded by Professor Labouret.[1] Or it may be combined with the custom of avoidance. Thus in the Andaman Islands the parents of a man and the parents of his wife avoid all contact with each other and do not speak; at the same time it is the custom that they should frequently exchange presents through the medium of the younger married couple. But the exchange of gifts may also exist without either joking or avoidance, as in Samoa, in the exchange of gifts between the family of a man and the family of the woman he marries or the very similar exchange between a chief and his 'talking chief'.

So also in an alliance by blood-brotherhood there may be a joking relationship as amongst the Zande;[2] and in the somewhat similar alliance formed by exchange of names there may also be mutual teasing. But in alliances of this kind there may be a relation of extreme respect and even of avoidance. Thus in the Yaralde and neighbouring tribes of South Australia two boys belonging to communities distant from one another, and therefore more or less hostile, are brought into an alliance by the exchange of their respective umbilical cords. The relationship thus established is a sacred one; the two boys may never speak to one another. But when they grow up they enter upon a regular exchange of gifts, which provides the machinery for a sort of commerce between the two groups to which they belong.

Thus the four modes of alliance or consociation, (1) through intermarriage, (2) by exchange of goods or services, (3) by blood-brotherhood or exchanges of names or sacra, and (4) by the joking relationship, may exist separately or combined in several different ways. The comparative study of these combinations presents a number of interesting but complex problems. The facts recorded from West Africa by Professor Labouret and Mademoiselle Paulme afford us valuable material. But a good deal more intensive

[1] *Africa*, Vol. II, p. 245.
[2] Evans-Pritchard, 'Zande Blood-brotherhood', *Africa*, Vol. VI, 1933, pp. 369–401.

field research is needed before these problems of social structure can be satisfactorily dealt with.

What I have called relations by alliance need to be compared with true contractual relations. The latter are specific jural relations entered into by two persons or two groups, in which either party has definite positive obligations towards the other, and failure to carry out the obligations is subject to a legal sanction. In an alliance by blood-brotherhood there are general obligations of mutual aid, and the sanction for the carrying out of these, as shown by Dr. Evans-Pritchard, is of a kind that can be called magical or ritual. In the alliance by exchange of gifts failure to fulfil the obligation to make an equivalent return for a gift received breaks the alliance and substitutes a state of hostility and may also cause a loss of prestige for the defaulting party. Professor Mauss[1] has argued that in this kind of alliance also there is a magical sanction, but it is very doubtful if such is always present, and even when it is it may often be of secondary importance.

The joking relationship is in some ways the exact opposite of a contractual relation. Instead of specific duties to be fulfilled there is privileged disrespect and freedom or even licence, and the only obligation is not to take offence at the disrespect so long as it is kept within certain bounds defined by custom, and not to go beyond those bounds. Any default in the relationship is like a breach of the rules of etiquette; the person concerned is regarded as not knowing how to behave himself.

In a true contractual relationship the two parties are conjoined by a definite common interest in reference to which each of them accepts specific obligations. It makes no difference that in other matters their interests may be divergent. In the joking relationship and in some avoidance relationships, such as that between a man and his wife's mother, one basic determinant is that the social structure separates them in such a way as to make many of their interests divergent, so that conflict or hostility might result. The alliance by extreme respect, by partial or complete avoidance, prevents such conflict but keeps the parties conjoined. The alliance by joking does the same thing in a different way.

All that has been, or could be, attempted in this paper is to show the place of the joking relationship in a general comparative

[1] 'Essai sur le Don'.

study of social structure. What I have called, provisionally, relations of consociation or alliance are distinguished from the relations set up by common membership of a political society which are defined in terms of general obligations, of etiquette, or morals, or of law. They are distinguished also from true contractual relations, defined by some specific obligation for each contracting party, into which the individual enters of his own volition. They are further to be distinguished from the relations set up by common membership of a domestic group, a lineage or a clan, each of which has to be defined in terms of a whole set of socially recognised rights and duties. Relations of consociation can only exist between individuals or groups which are in some way socially separated.

This paper deals only with formalised or standardised joking relations. Teasing or making fun of other persons is of course a common mode of behaviour in any human society. It tends to occur in certain kinds of social situations. Thus I have observed in certain classes in English-speaking countries the occurrence of horse-play between young men and women as a preliminary to courtship, very similar to the way in which a Cherokee Indian jokes with his 'grandmothers'. Certainly these unformalised modes of behaviour need to be studied by the sociologist. For the purpose of this paper it is sufficient to note that teasing is always a compound of friendliness and antagonism.

The scientific explanation of the institution in the particular form in which it occurs in a given society can only be reached by an intensive study which enables us to see it as a particular example of a widespread phenomenon of a definite class. This means that the whole social structure has to be thoroughly examined in order that the particular form and incidence of joking relationships can be understood as part of a consistent system. If it be asked why that society has the structure that it does have, the only possible answer would lie in its history. When the history is unrecorded, as it is for the native societies of Africa, we can only indulge in conjecture, and conjecture gives us neither scientific nor historical knowledge.[1]

[1] The general theory outlined in this paper is one that I have presented in lectures at various universities since 1909 as part of the general study of the forms of social structure. In arriving at the present formulation of it I have been helped by discussions with Dr. Meyer Fortes.

CHAPTER V

A FURTHER NOTE ON JOKING RELATIONSHIPS[1]

PROFESSOR GRIAULE'S article on 'L'Alliance cathartique' in *Africa* of October 1948 raises a methodological point of considerable importance. If we wish to understand a custom or institution that we find in a particular society there are two ways of dealing with it. One is to examine the part it plays in the system or complex of customs and institutions in which it is found and the meaning that it has within this complex for the people themselves. Professor Griaule deals in this way with the custom by which the Bozo and the Dogon exchange insults with each other. He considers it as an element in a complex of customs, institutions, myths, and ideas to which the Dogon themselves refer by the term *mangou*. He shows us also what meaning the natives themselves attribute to this exchange of insults (p. 253). As a piece of analysis the article is admirable, and is a most important contribution to our growing knowledge of West African society.

But there is another method open to us, namely, to make a wide comparative study of all those types of social relationship in which two persons are by custom permitted, or even required, to use speech or behaviour which in other relationships would be grievously offensive. To the use of this method it would seem that Professor Griaule objects. Referring to what has already been written on the comparative study of what are called 'joking relationships' or *parentés à plaisanterie* he writes: 'Nous adoptons, vis-à-vis travaux parus sur cette question, une attitude négative.'

Ethnographers had reported from North America, Oceania, and Africa instances of a custom by which persons standing in certain relationships resulting either from kinship, or more usually from marriage, were permitted or required to behave towards one another in a disrespectful or insulting way at which no offence might be taken. Such relationships came to be called 'joking relationships', admittedly not a very good name. The most numerous and widespread examples of this custom were in the relationship of a man to the brothers and sisters of his wife. But it was also found in some instances between cross-cousins, between mother's brother and sister's son, and in a somewhat milder form between grandparents and grandchildren. There thus arose a problem of comparative sociology: What is there in all these relationships that makes this type of behaviour appropriate, meaningful, and functional?

One of the first facts that strikes the sociological enquirer is that the custom of 'joking' with the wife's brothers and sisters is very commonly associated with a custom of strict avoidance of the wife's mother, frequently of the wife's father, and more occasionally the wife's mother's brother. Since it is clear that the avoidance custom and the joking custom are direct contraries, or polar opposites, the problem immediately became one of dealing with both these types of custom. And this in turn made it necessary to consider certain other kinds of relationships.

I became interested in this whole set of problems in 1908 when I was trying to find an explanation of customs of avoidance in the Andaman Islands. There the parents of a man and the parents of his wife must avoid each other. Their relationship is described by the term *aka-yat*, from a stem meaning 'forbidden' and a prefix referring to the mouth, and, therefore, to speech. Persons in such a relationship might not speak to each other. On the other hand I was told that they will regularly send each other presents. The explanation given by the Andamanese is: 'They are great friends because their children have married.' This conception of avoidance relationships as relationships of friendship I have found elsewhere. Thus in Australia, where a man carefully avoids all social contact with his wife's mother, I have more than once been told that she is the greatest friend he has since she has provided him with a wife. Again, the joking relationship is commonly referred to as one of friendship. 'I can tease my mother's brother and take his property because we are great friends; I am the son of his sister.' 'I can joke with my grandfather or grandmother, and they will joke with me because we are great friends.'

What does 'friendship' mean in these contexts? It is clearly something different from the relationship of solidarity and mutual help between two brothers or a father and son. On the basis of comparative analysis it seems to me that the assertion of 'friendship' means an obligation for the two persons not to enter into open quarrel or conflict with each other. It is sufficiently evident that one way of obviating open conflict between two persons is for them to avoid one another or treat each other with very marked respect. I think it is also fairly evident that a relationship in which insults are exchanged and there is an obligation not to take them seriously, is one which, by means of sham conflicts, avoids real ones.

This theory can be supported by reference to customs of other kinds, of which, to economise space, I will only mention two that are typical of one kind. In the Andamans I was told that two men who were initiated together at the same ceremony of initiation would be forbidden thereafter to speak to one another, but would regularly exchange gifts. Again the explanation was: 'They are great friends.' In South Australia there was a custom whereby two boys, born about the same time in two clans that were normally hostile, were united into a special relationship by the exchange of that portion of the umbilical cord which remains on the infant and later falls off. The two men who stand in this relationship may never speak to each other, but each may visit in safety the clan of the other carrying gifts to his friend and receiving gifts in exchange. Again the relationship is described as one of great friendship; through it each of the persons is safe in what would otherwise be hostile territory.

A careful examination of a great many instances from all over the world seems to me to justify the formulation of a general theory. But these special forms of 'friendship' can, of course, only be fully dealt with in terms of a study of forms of social relationship in general, and this is not the place in which to take up that very wide subject. Some social relationships are required by custom to be based on respect, of different degrees and expressed in different ways; others are such as to permit a certain degree of familiarity, and in extreme cases of licence. The rules of etiquette are one method of standardising these features of social relations. The respect required of a son to his father in many African tribes must be exhibited in this way. The avoidance relationship is in one sense an extreme form of respect, while the joking relationship is a form of familiarity, permitting disrespectful behaviour, and in extreme instances, licence. It is, for example, a relationship in which, in some cases, obscenity may be freely indulged in, as between the Dogon and the Bozo. Obscene talk, in all or most societies, is only permissible in ordinary social intercourse between persons standing in a specially familiar relationship. The prohibition against any reference to sexual matters before a father, and still more before a father-in-law, in many African societies, exemplifies this contrast between respectful and familiar or licentious behaviour.

The theory, of which I gave a brief outline in an earlier number of *Africa*[1] and to which M. Griaule adopts a negative attitude, starts from the position that the customs of avoidance or extreme respect towards the wife's parents, and of privileged 'joking' with the wife's brothers and sisters, can be regarded as the means of establishing and maintaining social equilibrium in a type of structural situation that results in many societies from marriage. In this situation we have two separate and distinct social groups, families or lineages, which are brought into connection with one another through the union of a man of one with a woman of the other. The husband is outside, and socially separated from, his wife's group. Through his relationship with her he is in an indirect or mediated relationship with individuals of her group. What is required for social equilibrium is that, as far as possible, he should not enter into conflict with his wife's group, but be obliged to maintain with that group or its members a 'friendly' relation. Both the avoidance customs and the 'joking' customs are the means by which this situation is socially regulated.

Why the difference, then, between the behaviour towards the wife's parents and that towards her brothers and sisters? The answer lies in the general principle, widely recognised, that towards relatives of the first ascending generation respect is required, whereas relations of familiarity and equality are appropriate between persons of the same generation. There are, of course, examples of exceptions to this rule, such as joking relations or privileged familiarity towards the father's sister's husband or the mother's brother.

Thus the special structural situation considered in this theory is one of groups which maintain their separateness, each having its own system of internal relationships between its members, and an indirect connection of a person of one group with the other

[1] *Africa*, Vol. XIII, No. 3, 1940, pp. 195–210. See Chapter IV.

group through a particular personal relation. In the instance of marriage the indirect relation is that of a man through his wife. The custom of a joking relationship with the mother's brother is found in societies in which an individual belongs to a patrilineal group, and therefore has an indirect relation to his mother's group through his mother. The widespread custom of relationships of familiarity with grandparents, often taking the form of a joking relationship (in Australia, Africa, North America, the Oraons of India), emphasises the relation of the two generations as being socially separated. The grandparents are thus placed in contrast with the relatives of the parents' generation, and the relation to one's own grandparent is an indirect one through a parent. The joking relationship between cross-cousins (Fiji, Ojibwa, etc.) is frequently a relation between possible relatives by marriage, but the relation is an indirect one through the mother or through the father's sister.

An interesting crucial instance for the theory is provided by the Crow Indians, who have matrilineal clans. A man must be respectful to all the members of his father's clan; though he is not a member of that clan his relation to its members is one of close solidarity. In the other clans of the tribe there are to be found some men who are sons of men of his father's clan. They belong to clans that are separate and distinct, not only from his own clan but also from his father's clan. With such men, with whom his personal relation is an indirect one through his father's clan, he has a joking relationship; he may make offensive remarks to them or receive such from them without offence. In the Crow tribe this relationship has been developed into an instrument of social control of conduct, since the joking relative may call public attention to the shortcomings of his relative.

The Cherokee also had a system of matrilineal clans, and a man was required to show respect to all the members of his father's clan. But with the clans of his father's father and his mother's father he had only an indirect connection through a parent. He called all the women of these clans 'grandmother' and could be on a relationship of familiarity or joking with them. Since marriage with such a 'grandmother' was approved they were possible wives or sisters-in-law.

The theory that I have offered of joking relationships between persons related through marriage or by kinship is that they occur as social institutions in structural situations of a certain general kind in which there are two groups, the separateness of which is emphasised, and relations are established indirectly between a person in one group and the members or some of the members of the other. The relationship may be said to be one which expresses and emphasises both detachment (as belonging to separated groups) and attachment (through the indirect personal relation). These relationships of 'friendship', by avoidance or joking, contrast in a marked way with the relationships of solidarity, involving a complex system of obligations, that exist within a group such as a lineage or a clan. For the further development of the theory they need to be compared also with those relations which are set up, between persons belonging to different groups, by the regular exchange of gifts. Thus the theory is only one part of an attempt to deal systematically with the types of social relationship that are to be found in primitive societies.

The great majority of instances of joking relationships that were recorded by ethnographers were relationships between individuals connected through marriage or by kinship. Hence the reference to them in French as relations of *parenté*. But there were also found instances of a similar relation between groups of persons, by which a member of one group was permitted and expected to offer insulting or derogatory remarks to any member of the other. A good example is provided by the 'coyote' and 'wild cat' moieties of Californian tribes. More recently similarcu stoms have been reported from Africa (Northern Rhodesia, Tanganyika, West Africa)[1] in which this kind of relationship exists between two clans of a tribe or between two tribes. These obviously present a problem of a somewhat different kind. But it is obvious that any valid general theory of joking relationships must take into account these relations between groups.

Tribes and clans are distinct separated groups each maintaining its own identity and separateness. Within a clan the relations of its members are those of solidarity in the special sense in which I have been using that term in this note. Two clans may, in some instances, be united in a way in which there is a permanent union of solidarity between the clans as groups and the members thereof. On the other hand there may also be a relation between two clans of active or latent hostility. There is a third possibility, that between two particular clans there may be a relation neither of solidarity nor of hostility but of 'friendship' in which the separateness of the groups is emphasised, but open conflict between the groups or the members on the two sides is avoided by establishing a relation in which they may insult each other without giving or taking offence. This kind of thing is well illustrated in the account of the clans of the Tallensi given by Dr. Meyer Fortes.[1] A similar relationship, whereby hostility is avoided, may exist between two tribes, as in the instances known from Tanganyika.[2] It seems to me that in this way the joking relationship between clans and tribes recorded from Africa can be brought within the scope of a single theory that refers all instances of these relationships to a certain general type of structural situation. It should be made clear that what such a theory attempts to do is to deal with all the known examples of a certain recognisable type of institutionalised relationships in order to discover what common social feature makes this type of behaviour appropriate, meaningful, and functional.

It is evident that in one particular respect the relation between the Dogon and the Bozo is similar to the relations that have been described from other parts of Africa, namely, in the exchange of insults. There is no evidence that they are similar in other respects, and they certainly are not so in all. The relation is spoken of as an 'alliance', but it is something very different from an alliance between two nations which co-operate in fighting a war against another. The term 'alliance' is therefore not entirely suitable, nor have I been able to find a really suitable term. I have used the term 'friendship' and there is justification for this in the way in which native peoples themselves speak of friendship. In Australian tribes a man may have a 'friend', that is, a person with whom he has a special personal relationship. In one region a wife's own sister's husband, if he is not a near kinsman, is such a friend. In other regions a man may not select a 'friend' from amongst the men to whom he applies the classificatory term for 'brother'. Between 'brothers' relations are fixed by the kinship system. He may choose a man who stands to him in the

[1] Fortes, M., The Dynamics of Clanship among the Tallensi, London: Oxford University Press, 1945.
[2] See Bibliography, p. 115.

classificatory relation of 'brother-in-law' but not his own brother-in-law. For brothers-in-law always necessarily belong to separated groups. There is a clear distinction made between friendship and relationships by kinship.

I am distinguishing, therefore, a certain class of what I call 'friendship' relations, from what I have called relations of 'solidarity' established by kinship or by membership of a group such as a lineage or clan. These terms are used only for the purposes of the present analysis because in this matter, as in so many others in social anthropology, no precise technical terms are yet available.

We may regard as one type of 'friendship' in this sense the relation set up between persons or groups on the basis of a continued exchange of goods and services. The world-wide custom of gift-exchange has to be considered in this connection. But there are other varieties; one group may bury the dead of the other or perform other ritual services. In North-West America one group would call in a 'friend' group to erect a totem-pole for them. A component of the relationship between groups is very commonly a certain amount and kind of opposition, meaning by that term socially controlled and regulated antagonism. The two groups may regularly engage in competitive games such as football. In *potlatch* in North America there is competition or rivalry in exchange of valuables. Social relations of friendly rivalry are of considerable theoretical importance. The universities of Oxford and Cambridge maintain a certain relation by competing regularly in rowing, football, etc. The joking relationship is thus one example of a wider kind; for it is a relation of friendship in which there is an appearance of antagonism, controlled by conventional rules.

The 'alliance' between the Dogon and the Bozo described and analysed by M. Griaule is clearly an example of what I have been referring to as 'friendship'. The Dogon and the Bozo are separate peoples distinguished by language and by their mode of life. The prohibition against intermarriage maintains this separation by preventing the creation of relations of kinship between members of the two groups. The 'friendship' appears in the prohibition, under supernatural sanction, against the shedding of the blood of a member of the allied people, and in the regular exchange of gifts and services, for example, the services that individuals of one group perform in the ritual purification of those of the other. To these is added a 'joking relationship', the exchange of insults between members of the two groups. It is with this last feature that we are concerned here.

This alliance is conceived by the two peoples concerned in terms of their own cosmological system of myths and ideas, and M. Griaule's article is an important addition to the series of publications in which he and his co-workers have given the results of their investigation of this cosmology. It is in terms of these ideas that the Dogon interpret the exchange of insults.[1] The exchange of insults is 'cathartic' because it rids the livers of both parties of impurities. M. Griaule has thus given us an explanation of the exchange of insults between Dogon and Bozo by showing what meaning it has to the natives themselves and also by showing its interconnections within a complex system of institutions, ideas, and myths. He finds that the most important function of the alliance is to provide what he calls, for lack of a more suitable term, 'purification'. So, provisionally, he proposes to call this type of alliance, as found in an extensive region of Africa, 'cathartic alliance'. Doubtless he would not suggest that we should apply this name to the exchange of insults between clans among the Tallensi or Bemba, or between tribes in Tanganyika.

M. Marcel Mauss and I have both been seeking for many years to find a satisfactory general theory of what I have been calling relations of 'friendship' between separate groups of persons belonging to separate groups. One part of such a theory must be a study of prestations or exchanges of goods or services. Another must be a study of 'joking relationships'. It is towards such studies that M. Griaule adopts, as he says, 'a negative attitude'. He suggests that to classify together the various examples of 'joking relationships' and to look for a general explanation, is like classifying together the ceremonies at which church bells are rung, such as funerals and weddings, calling them all *cérémonies à cloches*. This is the question of methodology in social anthropology that seems to me so important. For M. Griaule seems to be questioning the scientific validity of the comparative method as a means of arriving at general theoretical interpretations of social institutions.

It is only by the use of a comparative method that we can arrive

[1] *Africa*, Vol. XVIII, No. 4, pp. 253–4.

at general explanations. The alternative is to confine ourselves to particularistic explanations similar to those of the historians. The two kinds of explanation are both legitimate and do not conflict; but both are needed for the understanding of societies and their institutions. That the Dogon explain the exchange of insults as a means of purifying the liver does not prevent us from treating the Dogon institution as one example of a very widespread form of 'friendship' in which such exchange is a distinctive feature.

It is not a question of whether my theory, or any other general theory, of joking relationships is or is not satisfactory. It is the different question of whether such a general theory is possible, or whether attempts to arrive at one should be abandoned in favour of resting content with particularistic explanations.

The same question of methodology arises in connection with the conclusion of M. Griaule's article. He touches briefly on the need for an explanation of the Dogon-Bozo alliance 'en tant que système de groupes couplés et dont les deux parties ont des prérogatives et devoirs complémentaires'. He finds the explanation in 'les fondements même de la métaphysique dogon. En effet, dès l'origine du monde, la règle était de gémelléité. Les êtres devaient naître par couple.' This is therefore a particularistic explanation in terms of Dogon ideas about twins.

Relations of this kind between paired groups are to be found in many parts of the world. Outstanding examples are provided by the moiety organisations of North and South America, Melanesia, and Australia. The most usual way of representing this unity in duality, linking two groups into one society, is by pairs of opposites, such as heaven and earth, war and peace, red and white, land and water, coyote and wild cat, eaglehawk and crow. The underlying conception is therefore that of the union of opposites, as in the philosophy of Heraclitus. It was highly elaborated by the Chinese in the philosophy of *Yin* and *Yang*; *yang* and *yin* are male and female, day and night, summer and winter, activity and passivity, etc., and the dictum is that *yang* and *yin* together are required to make a unity or harmony (*tao*) as in the union of husband and wife, or the union of winter and summer to make a year

The Dogon are therefore unusual when they represent the relation between paired groups by reference to human twins.

But this can be seen to be only a special development of a conception that is very widespread in Africa, by which twins are regarded as a single entity divided into two parts. A comparative study of African customs concerning twins shows this conception developed in a number of different ways.

In the Dogon cosmology as recorded by M. Griaule and his associates the most fundamental conception of unity in duality seems to be not that of twin births but rather the opposition of the masculine and feminine principles, just as in the *yin* and *yang* of China. Human beings are born endowed with both principles and it is by operations of circumcision and clitoridectomy that they become truly male and female, so that there is again a Heraclitean union of opposites in the sexual union of husband and wife. One useful clue to the understanding of Dogon cosmological ideas, or certain of them, is the way in which this duality of male and female is combined with the duality in unity of twins. The latter form of duality corresponds to the number 2; the former to the opposition between 3, masculine symbol, and 4, feminine, which being added together give 7, the symbol of the complete being.

The symbolic representations of the Dogon present striking similarities to those found in other parts of the world besides West Africa. The basis of any scientific understanding of them must be such a particularistic study as is being made by M. Griaule and his co-workers; but it is suggested that it will need to be supplemented by a systematic comparative study extended as widely as possible. The conception of unity in duality has been used by man not only in the establishment of systems of cosmology but also in organising social structures. A comparative study of this, as of joking relationships, may be expected to aid in most important ways the understanding of the Dogon system which, without it, would seem to be only a peculiar product of a particular people.

BIBLIOGRAPHY

Fortes, M. *The Dynamics of Clanship among the Tallensi*. London Oxford University Press, 1945.

Moreau, R. E. 'The Joking Relationship (*utani*) in Tanganyika', *Tanganyika Notes and Records*, 12, 1941, pp. 1–10.

— 'Joking Relationships in Tanganyika', *Africa*, Vol. XIV, No. 3, 1944, pp. 386–400.

Paulme, Denise. 'Parenté à plaisanteries et alliance par le sang en Afrique occidentale', *Africa*, Vol. XII, No. 4, 1939, pp. 433-44.

Pedler, F. J. 'Joking Relationships in East Africa', *Africa*, Vol. XIII, No. 2, 1940, pp. 170-3.

Radcliffe-Brown, A. R. 'On Joking Relationships', *Africa*, Vol. XII, No. 3, 1940, pp. 195-210.

Richards, A. I. 'Reciprocal Clan Relationships among the Bemba of N. Rhodesia', *Man*, Vol. XXXVII, p. 222, 1927.

Schapera, I. 'Customs relating to twins in South Africa', *Journal Afr. Soc.*, Vol. XXVI, cii, pp. 117-37.

CHAPTER VI

THE SOCIOLOGICAL THEORY OF TOTEMISM[1]

THERE has been in the past some disagreement and discussion as to the definition of totemism. I wish to avoid as far as possible entering into any such discussion. The purpose of preliminary definitions in science is to mark off a class of phenomena for special study. A term is useful if and in so far as it brings together for our attention a number of phenomena which are in reality, and not merely in appearance, closely related to one another. It will be part of my thesis in this paper that however widely or narrowly we may define totemism, we cannot reach an understanding of the phenomena we so name unless we study systematically a much wider group of phenomena, namely, the general relation between man and natural species in mythology and ritual. It may well be asked if 'totemism' as a technical term has not outlived its usefulness.

It is necessary, however, to have some definition to guide and control our discussion. I shall use the term in the wider sense to apply wherever a society is divided into groups and there is a special relation between each group and one or more classes of objects that are usually natural species of animals or plants but may occasionally be artificial objects or parts of an animal. The word is sometimes used in a narrower sense and applied only when the groups in question are clans, i.e. exogamous groups of which all the members are regarded as being closely related by descent in one line. I shall regard 'clan totemism' as only one variety of totemism, in the wider sense.[2]

Even in the narrower sense of clan totemism, and still more in the wider sense, totemism is not one thing but is a general name

[1] Reprinted from *Proceedings of the Fourth Pacific Science Congress*, Java, 1929.
[2] It is sometimes said that totemism has two aspects, a social aspect and a religious or ritual aspect. What is referred to as the 'social aspect' of totemism is simply the clan organisation. But exogamous clans similar in all essentials to totemic clans so far as economic or juridical functions go, can, as we well know, exist without totemism. The so-called 'social aspect' of clan totemism is simply the social aspect of the clan.

given to a number of diverse institutions which all have, or seem to have, something in common. Thus even in the limited region of Australia, which has a single homogeneous culture throughout, there have been recorded a number of different varieties of totemism, and new varieties are being discovered by systematic researches now in progress.

In the south-east of the continent is found sex-totemism, i.e. an association of the two sex-groups, men and women, with two animal species. In the coastal districts of New South Wales, for example, the bat is the totem or animal representative of the men and the tree-creeper (*Climacteris sp.*) is that of the women.

In many parts of Australia the tribe is divided into two exogamous moieties, patrilineal in some regions, matrilineal in others. In some instances the moieties are named after species of animals, generally birds. Amongst such names are the following pairs: crow and white cockatoo, white cockatoo and black cockatoo, eaglehawk and crow, native companion and turkey, hill kangaroo and long-legged kangaroo. In other instances the meanings of the moiety names have not been discovered, and in some of them, at any rate, it seems certain that they are not animal names.

In many of the tribes that have this dual division, independently of whether the moieties are named after animals or not, there is a classification of animals and frequently of other natural objects whereby some are regarded as belonging to one moiety and others to the other.

Such moiety totemism, if we may use that term for any such association between the moiety and one or more natural species, is found in a number of different varieties in Australia, and still other varieties are found in Melanesia and in North America.

Over a large part of Australia the tribe is divided into four groups which have often been called 'classes' but which I prefer to call 'sections'. The easiest way to understand this division into four is to regard it as constituted by the intersection of a pair of patrilineal moieties and a pair of matrilineal moieties.[1]

---

[1] If we denote the four sections as A, B, C, and D, the matrilineal moieties are A + C and B + D; the patrilineal moieties are A + D and B + C. Since a man may not marry within his own patrilineal moiety or within his own matrilineal moiety it will follow that a man of A can only marry a woman of B and their children must belong to section D, i.e. to the patrilineal moiety of the father (A) and to the matrilineal moiety of the mother (B).

These sections are not as a rule named after species of animals, though there are one or two instances in which a section name is also the name of an animal. Thus Bandjur in Yukumbil is the name of a section and also of the native bear. In some tribes, however, there is a definite association between each section and one or more species of animal. Thus in the Nigena tribe of the Kimberley district of Western Australia the four sections are associated with four species of hawk. In some regions this association does not carry with it any prohibition against killing or eating the animal associated with one's own or any other section. In part of Queensland, however, each section has associated with it a number of species of animals and there is a rule that the members of a section may not eat the animals so associated with their section.

This 'section totemism' requires further investigation. We may distinguish, however, three varieties. In one each section has associated with it a single species of animal which is representative of the section in somewhat the same way as the sex-totem is the representative of the sex-group. In a second variety each section stands in a special ritual relation to a certain limited number of species which may not be eaten by the members of the section. In the third variety a great number of species of animals are classified as belonging to one or other of the four sections but there is no rule against eating the animals belonging to one's own section. The one thing that is common to these varieties is that each section is differentiated from the others and given its own individuality by being associated with one or more animal species.

In some tribes the four sections are again subdivided each into two parts, giving a division of the tribe into eight sub-sections. In some of these tribes there exist special associations between the sub-sections and certain natural species. Further investigation is needed before we can profitably discuss this subject.

If now we turn to clan-totemism we find a number of different varieties of this in Australia, too many, in fact, to be even enumerated in a short paper. Matrilineal clan totemism of different varieties occurs in three, or possibly four, separate areas in the east, north, and west of the continent. In Melville and Bathurst Islands there are three matrilineal phratries subdivided into twenty-two clans. Each clan is associated with one natural species, usually a species of animal or plant, though one or two clans have two totems and one has three. The association between the clan and its totem is apparently of very little importance in the life of the tribe. There is no prohibition against eating or using the totem, there are no totemic ceremonies, and totemism has little influence on the mythology.

The matrilineal clan totemism of some tribes of New South Wales, Victoria and South Australia seems to be of somewhat more importance. Here we find matrilineal moieties sometimes named totemically, sometimes not, and each moiety is divided into a number of clans. Each clan has one or more natural species regarded as belonging to it. Where there are several species associated with each clan, as is the case in many tribes, one of them is regarded as more important than the others and the clan is named after it. Throughout this region there is, so far as we know, no prohibition against killing or eating the totem.

Totemic ceremonial is apparently little developed nor have we any evidence of any elaborate totemic mythology connected with matrilineal totemism.

It should be noted that throughout Australia the most important group for social purposes is the horde, i.e. a small group occupying and owning a certain defined territory, and that the horde is normally strictly patrilineal. It follows that wherever there is a system of matrilineal totemic clans the clan consists of individuals scattered through a number of hordes. We thus get a double grouping of individuals. For most social purposes the individual is dependent on the local group, i.e. the horde, to which he is connected through his father, while at the same time he is also connected through his mother to a totemic group the members of which are scattered throughout the tribe.

Patrilineal totemism in Australia is more difficult to describe briefly than is matrilineal totemism. Where it exists the primary totemic group is usually the horde, i.e. the small patrilineal local group. In some regions the horde is a clan, i.e. it consists of close relatives in the male line and is therefore exogamous. But in a few regions the horde is not a clan in this sense.

As an example of one variety of patrilineal totemism we may take the tribes at the mouth of the Murray River (Yaralde, etc.). Here each horde is a local clan and each clan has one or more species of natural object associated with it. There is no prohibition against eating the totem of one's clan, but it is regarded with some respect. There is no evidence of totemic ceremonial or of any elaborate totemic mythology. The function of the totem seems to be merely to act as the representative of the group.

Perhaps the most important, and certainly the most interesting, form of totemism in Australia is that to a brief consideration of which we now pass. This consists of a fourfold association between (1) the horde, i.e. the patrilineal local group, (2) a certain number of classes of objects, animals, plants, and other things such as rain, sun and hot weather, cold weather, babies, etc., (3) certain sacred spots within the territory of the horde, frequently water-holes, each one of which is specially associated with one or more of the 'totems' of the group, and (4) certain mythical beings who are supposed to have given rise to these sacred spots in the mythical period of the beginning of the world. This system of totemism is now being traced and studied in a number of variant forms over a very large part of the Australian continent. It was formerly known best from the centre of the continent, where, however, the Aranda have it in a somewhat modified or anomalous form. We now know that it exists or existed over a large part of Western Australia. Recently it has been discovered and studied in the Cape York Peninsula by Miss McConnel. At the beginning of this year I was able to demonstrate its former existence on the east coast of Australia in the north of New South Wales and in southern Queensland.

Where this type of totemism is found it is usually accompanied by a system of ceremonies for the increase of natural species. The members of the horde, or some of them, proceed to the totem centre or sacred spot connected with a natural species and perform there a ceremony which is believed to result in an increase of that species. There is also an elaborate mythology dealing with the sacred totem centres and with the mythical beings who gave rise to them.

It may be noted that this kind of totemism may coexist in the same tribe with other kinds. Thus in the Dieri tribe it exists together with a system of matrilineal clan totemism. In some parts it coexists with section totemism.

Finally, we may note that in some parts of Australia there exists what is sometimes called individual or personal totemism. This is a special relation between an individual and some one or more species of animal. A good example is found in some tribes of New South Wales where every medicine-man has one or more of such personal totems. It is through his association with the animal species that he acquires his power to perform magic. Whether we call this totemism or not, it is quite evident that it is closely related to totemism and that any theory of totemism, to be satisfactory, must take it into account.

This brief and very incomplete survey of Australian institutions has shown us that special associations of groups or individuals with natural species exist in that region in a number of different forms. We find all gradations from a tribe with no form of totemism at all (such as the Bad of northern Dampier Land) through tribes such as the Melville Islanders where totemism of a simple form exists but is of comparatively little importance in the life of the tribe, to a tribe such as the Dieri which combines in a complex system two forms of totemism, one of matrilineal clans and the other of patrilineal hordes, with a highly elaborated totemic ritual and mythology. The only thing that these totemic systems have in common is the general tendency to characterise the segments into which society is divided by an association between each segment and some natural species or some portion of nature. The association may take any one of a number of different forms.

In the past the theoretical discussion of totemism was almost entirely concerned with speculations as to its possible origin. If we use the word origin to mean the historical process by which an institution or custom or a state of culture comes into existence, then it is clear that the very diverse forms of totemism that exist all over the world must have had very diverse origins. To be able to speak of an origin of totemism we must assume that all these diverse institutions that we include under the one general term have been derived by successive modifications from a single form. There does not seem to me to be a particle of evidence to justify such an assumption. But even if we make it we can still only speculate as to what this original form of totemism may have been, as to the enormously complex series of events which could have produced from it the various existing totemic systems, and as to where, when, and how that hypothetical original form of totemism came into existence. And such speculations, being for ever incapable of inductive verification, can be nothing more than speculations and can have no value for a science of culture.

For sociology, or social anthropology, by which I understand the study of the phenomena of culture by the same inductive methods that are in use in the natural sciences, the phenomena of totemism present a problem of a different kind. The task of the inductive sciences is to discover the universal or the general in the particular. That of a science of culture is to reduce the complex data with which it deals to a limited number of general laws or principles. Approaching totemism in this way we may formulate the problem that it presents in the form of the question, 'Can we show that totemism is a special form of a phenomenon which is universal in human society and is therefore present in different forms in all cultures?'

The most important attempt to arrive at a sociological theory of totemism is that of the late Professor Durkheim in his work *Les Formes élémentaires de la Vie religieuse*. I think that that work is an important and permanent contribution to sociological theory, but that it does not provide a complete and satisfactory theory of totemism. I shall attempt to point out, in the briefest possible way, where Durkheim's theory seems to me to fail.

Durkheim speaks of the totem as being 'sacred' to the members of the group of which it is the totem. This is to use the term 'sacred' in a sense somewhat different from that which it has at the present day in English or even in French, and not even identical with, though somewhat nearer to, the meaning that *sacer* had in Latin. I prefer to use a term which is as free as possible from special connotations, and therefore instead of saying that the totem is sacred I find it preferable to say that there is a 'ritual relation' between persons and their totem. There exists a ritual relation whenever a society imposes on its members a certain attitude towards an object, which attitude involves some measure of respect expressed in a traditional mode of behaviour with reference to that object. Thus the relation between a Christian and the first day of the week is a typical example of a ritual relation.

Every society adopts, and imposes upon its members, towards certain objects, this attitude of mind and behaviour which I am calling the ritual attitude. There are, not only in different societies, but in the same society in different references, many different varieties of this attitude, but all the varieties have something in common. Moreover the ritual attitude may vary from a very indefinite one to a definite and highly organised one.

One of the important problems of sociology is therefore to discover the function of this universal element of culture and to formulate its laws. This general problem obviously includes a vast number of partial problems of which the problem of totemism is one. That problem may be stated as being that of discovering why in certain societies a ritual attitude towards a certain species of natural object is imposed upon the members of a particular social group. It is obvious that no solution of the lesser problem of totemism can be satisfactory unless it conforms with or is part of a general solution of the wider problem, i.e. a theory of ritual relations in general.

With regard to the general problem Durkheim's theory is that the primary object of the ritual attitude is the social order itself, and that any thing becomes an object of that attitude when it stands in a certain relation to the social order. This general theory, with which I agree, obviously amounts to very little until we have succeeded in defining the more important types of relation to the social order which result in the object which stands in such a relation becoming an object of ritual attitude.

If I may restate in my own terms Durkheim's theory of totemism it is as follows. A social group such as a clan can only possess solidarity and permanence if it is the object of sentiments of attachment in the minds of its members. For such sentiments to be maintained in existence they must be given occasional collective expression. By a law that can be, I think, readily verified, all regular collective expressions of social sentiments tend to take on a ritual form. And in ritual, again by a necessary law, some more or less concrete object is required which can act as the representative of the group. So that it is a normal procedure that the sentiment of attachment to a group shall be expressed in some formalised collective behaviour having reference to an object that represents the group itself.

A typical example is to be found in our own society. National solidarity depends on a sentiment of patriotism in the minds of the nation. This sentiment, in conformity with the laws stated above, tends to find some of its chief expressions in reference to such concrete objects as flags, or kings and presidents, and such objects become in this way objects of the ritual attitude.

Part of a king's sacredness, whether in Africa or in Europe, is due to the fact that he is the representative of the national solidarity and unity, and the ritual that surrounds him is the means by which patriotic sentiments are maintained. In the same way in the flag we have an object which is 'sacred' because it is the concrete material representative or emblem of a social group and its solidarity.

Durkheim compares the totem of a clan with the flag of a nation. The comparison is valid, in a very general sense, for some forms of totemism, if not for all. But putting the comparison aside, the theory is that the totem is 'sacred' as Durkheim says, or is an object of ritual attitude, as I prefer to say, because it is the concrete representative or emblem of a social group. And the function of the ritual attitude towards the totem is to express and so to maintain in existence the solidarity of the social group.

With Durkheim's theory as stated above in my own terms I am in agreement, but I do not regard it as complete. In the first place it seems to me that totemism has other functions besides the one indicated above. Secondly, the theory so far as stated above does not explain why so many peoples in America, Asia, Africa and Australasia should select as emblems or representatives of clans or other social groups species of animals or plants. It is true that Durkheim offers an answer to this question, but it is an entirely unsatisfactory one. He regards as an essential part of totemism the use of totemic emblems or designs, i.e. figured representations of the totemic animal or plant, and suggests that the reason for selecting natural objects as emblems of social groups is because they are capable of being used in this way.

This hypothesis fails as soon as we apply it to the facts. In Australia no designs are made of the sex totems or of the totems of the moieties or sections, and even for clan totemism there are many tribes that do not make any representations of their totems. Totemic designs, which for Durkheim are so important or indeed so essential a part of totemism, are characteristic of central and northern Australia but not of the continent as a whole.

Moreover, the reason suggested for the selection of natural objects as emblems of social groups is of too accidental a character to give a satisfying explanation of an institution that is so widespread as totemism. There must surely be some much more important reason why all these peoples all over the world find it appropriate to represent social groups in this way by associating each one with some animal or plant.

This, then, is where I think Durkheim's theory of totemism fails. It implies that the totem owes its sacred or ritual character solely to its position as the emblem of a group. Now there are a number of peoples who have no form of totemism amongst whom we still find that natural species such as animals and plants are objects of ritual or of the ritual attitude expressed in mythology. And even amongst totemic peoples such as the Australian tribes the ritual customs relating to natural species are not all totemic. In other words the phenomena which we have agreed to denote by the term totemism are merely a part of a much larger class of phenomena which includes all sorts of ritual relations between man and natural species. No theory of totemism is satisfactory unless it conforms with a more general theory providing an explanation of many other things besides totemism. Durkheim's theory fails to do this.

In a great number, and I believe probably in all, of the societies where man depends entirely or largely on the hunting of wild animals and the collection of wild plants, whether they have any form of totemism or not, the animals and plants are made objects of the ritual attitude. This is done frequently, though perhaps not quite universally, in mythology, in which animal species are personified and regarded as ancestors or culture heroes. It is done also by a mass of customs relating to animals and plants. This system of ritual and mythological relations between man and natural species can be best studied in non-totemic peoples such as the Eskimo or the Andaman Islanders. In such societies we find that the relation between the society and the natural species is a general one, all the most important animals and plants being treated as in some way sacred (either in ritual or in mythology) and some being regarded as more sacred than others, but any single species being equally sacred to every member of the whole community. The ritual attitude of the Andaman Islanders towards the turtle, of Californian Indians to the salmon, of the peoples of North America and northern Asia to the bear, constitutes a relation between the whole society and the sacred species.

Now totemism, I would suggest, arises from or is a special development of this general ritual relation between man and natural species. Let us assume for the moment that such a general ritual relation of man to nature is universal in hunting societies, as I believe it can be shown to be. When the society becomes differentiated into segmentary groups such as clans, a process of ritual specialisation takes place by which each segment acquires a special and particular relation to some one or more of the *sacra* of the community, i.e. to some one or more natural species. The totem of the clan or group is still sacred in some sense to the whole community, but is now specially sacred, and in some special way, to the segment of which it is the totem.

The process here suggested as the active principle in the development of totemism is one which I believe to be of great importance in social development, and which can be observed in other phenomena. Thus, to take only one example, and perhaps not the best, in the Roman Church the saints are sacred to all members of the church as a whole. But the church is segmented into local congregations and a congregation is often placed in a special relation to one particular saint to whom its chapel is dedicated. This is, I think, parallel to clan or group totemism. We might also draw a significant though not quite exact analogy between the patron saint of an individual and the personal totem or guardian animal of Australian and American tribes.

There is no space in this paper to discuss this process of ritual specialisation, and indeed any adequate treatment of the subject would require us to deal with the whole process of social differentiation and segmentation. I will refer to a single example that may help to illustrate the problem. Amongst the Eskimo of part of North America one of the most important features of their adaptation to their environment is the sharp division between winter and summer, and between the winter animals and the summer animals. There is a complex system of ritual relations between the society and all the most important of these animals and in this ritual the opposition between summer and winter is strongly expressed. Thus you may not eat reindeer meat (summer food) and walrus meat (winter food) on the same day. The Eskimo have made for themselves a segmentation into two groups, one consisting of all the persons born in the summer and the other of those born in the winter, and there is some slight ritual specialisation, the summer people being regarded as specially connected with the summer animals and the winter people with the winter animals. This is not quite totemism, but it is clearly related to it, and illustrates, I think, the process by which totemism arises.

In this way, I think, we can formulate a sociological theory of totemism which incorporates a great deal of Durkheim's analysis and is not open to the criticisms that can be levelled against Durkheim's own presentation. We start with the empirical generalisation that amongst hunting and collecting peoples the more important animals and plants and natural phenomena are treated, in custom and in myth, as being 'sacred', i.e. they are made, in various ways and in different degrees, objects of the ritual attitude. Primarily this ritual relation between man and nature is a general one between the society as a whole and its sacra. When the society is differentiated, i.e. divided into segments or social groups marked off from one another and each having its own solidarity and individuality, there comes into action a principle which is more widespread than totemism and is indeed an important part of the general process of social differentiation, a principle by which within the general relation of the society to its sacra there are established special relations between each group or segment and some one or more of those sacra.

This theory incorporates what I think is the most valuable part of Durkheim's analysis, in the recognition that the function of the ritual relation of the group to its totem is to express and so to maintain in existence the solidarity of the group. It gives moreover a reason, which can be shown, I think, to be grounded in the very nature of social organisation itself, for the selection of natural species as emblems or representatives of social groups.

Before leaving this part of the discussion I would like to touch on one further point. Durkheim, in reference to clan totemism, emphasises the clan and its solidarity. The totem, for him, is primarily the means by which the clan recognises and expresses its unity. But the matter is much more complex than this. The clan is merely a segment of a larger society which also has its solidarity. By its special relation to its totem or totems the clan recognises its unity and its individuality. This is simply a special example of the universal process by which solidarity is created and maintained by uniting a number of individuals in a collective relation to the same sacred object or objects. By the fact that each clan has its own totem there is expressed the differentiation and opposition between clan and clan. The kangaroo men not only recognise the bond that unites them as kangaroo men but also recognise their difference from the emu men and the bandicoot men and so on. But also the wider unity and solidarity of the whole totemic society is expressed by the fact that the society as a whole, through its segments, stands in a ritual relation to nature as a whole. This is seen very well in the system of increase ceremonies that is so widespread in Australia. Each group is responsible for the ritual care of a certain number of species by which the maintenance of that species is believed to be assured. For the tribe all these species are of importance, and the ceremonies are thus a sort of co-operative effort, involving a division of (ritual) labour, by which the normal processes of nature and the supply of food are provided for. One of the results of Durkheim's theory is that it over-emphasises the clan and clan solidarity. Totemism does more than express the unity of the clan; it also expresses the unity of totemic society as a whole in the relations of the clans to one another within that wider unity.

The result of my argument, if it is valid, is to substitute for the problem of totemism another problem. The question that now demands an answer is, 'Why do the majority of what are called primitive peoples adopt in their custom and myth a ritual attitude towards animals and other natural species?' My aim in this paper has simply been to exhibit as exactly as possible in a brief space the relation of the problem of totemism to this wider problem.

It is obvious that I cannot attempt in a mere conclusion to a paper to deal with this subject of the relation in myth and ritual of man and nature. I attempted some years ago to deal with it in reference to the customs and beliefs of one non-totemic people, the Andaman Islanders. As a result of that and other investigations I was led to formulate the following law: Any object or event which has important effects upon the well-being (material or spiritual) of a society, or any thing which stands for or represents any such object or event, tends to become an object of the ritual attitude.

I have given reasons for rejecting Durkheim's theory that in totemism natural species become sacred because they are selected as representatives of social groups, and I hold, on the contrary, that natural species are selected as representatives of social groups, such as clans, because they are already objects of the ritual attitude on quite another basis, by virtue of the general law of the ritual expression of social values stated above.

In modern thought we are accustomed to draw a distinction between the social order and the natural order. We regard society as consisting of certain human beings grouped in a social structure under certain moral principles or laws, and we place over against the society its environment, consisting of geographical features, flora and fauna, climate with its seasonal changes, and so on, governed by natural law.

For certain purposes this contrast of society and environment, of man and nature, is a useful one, but we must not let it mislead us. From another and very important point of view the natural order enters into and becomes part of the social order. The seasonal changes that control the rhythm of social life, the animals and plants that are used for food or other purposes, these enter into and become an essential part of the social life, the social order. I believe that it can be shown that it is just in so far as they thus enter into the social order that natural phenomena and natural objects become, either in themselves, or through things or beings that represent them, objects of the ritual attitude, and I have already tried to demonstrate this so far as the Andaman Islanders are concerned. Our own explicit conception of a natural order and of natural law does not exist amongst the more primitive peoples, though the germs out of which it develops do exist in the empirical control of causal processes in technical activities. For primitive man the universe as a whole is a moral or social order governed not by what we call natural law but rather by what we must call moral or ritual law. The recognition of this conception, implicit but not explicit, in ritual and in myth is, I believe, one of the most important steps towards the proper understanding not only of what is sometimes called 'primitive mentality' but also of all the phenomena that we group vaguely around the term religion.[1]

A study of primitive myth and ritual from this point of view is, I think, very illuminating. In Australia, for example, there are innumerable ways in which the natives have built up between themselves and the phenomena of nature a system of relations which are essentially similar to the relations that they have built up in their social structure between one human being and another.

---

[1] A more precise way of stating the view I am here suggesting is that in every human society there inevitably exist two different and in a certain sense conflicting conceptions of nature. One of them, the naturalistic, is implicit everywhere in technology, and in our twentieth century European culture, with its great development of control over natural phenomena, has become explicit and preponderant in our thought. The other, which might be called the mythological or spiritualistic conception, is implicit in myth and in religion, and often becomes explicit in philosophy.

I can do no more than mention examples. One is the personification of natural phenomena and of natural species. A species of animal is personified, i.e. treated for certain purposes as if it were a human being, and in the mythology such personified species are regarded as ancestors or culture heroes. The function of this process of personification is that it permits nature to be thought of as if it were a society of persons, and so makes of it a social or moral order. Another of the processes by which, in Australia, the world of nature is brought within the social order is to be found in the systems of classification of natural species, existing in a number of diverse forms in different parts of the continent with this one thing in common to them all, that the more important natural species are so classified that each one is regarded as belonging to a certain social group, and occupying a specific position in the social structure.

Although there is always a danger in short formulas I think it does not misrepresent Australian totemism to describe it as a mechanism by which a system of social solidarities is established between man and nature. The mechanism has been worked out in many different ways, and much more elaborately in some than in others, but everywhere it possesses this character.

The suggestion I put forward, therefore, is that totemism is part of a larger whole, and that one important way in which we can characterise this whole is that it provides a representation of the universe as a moral or social order. Durkheim, if he did not actually formulate this view, at any rate came near to it. But his conception seems to have been that the process by which this takes place is by a projection of society into external nature. On the contrary, I hold that the process is one by which, in the fashioning of culture, external nature, so called, comes to be incorporated in the social order as an essential part of it.

Now the conception of the universe as a moral order is not confined to primitive peoples, but is an essential part of every system of religion. It is, I think, a universal element in human culture. With the question of why this should be so I cannot now attempt to deal.

I may summarise what I have tried to say as follows: A sociological theory of totemism must be able to show that totemism is simply a special form taken in certain definite conditions by an element or process of culture that is universal and necessary.

Durkheim's attempt to provide such a theory fails in certain important respects. We can, however, incorporate a good deal of Durkheim's analysis in a theory which rests on the same general hypothesis of the nature and function of ritual or the 'sacred'.

Finally, my argument has brought out something of the conditions in which this universal element of culture is most likely to take the form of totemism. These are (1) dependence wholly or in part on natural productions for subsistence, and (2) the existence of a segmentary organisation into clans and moieties or other similar social units. The Andamanese and the Eskimo have (1) but not (2), and they have no totemism though they have the material out of which totemism could easily be made. There are, of course, apparent exceptions to this generalisation, in some of the tribes of Africa, America and Melanesia. The detailed examination of these, which of course cannot be undertaken in a brief paper, really serves, I believe, to confirm the rule.

I would not be understood to maintain the view that totemism, or rather the different institutions which in different parts of the world we call by this general term, have arisen independently of one another. I think that it is very likely. But it does not matter for the sociologist, at any rate in the present state of our knowledge. If anyone wishes to believe that all the existing forms of totemism have come into existence by a process of what is rather unsatisfactorily called 'diffusion' from a single centre, I have no objection. I would point out that totemism has not spread everywhere, or evenly, and that it has not survived equally in all regions. It is sufficient for my argument if we can say that it is only where certain other features of culture are present that totemism is likely to be accepted by a people when it is brought to them from outside, or is likely to remain in active existence after it has been introduced.

CHAPTER VII

TABOO[1]

THE purpose of this lecture, which you have done me the honour of inviting me to deliver, is to commemorate the work of Sir James Frazer, as an example of life-long single-minded devotion to scientific investigation and as having contributed, in as large a measure as that of any man, to laying the foundations of the science of social anthropology. It therefore seems to me appropriate to select as the subject of my discourse one which Sir James was the first to investigate systematically half a century ago, when he wrote the article on 'Taboo' for the ninth edition of the *Encyclopaedia Britannica*, and to the elucidation of which he has made many successive contributions in his writings since that time.

The English word 'taboo' is derived from the Polynesian word 'tabu' (with the accent on the first syllable). In the languages of Polynesia the word means simply 'to forbid', 'forbidden', and can be applied to any sort of prohibition. A rule of etiquette, an order issued by a chief, an injunction to children not to meddle with the possessions of their elders, may all be expressed by the use of the word tabu.

The early voyagers in Polynesia adopted the word to refer to prohibitions of a special kind, which may be illustrated by an example. Certain things such as a newly-born infant, a corpse or the person of a chief are said to be tabu. This means that one should, as far as possible, avoid touching them. A man who does touch one of these tabu objects immediately becomes tabu himself. This means two things. In the first place a man who is tabu in this sense must observe a number of special restrictions on his behaviour; for example, he may not use his hands to feed himself. He is regarded as being in a state of danger, and this is generally stated by saying that if he fails to observe the customary precautions he will be ill and perhaps die. In the second place he is also dangerous to other persons—he is tabu in the same sense as the thing he has touched. If he should come in contact with

[1] The Frazer Lecture, 1939.

utensils in which, or the fire at which, food is cooked, the dangerous influence would be communicated to the food and so injure anyone who partook of it. A person who is tabu in this way, as by touching a corpse, can be restored to his normal condition by rites of purification or desacralisation. He is then said to be *noa* again, this term being the contrary of tabu.

Sir James Frazer has told us that when he took up the study of taboo in 1886 the current view of anthropologists at the time was that the institution in question was confined to the brown and black races of the Pacific, but that as a result of his investigations he came to the conclusion that the Polynesian body of practices and beliefs 'is only one of a number of similar systems of superstition which among many, perhaps all the races of men have contributed in large measure, under many different names and with many variations of detail, to build up the complex fabric of society in all the various sides or elements of it which we describe as religious, social, political, moral and economic'.

The use of the word taboo in anthropology for customs all over the world which resemble in essentials the example given from Polynesia seems to me undesirable and inconvenient. There is the fact already mentioned that in the Polynesian language the word tabu has a much wider meaning, equivalent to our own word 'forbidden'. This has produced a good deal of confusion in the literature relating to Polynesia owing to the ambiguity resulting from two different uses of the same word. You will have noticed that I have used the word taboo (with the English spelling and pronunciation) in the meaning that it has for anthropologists, and tabu (with the Polynesian spelling and pronunciation) in special reference to Polynesia and in the Polynesian sense. But this is not entirely satisfactory.

I propose to refer to the customs we are considering as 'ritual avoidances' or 'ritual prohibitions' and to define them by reference to two fundamental concepts for which I have been in the habit of using the terms 'ritual status' and 'ritual value'. I am not suggesting that these are the best terms to be found; they are merely the best that I have been able to find up to the present. In such a science as ours words are the instruments of analysis and we should always be prepared to discard inferior tools for superior when opportunity arises.

A ritual prohibition is a rule of behaviour which is associated with a belief that an infraction will result in an undesirable change in the ritual status of the person who fails to keep to the rule. This change of ritual status is conceived in many different ways in different societies, but everywhere there is the idea that it involves the likelihood of some minor or major misfortune which will befall the person concerned.

We have already considered one example. The Polynesian who touches a corpse has, according to Polynesian belief, undergone what I am calling an undesirable change of ritual status. The misfortune of which he is considered to be in danger is illness, and he therefore takes precautions and goes through a ritual in order that he may escape the danger and be restored to his former ritual status.

Let us consider two examples of different kinds from contemporary England. There are some people who think that one should avoid spilling salt. The person who spills salt will have bad luck. But he can avoid this by throwing a pinch of the spilled salt over his shoulder. Putting this in my terminology it can be said that spilling salt produces an undesirable change in the ritual status of the person who does so, and that he is restored to his normal or previous ritual status by the positive rite of throwing salt over his shoulder.

A member of the Roman Catholic Church, unless granted a dispensation, is required by his religion to abstain from eating meat on Fridays and during Lent. If he fails to observe the rule he sins, and must proceed, as in any other sin, to confess and obtain absolution. Different as this is in important ways from the rule about spilling salt, it can and must for scientific purposes be regarded as belonging to the same general class. Eating meat on Friday produces in the person who does so an undesirable change of ritual status which requires to be remedied by fixed appropriate means.

We may add to these examples two others from other societies. If you turn to the fifth chapter of Leviticus you will find that amongst the Hebrews if a 'soul' touch the carcase of an unclean beast or of unclean cattle, or of unclean creeping things, even if he is unaware that he does so, then he is unclean and guilty and has sinned. When he becomes aware of his sin he must confess that he has sinned and must take a trespass offering—a female from the flock, a lamb or a kid of the goats—which the priest shall sacrifice to make an atonement for the sin so that it shall be forgiven him. Here the change in ritual status through touching an unclean carcase is described by the terms 'sin', 'unclean' and 'guilty'.

In the Kikuyu tribe of East Africa the word *thahu* denotes the undesirable ritual status that results from failure to observe rules of ritual avoidance. It is believed that a person who is *thahu* will be ill and will probably die unless he removes the *thahu* by the appropriate ritual remedies, which in all serious cases require the services of a priest or medicine man. Actions which produce this condition are touching or carrying a corpse, stepping over a corpse, eating food from a cracked pot, coming in contact with a woman's menstrual discharge, and many others. Just as among the Hebrews a soul may unwittingly be guilty of sin by touching in ignorance the carcase of an unclean animal, so amongst the Kikuyu a man may become *thahu* without any voluntary act on his part. If an elder or a woman when coming out of the hut slips and falls down on the ground, he or she is *thahu* and lies there until some of the elders of the neighbourhood come and sacrifice a sheep. If the side-pole of a bedstead breaks, the person lying on it is *thahu* and must be purified. If the droppings of a kite or crow fall on a person he is *thahu*, and if a hyaena defaecates in a village, or a jackal barks therein, the village and its inhabitants are *thahu*.

I have purposely chosen from our society two examples of ritual avoidances which are of very different kinds. The rule against eating meat on Friday or in Lent is a rule of religion, as is the rule, where it is recognised, against playing golf or tennis on Sunday. The rule against spilling salt, I suppose it will be agreed, is non-religious. Our language permits us to make this distinction very clearly, for infractions of the rules of religion are sins, while the non-religious avoidances are concerned with good and bad luck. Since this distinction is so obvious to us it might be thought that we should find it in other societies. My own experience is that in some of the societies with which I am acquainted this distinction between sinful acts and acts that bring bad luck cannot be made. Several anthropologists, however, have attempted to classify rites into two classes, religious rites and magical rites.

For Emile Durkheim the essential distinction is that religious rites are obligatory within a religious society or church, while

magical rites are optional. A person who fails in religious observances is guilty of wrong-doing, whereas one who does not observe
the precautions of magic or those relating to luck is simply acting
foolishly. This distinction is of considerable theoretical importance. It is difficult to apply in the study of the rites of
simple societies.

Sir James Frazer defines religion as 'a propitiation or con-
ciliation of superhuman powers which are believed to control
nature and man', and regards magic as the erroneous application
of the notion of causality. If we apply this to ritual prohibitions,
we may regard as belonging to religion those rules the infraction
of which produces a change of ritual status in the individual
by offending the superhuman powers, whereas the infraction
of a rule of magic would be regarded as resulting immediately
in a change of ritual status, or in the misfortune that follows, by a
process of hidden causation. Spilling salt, by Sir James Frazer's
definition, is a question of magic, while eating meat on Friday is a
question of religion.

An attempt to apply this distinction systematically meets with
certain difficulties. Thus with regard to the Maori Sir James
Frazer states that 'the ultimate sanction of the taboo, in other
words, that which engaged the people to observe its command-
ments, was a firm persuasion that any breach of those command-
ments would surely and speedily be punished by an *atua* or ghost,
who would afflict the sinner with a painful malady till he died'.
This would seem to make the Polynesian taboo a matter of religion,
not of magic. But my own observation of the Polynesians suggests
to me that in general the native conceives of the change in his
ritual status as taking place as the immediate result of such an act
as touching a corpse, and that it is only when he proceeds to
rationalise the whole system of taboos that he thinks of the gods
and spirits—the *atua*—as being concerned. Incidentally it should
not be assumed that the Polynesian word *atua* or *otua* always
refers to a personal spiritual being.

Of the various ways of distinguishing magic and religion I
will mention only one more. For Professor Malinowski a rite is
magical when 'it has a definite practical purpose which is known
to all who practise it and can be easily elicited from any native
informant', while a rite is religious if it is simply expressive and
has no purpose, being not a means to an end but an end in itself.

A difficulty in applying this criterion is due to uncertainty as to what is meant by 'definite practical purpose'. To avoid the bad luck which results from spilling salt is, I suppose, a practical purpose though not very definite. The desire to please God in all our actions and thus escape some period of Purgatory is perhaps definite enough, but Professor Malinowski may regard it as not practical. What shall we say of the desire of the Polynesian to avoid sickness and possible death which he gives as his reason for not touching chiefs, corpses and newly-born babies?

Seeing that there is this absence of agreement as to the definitions of magic and religion and the nature of the distinction between them, and seeing that in many instances whether we call a particular rite magical or religious depends on which of the various proposed definitions we accept, the only sound procedure, at any rate in the present state of anthropological knowledge, is to avoid as far as possible the use of the terms in question until there is some general agreement about them. Certainly the distinctions made by Durkheim and Frazer and Malinowski may be theoretically significant, even though they are difficult to apply universally. Certainly, also, there is need for a systematic classification of rites, but a satisfactory classification will be fairly complex and a simple dichotomy between magic and religion does not carry us very far towards it.

Another distinction which we make in our own society within the field of ritual avoidances is between the holy and the unclean. Certain things must be treated with respect because they are holy, others because they are unclean. But, as Robertson Smith and Sir James Frazer have shown, there are many societies in which this distinction is entirely unrecognised. The Polynesian, for example, does not think of a chief or a temple as holy and a corpse as unclean. He thinks of them all as things dangerous. An example from Hawaii will illustrate this fundamental identity of holiness and uncleanness. There, in former times, if a commoner committed incest with his sister he became *kapu* (the Hawaiian form of tabu). His presence was dangerous in the extreme for the whole community, and since he could not be purified he was put to death. But if a chief of high rank, who, by reason of his rank was, of course, sacred (*kapu*), married his sister he became still more so. An extreme sanctity or untouchability attached to a chief born of a brother and sister who were themselves the children of a brother and sister. The sanctity of such a chief and the uncleanness of the person put to death for incest have the same source and are the same thing. They are both denoted by saying that the person is *kapu*. In studying the simpler societies it is essential that we should carefully avoid thinking of their behaviour and ideas in terms of our own ideas of holiness and uncleanness. Since most people find this difficult it is desirable to have terms which we can use that do not convey this connotation. Durkheim and others have used the word 'sacred' as an inclusive term for the holy and the unclean together. This is easier to do in French than in English, and has some justification in the fact that the Latin *sacer* did apply to holy things such as the gods and also to accursed things such as persons guilty of certain crimes. But there is certainly a tendency in English to identify sacred with holy. I think that it will greatly aid clear thinking if we adopt some wide inclusive term which does not have any undesirable connotation. I venture to propose the term 'ritual value'.

Anything—a person, a material thing, a place, a word or name, an occasion or event, a day of the week or a period of the year— which is the object of a ritual avoidance or taboo can be said to have ritual value. Thus in Polynesia chiefs, corpses and newly-born babies have ritual value. For some people in England salt has ritual value. For Christians all Sundays and Good Friday have ritual value, and for Jews all Saturdays and the Day of Atonement. The ritual value is exhibited in the behaviour adopted towards the object or occasion in question. Ritual values are exhibited not only in negative ritual but also in positive ritual, being possessed by the objects towards which positive rites are directed and also by objects, words or places used in the rites. A large class of positive rites, those of consecration or sacralisation, have for their purpose to endow objects with ritual value. It may be noted that in general anything that has value in positive ritual is also the object of some sort of ritual avoidance or at the very least of ritual respect.

The word 'value', as I am using it, always refers to a relation between a subject and an object. The relation can be stated in two ways by saying either that the object has a value for the subject, or that the subject has an interest in the object. We can use the terms in this way to refer to any act of behaviour towards an object. The relation is exhibited in and defined by the behaviour. The words 'interest' and 'value' provide a convenient shorthand by which we can describe the reality, which consists of acts of behaviour and the actual relations between subjects and objects which those acts of behaviour reveal. If Jack loves Jill, then Jill has the value of a loved object for Jack, and Jack has a recognisable interest in Jill. When I am hungry I have an interest in food, and a good meal has an immediate value for me that it does not have at other times. My toothache has a value to me as something that I am interested in getting rid of as quickly as possible.

A social system can be conceived and studied as a system of values. A society consists of a number of individuals bound together in a network of social relations. A social relation exists between two or more persons when there is some harmonisation of their individual interests, by some convergence of interest and by limitation or adjustment of divergent interests. An interest is always the interest of an individual. Two individuals may have similar interests. Similar interests do not in themselves constitute a social relation; two dogs may have a similar interest in the same bone and the result may be a dog-fight. But a society cannot exist except on the basis of a certain measure of similarity in the interests of its members. Putting this in terms of value, the first necessary condition of the existence of a society is that the individual members shall agree in some measure in the values that they recognise.

Any particular society is characterised by a certain set of values—moral, aesthetic, economic, etc. In a simple society there is a fair amount of agreement amongst the members in their evaluations, though of course the agreement is never absolute. In a complex modern society we find much more disagreement if we consider the society as a whole, but we may find a closer measure of agreement amongst the members of a group or class within the society.

While some measure of agreement about values, some similarity of interests, is a prerequisite of a social system, social relations involve more than this. They require the existence of common interests and of social values. When two or more persons have a common interest in the same object and are aware of their community of interest a social relation is established. They form, whether for a moment or for a long period, an association, and the object may be said to have a social value. For a man and his wife the birth of a child, the child itself and its well-being and happiness or its death, are objects of a common interest which binds them together and they thus have, for the association formed by the two persons, social value. By this definition an object can only have a social value for an association of persons. In the simplest possible instance we have a triadic relation; Subject 1 and Subject 2 are both interested in the same way in the Object and each of the Subjects has an interest in the other, or at any rate in certain items of the behaviour of the other, namely those directed towards the object. To avoid cumbersome circumlocutions it is convenient to speak of the object as having a social value for any one subject involved in such a relation, but it must be remembered that this is a loose way of speaking.

It is perhaps necessary for the avoidance of misunderstanding to add that a social system also requires that persons should be objects of interest to other persons. In relations of friendship or love each of two persons has a value for the other. In certain kinds of groups each member is an object of interest for all the others, and each member therefore has a social value for the group as a whole. Further, since there are negative values as well as positive, persons may be united or associated by their antagonism to other persons. For the members of an anti-Comintern pact the Comintern has a specific social value.

Amongst the members of a society we find a certain measure of agreement as to the ritual value they attribute to objects of different kinds. We also find that most of these ritual values are social values as defined above. Thus for a local totemic clan in Australia the totem-centres, the natural species associated with them, i.e. the totems, and the myths and rites that relate thereto, have a specific social value for the clan; the common interest in them binds the individuals together into a firm and lasting association.

Ritual values exist in every known society, and show an immense diversity as we pass from one society to another. The problem of a natural science of society (and it is as such that I regard social anthropology) is to discover the deeper, not immediately perceptible, uniformities beneath the superficial differences. This is, of course, a highly complex problem which will require the studies begun by Sir James Frazer and others to be continued by many investigators over many years. The ultimate aim should be, I think, to find some relatively adequate answer to the question—*What is the relation of ritual and ritual values to the essential constitution of human society?* I have chosen a particular approach to this study which I believe to be promising— to investigate in a few societies studied as thoroughly as possible the relations of ritual values to other values including moral and aesthetic values. In the present lecture, however, it is only one small part of this study in which I seek to interest you—the question of a relation between ritual values and social values.

One way of approaching the study of ritual is by the consideration of the purposes or reasons for the rites. If one examines the literature of anthropology one finds this approach very frequently adopted. It is by far the least profitable, though the one that appeals most to common sense. Sometimes the purpose of a rite is obvious, or a reason may be volunteered by those who practise it. Sometimes the anthropologist has to ask the reason, and in such circumstances it may happen that different reasons are given by different informants. What is fundamentally the same rite in two different societies may have different purposes or reasons in the one and in the other. The reasons given by the members of a community for any custom they observe are important data for the anthropologist. But it is to fall into grievous error to suppose that they give a valid explanation of the custom. What is entirely inexcusable is for the anthropologist, when he cannot get from the people themselves a reason for their behaviour which seems to him satisfactory, to attribute to them some purpose or reason on the basis of his own preconceptions about human motives. I could adduce many instances of this from the literature of ethnography, but I prefer to illustrate what I mean by an anecdote.

A Queenslander met a Chinese who was taking a bowl of cooked rice to place on his brother's grave. The Australian in jocular tones asked if he supposed that his brother would come and eat the rice. The reply was 'No! We offer rice to people as an expression of friendship and affection. But since you speak as you do I suppose that you in this country place flowers on the graves of your dead in the belief that they will enjoy looking at them and smelling their sweet perfume.'

So far as ritual avoidances are concerned the reasons for them may vary from a very vague idea that some sort of misfortune or ill-luck, not defined as to its kind, is likely to befall anyone who fails to observe the taboo, to a belief that non-observance will produce some quite specific and undesirable result. Thus an Australian aborigine told me that if he spoke to any woman who stood in the relation of mother-in-law to him his hair would turn grey.[1]

The very common tendency to look for the explanation of ritual actions in their purpose is the result of a false assimilation of them to what may be called technical acts. In any technical activity an adequate statement of the purpose of any particular act or series of acts constitutes by itself a sufficient explanation. But ritual acts differ from technical acts in having in all instances some expressive or symbolic element in them.

A second approach to the study of ritual is therefore by a consideration not of their purpose or reason but of their meaning. I am here using the words symbol and meaning as coincident. Whatever has a meaning is a symbol and the meaning is whatever is expressed by the symbol.

But how are we to discover meanings? They do not lie on the surface. There is a sense in which people always know the meaning of their own symbols, but they do so intuitively and can rarely express their understanding in words. Shall we therefore be reduced to guessing at meanings as some anthropologists have guessed at reasons and purposes? I think not. For as long as we admit guess-work of any kind social anthropology cannot be a science. There are, I believe, methods of determining, with some fair degree of probability, the meanings of rites and other symbols.

There is still a third approach to the study of rites. We can consider the effects of the rite—not the effects that it is supposed to produce by the people who practise it but the effects that it does actually produce. A rite has immediate or direct effects on the persons who are in any way directly concerned in it, which we may call, for lack of a better term, the psychological effects. But there

[1] In case it may be thought that this is an inadequate supernatural punishment for a serious breach of rules of proper behaviour a few words of explanation are necessary. Grey hair comes with old age and is thought to be usually associated with loss of sexual potency. It is thus premature old age with its disadvantages but without the advantages that usually accompany seniority that threatens the man who fails to observe the rules of avoidance. On the other hand when a man's hair is grey and his wife's mother has passed the age of child-bearing the taboo is relaxed so that the relatives may talk together if they wish.

are also secondary effects upon the social structure, i.e. the network of social relations binding individuals together in an ordered life. These we may call the social effects. By considering the psychological effects of a rite we may succeed in defining its psychological function; by considering the social effects we may discover its social function. Clearly it is impossible to discover the social function of a rite without taking into account its usual or average psychological effects. But it is possible to discuss the psychological effects while more or less completely ignoring the more remote sociological effects, and this is often done in what is called 'functional anthropology'.

Let us suppose that we wish to investigate in Australian tribes the totemic rites of a kind widely distributed over a large part of the continent. The ostensible purpose of these rites, as stated by the natives themselves, is to renew or maintain some part of nature, such as a species of animal or plant, or rain, or hot or cold weather. With reference to this purpose we have to say that from our point of view the natives are mistaken, that the rites do not actually do what they are believed to do. The rain-making ceremony does not, we think, actually bring rain. In so far as the rites are performed for a purpose they are futile, based on erroneous belief. I do not believe that there is any scientific value in attempts to conjecture processes of reasoning which might be supposed to have led to these errors.

The rites are easily perceived to be symbolic, and we may therefore investigate their meaning. To do this we have to examine a considerable number of them and we then discover that there is a certain body of ritual idiom extending from the west coast of the continent to the east coast with some local variations. Since each rite has a myth associated with it we have similarly to investigate the meanings of the myths. As a result we find that the meaning of any single rite becomes clear in the light of a cosmology, a body of ideas and beliefs about nature and human society, which, so far as its most general features are concerned, is current in all Australian tribes.

The immediate psychological effects of the rites can be to some extent observed by watching and talking to the performers. The ostensible purpose of the rite is certainly present in their minds, but so also is that complex set of cosmological beliefs by reference to which the rite has a meaning. Certainly a person performing the rite, even if, as sometimes happens, he performs it alone, derives therefrom a definite feeling of satisfaction, but it would be entirely false to imagine that this is simply because he believes that he has helped to provide a more abundant supply of food for himself and his fellow-tribesmen. His satisfaction is in having performed a ritual duty, we might say a religious duty. Putting in my own words what I judge, from my own observations, to express what the native feels, I would say that in the performance of the rite he has made that small contribution, which it is both his privilege and his duty to do, to the maintenance of that order of the universe of which man and nature are interdependent parts. The satisfaction which he thus receives gives the rite a special value for him. In some instances with which I am acquainted of the last survivor of a totemic group who still continues to perform the totemic rites by himself, it is this satisfaction that constitutes apparently the sole motive for his action.

To discover the social function of the totemic rites we have to consider the whole body of cosmological ideas of which each rite is a partial expression. I believe that it is possible to show that the social structure of an Australian tribe is connected in a very special way with these cosmological ideas and that the maintenance of its continuity depends on keeping them alive, by their regular expression in myth and rite.

Thus any satisfactory study of the totemic rites of Australia must be based not simply on the consideration of their ostensible purpose and their psychological function, or on an analysis of the motives of the individuals who perform the rites, but on the discovery of their meaning and of their social function.

It may be that some rites have no social function. This may be the case with such taboos as that against spilling salt in our own society. Nevertheless, the method of investigating rites and ritual values that I have found most profitable during work extending over more than thirty years is to study rites as symbolic expressions and to seek to discover their social functions. This method is not new except in so far as it is applied to the comparative study of many societies of diverse types. It was applied by Chinese thinkers to their own ritual more than twenty centuries ago.

In China, in the fifth and sixth centuries B.C., Confucius and his followers insisted on the great importance of the proper performance of ritual, such as funeral and mourning rites and sacrifices. After Confucius there came the reformer Mo Ti who taught a combination of altruism—love for all men—and utilitarianism. He held that funeral and mourning rites were useless and interfered with useful activities and should therefore be abolished or reduced to a minimum. In the third and second centuries B.C., the Confucians, Hsün Tze and the compilers of the *Li Chi* (Book of Rites), replied to Mo Ti to the effect that though these rites might have no utilitarian purpose they none the less had a very important social function. Briefly the theory is that the rites are the orderly (the *Li Chi* says the beautified) expression of feelings appropriate to a social situation. They thus serve to regulate and refine human emotions. We may say that partaking in the performance of rites serves to cultivate in the individual sentiments on whose existence the social order itself depends.

Let us consider the meaning and social function of an extremely simple example of ritual. In the Andaman Islands when a woman is expecting a baby a name is given to it while it is still in the womb. From that time until some weeks after the baby is born nobody is allowed to use the personal name of either the father or the mother; they can be referred to by teknonymy, i.e. in terms of their relation to the child. During this period both the parents are required to abstain from eating certain foods which they may freely eat at other times.

I did not obtain from the Andamanese any statement of the purpose or reason for this avoidance of names. Assuming that the act is symbolic, what method, other than that of guessing, is there of arriving at the meaning? I suggest that we may start with a general working hypothesis that when, in a single society, the same symbol is used in different contexts or on different kinds of occasions there is some common element of meaning, and that by comparing together the various uses of the symbol we may be able to discover what the common element is. This is precisely the method that we adopt in studying an unrecorded spoken language in order to discover the meanings of words and morphemes.

In the Andamans the name of a dead person is avoided from the occurrence of the death to the conclusion of mourning; the name of a person mourning for a dead relative is not used; there is avoidance of the name of a youth or girl who is passing through the ceremonies that take place at adolescence; a bride or bridegroom is not spoken of or to by his or her own name for a short time after the marriage. For the Andamanese the personal name is a symbol of the social personality, i.e. of the position that an individual occupies in the social structure and the social life. The avoidance of a personal name is a symbolic recognition of the fact that at the time the person is not occupying a normal position in the social life. It may be added that a person whose name is thus temporarily out of use is regarded as having for the time an abnormal ritual status.

Turning now to the rule as to avoiding certain foods, if the Andaman Islanders are asked what would happen if the father or mother broke his taboo the usual answer is that he or she would be ill, though one or two of my informants thought it might perhaps also affect the child. This is simply one instance of a standard formula which applies to a number of ritual prohibitions. Thus persons in mourning for a relative may not eat pork and turtle, the most important flesh foods, and the reason given is that if they did they would be ill.

To discover the meaning of this avoidance of foods by the parents we can apply the same method as in reference to the avoidance of their names. There are similar rules for mourners, for women during menstruation, and for youths and girls during the period of adolescence. But for a full demonstration we have to consider the place of foods in Andamanese ritual as a whole, and for an examination of this I must refer to what I have already written on the subject.

I should like to draw your attention to another point in the method by which it is possible to test our hypotheses as to the meanings of rites. We take the different occasions on which two rites are associated together, for example the association of the avoidance of a person's name with the avoidance by that person of certain foods, which we find in the instance of mourners on the one hand and the expectant mother and father on the other. We must assume that for the Andamanese there is some important similarity between these two kinds of occasions—birth and death—by virtue of which they have similar ritual values. We cannot rest content with any interpretation of the taboos at childbirth unless there is a parallel interpretation of those relating to mourners. In the terms I am using here we can say that in the Andamans the relatives of a recently dead person, and the father and mother of a child that is about to be, or has recently been, born, are in an abnormal ritual status. This is recognised or indicated by the avoidance of their names. They are regarded as likely to suffer some misfortune, some bad luck, if you will, unless they observe certain prescribed ritual precautions of which the avoidance of certain foods is one. In the Andaman Islands the danger in such instances is thought of as the danger of illness. This is the case also with the Polynesian belief about the ritual status of anyone who has touched a corpse or a newly-born baby. It is to be noted that for the Polynesians as well as for the Andamanese the occasion of a birth has a similar ritual value to that of a death.

The interpretation of the taboos at childbirth at which we arrive by studying it in relation to the whole system of ritual values of the Andamanese is too complex to be stated here in full. Clearly, however, they express, in accordance with Andamanese ritual idiom, a common concern in the event. The parents show their concern by avoiding certain foods; their friends show theirs by avoiding the parents' personal names. By virtue of these taboos the occasion acquires a certain social value, as that term has been defined above.

There is one theory that might seem to be applicable to our example. It is based on a hypothesis as to the psychological function of a class of rites. The theory is that in certain circumstances the individual human being is anxious about the outcome of some event or activity because it depends to some extent on conditions that he cannot control by any technical means. He therefore observes some rite which, since he believes it will ensure good luck, serves to reassure him. Thus an aeronaut takes with him in a plane a mascot which he believes will protect him from accident and thus carries out his flight with confidence.

The theory has a respectable antiquity. It was perhaps implied in the *Primus in orbe deos fecit timor* of Petronius and Statius. It has taken various forms from Hume's explanation of religion to Malinowski's explanation of Trobriand magic. It can be made so plausible by a suitable selection of illustrations that it is necessary to examine it with particular care and treat it with reasonable scepticism. For there is always the danger that we may be taken in by ·the plausibility of a theory that ultimately proves to be unsound.

I think that for certain rites it would be easy to maintain with equal plausibility an exactly contrary theory, namely, that if it were not for the existence of the rite and the beliefs associated with it the individual would feel no anxiety, and that the psychological effect of the rite is to create in him a sense of insecurity or danger. It seems very unlikely that an Andaman Islander would think that it is dangerous to eat dugong or pork or turtle meat if it were not for the existence of a specific body of ritual the ostensible purpose of which is to protect him from those dangers. Many hundreds of similar instances could be mentioned from all over the world.

Thus, while one anthropological theory is that magic and religion give men confidence, comfort and a sense of security,[1] it could equally well be argued that they give men fears and anxieties from which they would otherwise be free—the fear of black magic or of spirits, fear of God, of the Devil, of Hell.

Actually in our fears or anxieties as well as in our hopes we are conditioned (as the phrase goes) by the community in which we live. And it is largely by the sharing of hopes and fears, by what I have called common concern in events or eventualities, that human beings are linked together in temporary or permanent associations.

To return to the Andamanese taboos at childbirth, there are difficulties in supposing that they are means by which parents reassure themselves against the accidents that may interfere with a successful delivery. If the prospective father fails to observe the food taboo it is he who will be sick, according to the general Andamanese opinion. Moreover, he must continue to observe the taboos after the child is safely delivered. Further, how are we to provide a parallel explanation of the similar taboos observed by a person mourning for a dead relative?

The taboos associated with pregnancy and parturition are often explained in terms of the hypothesis I have mentioned. A father, naturally anxious at the outcome of an event over which he does not have a technical control and which is subject to hazard, reassures himself by observing some taboo or carrying out some magical action. He may avoid certain foods. He may avoid making nets or tying knots, or he may go round the house untying all knots and opening any locked or closed boxes or containers.

I wish to arouse in your minds, if it is not already there, a suspicion that both the general theory and this special application

---

[1] This theory has been formulated by Loisy, and for magic has been adopted by Malinowski.

of it do not give the whole truth and indeed may not be true at all. Scepticism of plausible but unproved hypotheses is essential in every science. There is at least good ground for suspicion in the fact that the theory has so far been considered in reference to facts that seem to fit it, and no systematic attempt has been made, so far as I am aware, to look for facts that do not fit. That there are many such I am satisfied from my own studies.

The alternative hypothesis which I am presenting for consideration is as follows. In a given community it is appropriate that an expectant father should feel concern or at least should make an appearance of doing so. Some suitable symbolic expression of his concern is found in terms of the general ritual or symbolic idiom of the society, and it is felt generally that a man in that situation ought to carry out the symbolic or ritual actions or abstentions. For every rule that *ought* to be observed there must be some sort of sanction or reason. For acts that patently affect other persons the moral and legal sanctions provide a generally sufficient controlling force upon the individual. For ritual obligations conformity and rationalisation are provided by the ritual sanctions. The simplest form of ritual sanction is an accepted belief that if rules of ritual are not observed some undefined misfortune is likely to occur. In many societies the expected danger is somewhat more definitely conceived as a danger of sickness or, in extreme cases, death. In the more specialised forms of ritual sanction the good results to be hoped for or the bad results to be feared are more specifically defined in reference to the occasion or meaning of the ritual.

The theory is not concerned with the historical origin of ritual, nor is it another attempt to explain ritual in terms of human psychology; it is a hypothesis as to the relation of ritual and ritual values to the essential constitution of human society, i.e. to those invariant general characters which belong to all human societies, past, present and future. It rests on the recognition of the fact that while in animal societies social coaptation depends on instinct, in human societies it depends upon the efficacy of symbols of many different kinds. The theory I am advancing must therefore, for a just estimation of its value, be considered in its place in a general theory of symbols and their social efficacy.

By this theory the Andamanese taboos relating to childbirth are the obligatory recognition in a standardised symbolic form

of the significance and importance of the event to the parents and
to the community at large. They thus serve to fix the social value
of occasions of this kind. Similarly I have argued in another place
that the Andamanese taboos relating to the animals and plants
used for food are means of affixing a definite social value to food,
based on its social importance: The *social* importance of food is
not that it satisfies hunger, but that in such a community as an
Andamanese camp or village an enormously large proportion
of the activities are concerned with the getting and consuming of
food, and that in these activities, with their daily instances of
collaboration and mutual aid, there continuously occur those
inter-relations of interests which bind the individual men, women
and children into a society.

I believe that this theory can be generalised and with suitable
modifications will be found to apply to a vast number of the taboos
of different societies. My theory would go further for I would hold,
as a reasonable working hypothesis, that we have here the primary
basis of all ritual and therefore of religion and magic, however
those may be distinguished. The primary basis of ritual, so the
formulation would run, is the attribution of ritual value to objects
and occasions which are either themselves objects of important
common interests linking together the persons of a community
or are symbolically representative of such objects. To illustrate
what is meant by the last part of this statement two illustrations
may be offered. In the Andamans ritual value is attributed to the
cicada, not because it has any social importance itself but because
it symbolically represents the seasons of the year which do have
importance. In some tribes of Eastern Australia the god Baiame
is the personification, i.e. the symbolical representative, of the
moral law of the tribe, and the rainbow-serpent (the Australian
equivalent of the Chinese dragon) is a symbol representing
growth and fertility in nature. Baiame and the rainbow-serpent
in their turn are represented by the figures of earth which are
made on the sacred ceremonial ground of the initiation ceremonies and at which rites are performed. The reverence that the
Australian shows to the image of Baiame or towards his name is
the symbolic method of fixing the social value of the moral law,
particularly the laws relating to marriage.

In conclusion let me return once more to the work of the
anthropologist whom we are here to honour. Sir James Frazer, in

his *Psyche's Task* and in his other works, set himself to show how, in his own words, taboos have contributed to build up the complex fabric of society. He thus initiated that functional study of ritual to which I have in this lecture and elsewhere attempted to make some contribution. But there has been a shift of emphasis. Sir James accounted for the taboos of savage tribes as the application in practice of beliefs arrived at by erroneous processes of reasoning, and he seems to have thought of the effects of these beliefs in creating or maintaining a stable orderly society as being accidental. My own view is that the negative and positive rites of savages exist and persist because they are part of the mechanism by which an orderly society maintains itself in existence, serving as they do to establish certain fundamental social values. The beliefs by which the rites themselves are justified and given some sort of consistency are the rationalisations of symbolic actions and of the sentiments associated with them. I would suggest that what Sir James Frazer seems to regard as the accidental results of magical and religious beliefs really constitute their essential function and the ultimate reason for their existence.

NOTE

The theory of ritual outlined in this lecture was first worked out in 1908 in a thesis on the Andaman Islanders. It was written out again in a revised and extended form in 1913 and appeared in print in 1922. Unfortunately the exposition contained in *The Andaman Islanders* is evidently not clear, since some of my critics have failed to understand what the theory is. For example, it has been assumed that by 'social value' I mean 'utility'.

The best treatment of the subject of value with which I am acquainted is Ralph Barton Perry's *General Theory of Value*, 1926. For the Chinese theory of ritual the most easily accessible account is in chapter xiv of Fung Yu-lan's *History of Chinese Philosophy*, 1937. The third chapter, on the uses of symbolism, of Whitehead's *Symbolism, its Meaning and Effect*, is an admirable brief introduction to the sociological theory of symbolism.

One very important point that could not be dealt with in the lecture is that indicated by Whitehead in the following sentence— 'No account of the uses of symbolism is complete without the recognition that the symbolic elements in life have a tendency to run wild, like the vegetation in a tropical forest.'

CHAPTER VIII

RELIGION AND SOCIETY[1]

THE Royal Anthropological Institute has honoured me with an invitation to deliver the Henry Myers Lecture on the rôle of religion in the development of human society. That is an important and complex subject, about which it is not possible to say very much in a single lecture, but as it is hoped that this may be only the first of a continuing series of lectures, in which different lecturers will each offer some contribution, I think that the most useful thing I can do is to indicate certain lines along which I believe that an enquiry into this problem can be profitably pursued.

The usual way of looking at religions is to regard all of them, or all except one, as bodies of erroneous beliefs and illusory practices. There is no doubt that the history of religions has been in great part a history of error and illusion. In all ages men have hoped that by the proper performance of religious actions or observances they would obtain some specific benefit: health and long life, children to carry on their line, material well-being, success in hunting, rain, the growth of crops and the multiplication of cattle, victory in war, admission of their souls after death to a paradise, or inversely, release by the extinction of personality from the round of reincarnation. We do not believe that the rain-making rites of savage tribes really produce rain. Nor do we believe that the initiates of the ancient mysteries did actually attain through their initiation an immortality denied to other men.

When we regard the religions of other peoples, or at least those of what are called primitive peoples, as systems of erroneous and illusory beliefs, we are confronted with the problem of how these beliefs came to be formulated and accepted. It is to this problem that anthropologists have given most attention. My personal opinion is that this method of approach, even though it may seem the most direct, is not the one most likely to lead to a real understanding of the nature of religions.

[1] The Henry Myers Lecture, 1945.

There is another way in which we may approach the study of religions. We may entertain as at least a possibility the theory that any religion is an important or even essential part of the social machinery, as are morality and law, part of the complex system by which human beings are enabled to live together in an orderly arrangement of social relations. From this point of view we deal not with the origins but with the social functions of religions, i.e. the contribution that they make to the formation and maintenance of a social order. There are many persons who would say that it is only *true* religion (i.e. one's own) that can provide the foundation of an orderly social life. The hypothesis we are considering is that the social function of a religion is independent of its truth or falsity, that religions which we think to be erroneous or even absurd and repulsive, such as those of some savage tribes, may be important and effective parts of the social machinery, and that without these 'false' religions social evolution and the development of modern civilisation would have been impossible.

The hypothesis, therefore, is that in what we regard as false religions, though the performance of religious rites does not actually produce the effects that are expected or hoped for by those who perform or take part in them, they have other effects, some at least of which may be socially valuable.

How are we to set to work to test this hypothesis? It is of no use thinking in terms of religion in general, in the abstract, and society in the abstract. Nor is it adequate to consider some one religion, particularly if it is the one in which we have been brought up and about which we are likely to be prejudiced one way or another. The only method is the experimental method of social anthropology, and that means that we must study in the light of our hypothesis a sufficient number of diverse particular religions or religious cults in their relation to the particular societies in which they are found. This is a task not for one person but for a number.

Anthropologists and others have discussed at length the question of the proper definition of religion. I do not intend to deal with that controversial subject on this occasion. But there are some points that must be considered. I shall assume that any religion or any religious cult normally involves certain ideas or beliefs on the one hand, and on the other certain observances.

These observances, positive and negative, i.e. actions and abstentions, I shall speak of as rites.

In European countries, and more particularly since the Reformation, religion has come to be considered as primarily a matter of belief. This is itself a phenomenon which needs to be explained, I think, in terms of social development. We are concerned here only with its effects on the thinking of anthropologists. Among many of them there is a tendency to treat belief as primary: rites are considered as the results of beliefs. They therefore concentrate their attention on trying to explain the beliefs by hypotheses as to how they may have been formed and adopted.

To my mind this is the product of false psychology. For example, it is sometimes held that funeral and mourning rites are the result of a belief in a soul surviving death. If we must talk in terms of cause and effect, I would rather hold the view that the belief in a surviving soul is not the cause but the effect of the rites. Actually the cause-effect analysis is misleading. What really happens is that the rites and the justifying or rationalising beliefs develop together as parts of a coherent whole. But in this development it is action or the need of action that controls or determines belief rather than the other way about. The actions themselves are symbolic expressions of sentiments.

My suggestion is that in attempting to understand a religion it is on the rites rather than on the beliefs that we should first concentrate our attention. Much the same view is taken by Loisy, who justifies his selection of sacrificial rites as the subject of his analysis of religion by saying that rites are in all religions the most stable and lasting element, and consequently that in which we can best discover the spirit of ancient cults.[1]

That great pioneer of the science of religion, Robertson Smith, took this view. He wrote as follows:

In connection with every religion, whether ancient or modern, we find on the one hand certain beliefs, and on the other certain institutions, ritual practices and rules of conduct. Our modern habit is to look at religion from the side of belief rather than that of practice; for, down to comparatively recent times, almost the only forms of religion seriously studied in Europe have been those of the various Christian Churches, and all parts of Christendom are agreed that ritual is important

[1] 'Les rites étant dans toutes les religions l'élément le plus consistant et le plus durable, celui, par conséquent, où se découvre le mieux l'esprit des cultes anciens.'—*Essai historique sur le Sacrifice*, Paris, 1920, p. 1.

only in connection with its interpretation. Thus the study of religion has meant mainly the study of Christian beliefs, and instruction in religion has habitually begun with the creed, religious duties being presented to the learner as flowing from the dogmatic truths he is taught to accept. All this seems to us so much a matter of course that, when we approach some strange or antique religion, we naturally assume that here also our first business is to search for a creed, and find in it the key to ritual and practice. But the antique religions had for the most part no creed; they consisted entirely of institutions and practices. No doubt men will not habitually follow certain practices without attaching a meaning to them; but as a rule we find that while the practice was rigorously fixed, the meaning attached to it was extremely vague, and the same rite was explained by different people in different ways, without any question of orthodoxy or heterodoxy arising in consequence. In ancient Greece, for example, certain things were done at a temple, and people were agreed that it would be impious not to do them. But if you asked why they were done you would probably have had several mutually contradictory explanations from different persons, and no one would have thought it a matter of the least religious importance which of these you chose to adopt. Indeed, the explanations offered would not have been of a kind to stir any strong feeling; for in most cases they would have been merely different stories as to the circumstances under which the rite first came to be established, by the command or by the direct example of the god. The rite, in short, was connected not with dogma but with a myth.[1]

. . . It is of the first importance to realise clearly from the outset that ritual and practical usage were, strictly speaking, the sum-total of ancient religions. Religion in primitive times was not a system of belief with practical applications; it was a body of fixed traditional practices to which every member of society conformed as a matter of course. Men would not be men if they agreed to do certain things without having a reason for their action; but in ancient religion the reason was not first formulated as a doctrine and then expressed in practice, but conversely, practice preceded doctrinal theory. Men form general rules of conduct before they begin to express general principles in words; political institutions are older than political theories, and in like manner religious institutions are older than religious theories. This analogy is not arbitrarily chosen, for in fact the parallelism in ancient society between religious and political institutions is complete. In each sphere great importance was attached to form and precedent, but the explanation why the precedent was followed consisted merely of a legend as to its first establishment. That the precedent, once established, was authoritative did not appear to require any proof. The rules of society were based on precedent, and the continued existence of the society was sufficient reason why a precedent once set should continue to be followed.[2]

[1] W. Robertson Smith, *Lectures on the Religion of the Semites*, 1907, pp. 16–17.
[2] *op. cit.*, p. 20.

The relative stability of rites and the variability of doctrines can be illustrated from the Christian religions. The two essential rites of all Christian religions are baptism and the eucharist, and we know that the latter solemn sacrament is interpreted differently in the Orthodox Church, the Roman Church and the Anglican Church. The modern emphasis on the exact formulation of beliefs connected with the rites rather than on the rites themselves is demonstrated in the way in which Christians have fought with and killed one another over differences of doctrine.

Thirty-seven years ago (1908), in a fellowship thesis on the Andaman Islanders (which did not appear in print till 1922), I formulated briefly a general theory of the social function of rites and ceremonies. It is the same theory that underlies the remarks I shall offer on this occasion. Stated in the simplest possible terms the theory is that an orderly social life amongst human beings depends upon the presence in the minds of the members of a society of certain sentiments, which control the behaviour of the individual in his relation to others. Rites can be seen to be the regulated symbolic expressions of certain sentiments. Rites can therefore be shown to have a specific social function when, and to the extent that, they have for their effect to regulate, maintain and transmit from one generation to another sentiments on which the constitution of the society depends. I ventured to suggest as a general formula that religion is everywhere an expression in one form or another of a sense of dependence on a power outside ourselves, a power which we may speak of as a spiritual or moral power.

This theory is by no means new. It is to be found in the writings of the philosophers of ancient China. It is most explicit in the teachings of Hsün Tzŭ who lived in the third century B.C., and in the *Book of Rites* (the *Li Chi*), which was compiled some time later. The Chinese writers do not write about religion. I am doubtful if there is in Chinese any word which will convey just what we understand by the word religion. They write about *li*, and the word is variously translated as ceremonial, customary morality, rites, rules of good manners, propriety. But the character by which this word is written consists of two parts, of which one refers to spirits, sacrifice and prayer, and the other originally meant a vessel used in performing sacrifices. We may therefore appropriately translate *li* as 'ritual'. In any case what the ancient philosophers are chiefly concerned with are the rites of mourning and sacrificial rites.

There is no doubt that in China, as elsewhere, it was thought that many or all of the religious rites were efficacious in the sense of averting evils and bringing blessings. It was believed that the seasons would not follow one another in due order unless the Emperor, the Son of Heaven, performed the established rites at the appropriate times. Even under the Republic a reluctant magistrate of a *hsien* may be compelled by public opinion to take the leading part in a ceremony to bring rain. But there developed among the scholars an attitude which might perhaps be called rationalistic and agnostic. For the most part the question of the efficacy of rites was not considered. What was thought important was the social function of the rites, i.e. their effects in producing and maintaining an orderly human society.

In a text that is earlier than Confucius we read that 'sacrifice is that through which one can show one's filial piety and give peace to the people, pacify the country and make the people settled. . . . It is through the sacrifices that the unity of the people is strengthened' (*Ch'u Yü*, II, 2).

You know that one of the major points of the teaching of Confucius was the importance of the proper performance of rites. But it is said of Confucius that he would not discuss the supernatural.[1] In the Confucian philosophy, music and ritual are considered as means for the establishment and preservation of social order, and regarded as superior to laws and punishments as means to this end. We take a very different view of music, but I may remind you that Plato held somewhat similar ideas, and I suggest that an anthropological study of the relations between music (and dancing) and religious rituals would provide some interesting results. In the *Book of Rites* one section (the *Yüeh Chi*) is concerned with music. The third paragraph reads:

> The ancient kings were watchful in regard to the things by which the mind was affected. And so they instituted ceremonies to direct men's aims aright; music to give harmony to their voices; laws to unify their conduct; and punishments to guard against their tendencies to evil. The end to which ceremonies, music, punishments and laws conduct

---

[1] *Analects*, VII, 20. Waley translates this passage as: 'The Master never talked of prodigies, feats of strength, disorders or spirits.'

is one; they are the instruments by which the minds of the people are assimilated, and good order in government is made to appear.[1]

The view of religion that we are here concerned with might be summed up in the following sentence from the *Book of Rites*, 'Ceremonies are the bond that holds the multitudes together, and if the bond be removed, those multitudes fall into confusion.'

The later Confucian philosophers, beginning with Hsün Tzŭ, paid attention to the ways in which rites, particularly the mourning and sacrificial rites, performed their function of maintaining social order. The chief point of their theory is that the rites serve to 'regulate' and 'refine' human feelings. Hsün Tzŭ says:

> Sacrificial rites are the expressions of man's affectionate longings. They represent the height of altruism, faithfulness, love and reverence. They represent the completion of propriety and refinement.[2]

Of the mourning rites Hsün Tzŭ says:

> The rites (*li*) consist in being careful about the treatment of life and death. Life is the beginning of man, Death is the end of man. When the end and beginning are both good, the way of humanity is complete. Hence the Superior Man respects the beginning and venerates the end. To make the end and beginning uniform is the practice of the Superior man, and is that in which lies the beauty of *li* and standards of justice (*i*). For to pay over-attention to the living and belittle the dead would be to respect them when they have knowledge and disrespect them when they have not. . . .
>
> The way of death is this: once dead, a person cannot return again. [It is in realising this that] the minister most completely fulfils the honour due to his ruler, and the son the honour of his parents.
>
> Funeral rites are for the living to give beautified ceremonial to the dead; to send off the dead as if they were living; to render the same service to the dead as to the living; to the absent as to the present; and to make the end be the same as the beginning. . .
>
> Articles used in life are prepared so as to be put into the grave, as if [the deceased] were only moving house. Only a few things are taken, not all of them. They are to give the appearance, but are not for practical use. . . . Hence the things [such as were used] in life are adorned, but not completed, and the 'spiritual utensils' are for appearance but not use. . . .[3]

---

[1] Legge's translation. An alternative translation of the last sentence would be: 'Rites, music, punishments, laws have one and the same end, to unite hearts and establish order.'

[2] The translations from Hsün Tzŭ are those of Fung Yu Lan and are quoted from his *History of Chinese Philosophy*, Peiping, 1937.

[3] Fung Yu Lan translates by the term 'spiritual utensils' the Chinese *ming ch'i*, which Legge in the following passage from the *Book of Rites* translates as

Hence the funeral rites are for no other purpose than to make clear the meaning of death and life, to send off the dead with sorrow and reverence, and when the end comes, to prepare for storing the body away. . . . Service to the living is beautifying their beginning; sending off the dead is beautifying their end. When the end and the beginning are both attended to, the service of the filial son is ended and the way of the Sage is completed. Slighting the dead and over-emphasising the living is the way of Mo (Tzŭ).[1] Slighting the living and over-attention to the dead is the way of superstition. Killing the living to send off the dead is murder.[2] The method and manner of *li* and standards of justice (*i*) is to send off the dead as if they were alive, so that in death and life, the end and the beginning, there is nothing that is not appropriate and good. The Confucian does this.

The view taken by this school of ancient philosophers was that religious rites have important social functions which are independent of any beliefs that may be held as to the efficacy of the rites. The rites gave regulated expression to certain human feelings and sentiments and so kept these sentiments alive and active. In turn it was these sentiments which, by their control of or influence on the conduct of individuals, made possible the existence and continuance of an orderly social life.

It is this theory that I propose for your consideration. Applied, not to a single society such as ancient China, but to all human societies, it points to the correlation and co-variation of different characteristics or elements of social systems. Societies differ from one another in their structure and constitution and therefore in the customary rules of behaviour of persons one to another. The system of sentiments on which the social constitution depends must therefore vary in correspondence with the difference of constitution. In so far as religion has the kind of social function

'vessels to the eye of fancy': 'Confucius said, "In dealing with the dead, if we treat them as if they were entirely dead, that would show a want of affection, and should not be done; or, if we treat them as if they were entirely alive, that would show a want of wisdom, and should not be done. On this account the vessels of bamboo [used in connection with the burial of the dead] are not fit for actual use; those of earthenware cannot be used to wash in; those of wood are incapable of being carved; the lutes are strung, but not evenly; the pandean pipes are complete, but not in tune; the bells and musical stones are there, but they have no stands. They are called vessels to the eye of fancy; that is [the dead] are thus treated as if they were spiritual intelligencies."' Legge, *The Sacred Books of China*, Part III, The Lî Kî, I–X, Oxford, 1885, p. 148.

[1] Mo Tzŭ was a philosopher who criticised the mourning rites as being wasteful.

[2] Referring to the ancient practice of human sacrifice at the burial of important persons.

that the theory suggests, religion must also vary in correspondence with the manner in which the society is constituted. In a social system constituted on the basis of nations which make war on one another, or stand ready to do so, a well-developed sentiment of patriotism in its members is essential to maintain a strong nation. In such circumstances patriotism or national feeling may be given support by religion. Thus the Children of Israel, when they invaded the land of Canaan under the leadership of Joshua, were inspired by the religion that had been taught to them by Moses and was centred upon the Holy Tabernacle and its rites.

War or the envisaged possibility of war is an essential element in the constitution of great numbers of human societies, though the warlike spirit varies very much from one to another. It is thus in accordance with our theory that one of the social functions of religion is in connection with war. It can give men faith and confidence and devotion when they go out to do battle, whether they are the aggressors or are resisting aggression. In the recent conflict the German people seem to have prayed to God for victory not less fervently than the people of the allied nations.

It will be evident that to test our theory we must examine many societies to see if there is a demonstrable correspondence of the religion or religions of any one of them and the manner in which that society is constituted. If such a correspondence can be made out, we must then try to discover and as far as possible define the major sentiments that find their expression in the religion and at the same time contribute to the maintenance of stability in the society as constituted.

An important contribution to our study is to be found in a book that is undeservedly neglected by anthropologists, *La Cité antique*, by the historian Fustel de Coulanges. It is true that it was written some time ago (1864) and that in some matters it may need correction in the light of later historical research, but it remains a valuable contribution to the theory of the social function of religion.

The purpose of the book is to show the point-by-point correspondence between religion and the constitution of society in ancient Greece and Rome, and how in the course of history the two changed together. It is true that the author, in conformity with the ideas of the nineteenth century, conceived this cor-relation between two sets of social features in terms of cause and effect, those of one set being thought of as the cause producing those of the other set. The men of the ancient world, so the argument runs, came to hold certain beliefs about the souls of the dead. As the result of their beliefs they made offerings at their tombs.

> Since the dead had need of food and drink it appeared to be a duty of the living to satisfy this need. The care of supplying the dead with sustenance was not left to the caprice or to the variable sentiments of of men; it was obligatory. Thus a complete religion of the dead was established, whose dogmas might soon be effaced, but whose rites endured until the triumph of Christianity.[1]

It was a result of this religion that ancient society came to be constituted on the basis of the family, the agnatic lineage and the gens, with its laws of succession, property, authority and marriage.

> A comparison of beliefs and laws shows that a primitive religion constituted the Greek and Roman family, established marriage and paternal authority, fixed the order of relationship, and consecrated the right of property and the right of inheritance. This same religion, after having enlarged and extended the family, formed a still larger association, the city, and reigned in that as it had reigned in the family. From it came all the institutions, as well as all the private law, of the ancients. It was from this that the city received all its principles, its rules, its usages and its magistracies. But, in the course of time, this ancient religion became modified or effaced, and private law and political institutions were modified with it. Then came a series of revolutions, and social changes regularly followed the development of knowledge.[2]

In his final paragraph the author writes:

> We have written the history of a belief. It was established and human society was constituted. It was modified, and society underwent a series of revolutions. It disappeared and society changed its character.[3]

This idea of the primacy of belief and of a causal relation in which the religion is the cause and the other institutions are the effect is in accordance with a mode of thought that was common in the nineteenth century. We can, as I indeed do, completely reject this theory and yet retain as a valuable and permanent contribution to our subject a great deal of what Fustel de Coulanges wrote. We can say that he has produced evidence that in ancient Greece and Rome the religion on the one side and the many important institutions on the other are closely united as inter-

[1] *The Ancient City* (trans. Willard Small), p. 23.
[2] op cit., p. 12.   [3] op cit., p. 529.

dependent parts of a coherent and unified system. The religion was an essential part of the constitution of the society. The form of the religion and the form of the social structure correspond one with the other. We cannot, as Fustel de Coulanges says, understand the social, juridical and political institutions of the ancient societies unless we take the religion into account. But it is equally true that we cannot understand the religion except by an examination of its relation to the institutions.

A most important part of the religion of ancient Greece and Rome was the worship of ancestors. We may regard this as one instance of a certain type of religion. A religious cult of the same general kind has existed in China from ancient times to the present day. Cults of the same kind exist to-day and can be studied in many parts of Africa and Asia. It is therefore possible to make a wide comparative study of this type of religion. In my own experience it is in ancestor-worship that we can most easily discover and demonstrate the social function of a religious cult.

The term 'ancestor-worship' is sometimes used in a wide, loose sense to refer to any sort of rites referring to dead persons. I propose to use it in a more limited and more precisely defined sense. The cult group in this religion consists solely of persons related to one another by descent in one line from the same ancestor or ancestors. In most instances descent is patrilineal, through males. But in some societies, such as the Bakongo in Africa and the Nayar in India, descent is matrilineal, and the cult group consists of descendants of a single ancestress. The rites in which the members of the group, and only they, participate have reference to their own ancestors, and normally they include the making of offerings or sacrifices to them.

A particular lineage consists of three or more generations. A lineage of four or five generations will normally be included as a part in one of six or seven generations. In a well-developed system related lineages are united into a larger body, such as the Roman gens, or what may be called the clan in China. In parts of China we can find a large body of persons, numbering in some instances as much as a thousand, all having the same name and tracing their descent in the male line from a single ancestor, the founder of the clan. The clan itself is divided into lineages.

A lineage, if it is of more than three or four generations, includes both living persons and dead persons. What is called ancestor-worship consists of rites carried out by members of a larger or smaller lineage (i.e. one consisting of more or fewer generations) with reference to the deceased members of the lineage. Such rites include the making of offerings, usually of food and drink, and such offerings are sometimes interpreted as the sharing of a meal by the dead and the living.

In such a society, what gives stability to the social structure is the solidarity and continuity of the lineage, and of the wider group (the clan) composed of related lineages. For the individual, his primary duties are those to his lineage. These include duties to the members now living, but also to those who have died and to those who are not yet born. In the carrying out of these duties he is controlled and inspired by the complex system of sentiments of which we may say that the object on which they are centred is the lineage itself, past, present and future. It is primarily this system of sentiments that is expressed in the rites of the cult of the ancestors. The social function of the rites is obvious: by giving solemn and collective expression to them the rites reaffirm, renew and strengthen those sentiments on which the social solidarity depends.

We have no means of studying how an ancestor-worshipping society comes into existence, but we can study the decay of this type of system in the past and in the present. Fustel de Coulanges deals with this in ancient Greece and Rome. It can be observed at the present time in various parts' of the world. The scanty information I have been able to gather suggests that the lineage and joint-family organisation of some parts of India is losing something of its former strength and solidarity and that what we should expect as the inevitable accompaniment of this, a weakening of the cult of ancestors, is also taking place. I can speak with more assurance about some African societies, particularly those of South Africa. The effect of the impact of European culture, including the teaching of the Christian missionaries, is to weaken in some individuals the sentiments that attach them to their lineage. The disintegration of the social structure and the decay of the ancestral cult proceed together.

Thus for one particular type of religion I am ready to affirm that the general theory of the social function of religions can be fully demonstrated.

A most important contribution to our subject is a work of

Emile Durkheim published in 1912. The title is *Les Formes élémentaires de la Vie religieuse*, but the sub-title reads: *La Système totémique en Australie*. It is worth while mentioning that Durkheim was a pupil of Fustel de Coulanges at the École Normale Supérieure and that he himself said that the most important influence on the development of his ideas about religion was that of Robertson Smith.

Durkheim's aim was to establish a general theory of the nature of religion. Instead of a wide comparative study of many religions, he preferred to take a simple type of society and carry out an intensive and detailed analysis, and for this purpose he selected the aboriginal tribes of Australia. He held the view that these tribes represent the simplest type of society surviving to our own times, but the value of his analysis is in no way affected if we refuse to accept this view, as I do myself.

The value of Durkheim's book is as an exposition of a general theory of religion which had been developed with the collaboration of Henri Hubert and Marcel Mauss, starting from the foundations provided by Robertson Smith. Durkheim's exposition of this theory has often been very much misunderstood. A clear, though very brief, statement of it is to be found in the Introduction written by Henri Hubert in 1904 for the French translation of the *Manuel d'Histoire des Religions* of Chantepie de la Saussaye. But it is not possible on this occasion to discuss this general theory. I wish only to deal with one part of Durkheim's work, namely his theory that religious ritual is an expression of the unity of society and that its function is to 're-create' the society or the social order by reaffirming and strengthening the sentiments on which the social solidarity and therefore the social order itself depend.[1] This theory he tests by an examination of the totemic ritual of the Australians. For while Frazer regarded the totemic rites of the Australian tribes as being a matter of magic, Durkheim treats them as religious because the rites themselves are sacred and have reference to sacred beings, sacred places and sacred objects.

In 1912 very much less was known about the Australian aborigines than is known at present. Some of the sources used by Durkheim have proved to be unreliable. The one tribe that was well known, through the writings of Spencer and Gillen and

[1] op cit., pp. 323, 497 and elsewhere.

Strehlow—the Aranda—is in some respects atypical. The information that Durkheim could use was therefore decidedly imperfect. Moreover, it cannot be said that his handling of this material was all that it might have been. Consequently there are many points in his exposition which I find unacceptable. Nevertheless, I think that Durkheim's major thesis as to the social function of the totemic rites is valid and only requires revision and correction in the light of the more extensive and more exact knowledge we now have.[1]

The beings to which the Australian cult refers are commonly spoken of as 'totemic ancestors', and I have myself used the term. But it is somewhat misleading, since they are mythical beings and not ancestors in the same sense as the dead persons commemorated in ancestor-worship. In the cosmology of the Australian natives the cosmos, the ordered universe, including both the order of nature and the social order, came into existence at a time in the past which I propose to speak of as the World-Dawn, for this name corresponds to certain ideas that I have found amongst the aborigines of some tribes. This order (of nature and of society) resulted from the doings and adventures of certain sacred beings. These beings, whom I shall call the Dawn Beings, are the totemic ancestors of ethnological literature. The explanations of topographical features, of natural species and their characteristics, and of social laws, customs and usages are given in the form of myths about the happenings of the World-Dawn.

The cosmos is ruled by law. But whereas we think of the laws of nature as statements of what invariably does happen (except, of course, in miracles), and of moral or social laws as what ought to be observed but are sometimes broken, the Australian does not make this distinction. For him men and women ought to observe the rules of behaviour that were fixed for all time by the events of the World-Dawn, and similarly the rain ought to fall in its proper season, plants should grow and produce fruit or seed, and animals should bear young. But there are irregularities in human society and in nature.

In what I shall venture to call the totemic religion of the Australian aborigines, there are two main types of ritual. One of these consists of rites carried out at certain spots which are com-

---

[1] For a criticism of some points in Durkheim's work, see 'The Sociological Theory of Totemism' in this volume.

monly referred to as 'totem centres'. A totem centre is a spot that is specially connected with some species of object, most commonly with a particular species of animal or plant, or with an aspect of nature such as rain or hot weather. Each centre is associated with one (or occasionally more than one) of the Dawn Beings. Frequently the Being is said to have gone into the ground at this spot. For each totem centre there is a myth connecting it with the events of the World-Dawn. The totem centre, the myth connected with it and the rites that are performed there, belong to the local group that owns the territory within which the totem centre lies. Each totem centre is thought of as containing, in a rock or a tree or a pool of water or a heap of stones, what we may perhaps call the life-spirit or life-force of the totem species.

The rites performed at the totem centre by the members of the local group to which it belongs, or under their leadership and direction, are thought to renew the vitality of this life-spirit of the species. In eastern Australia the totem centre is spoken of as the 'home' or 'dwelling-place' of the species, and the rites are called 'stirring up'. Thus, the rite at a rain totem centre brings the rain in its due season, that at a kangaroo totem centre ensures the supply of kangaroos, and that at the baby totem centre provides for the birth of children in the tribe.

These rites imply a certain conception, which I think we can call specifically a religious conception, of the place of man in the universe. Man is dependent upon what we call nature: on the regular successions of the seasons, on the rain falling when it should, on the growth of plants and the continuance of animal life. But, as I have already said, while for us the order of nature is one thing and the social order another, for the Australian they are two parts of a single order. Well-being, for the individual or for the society, depends on the continuance of this order free from serious disturbance. The Australians believe that they can ensure this continuance, or at least contribute to it, by their actions, including the regular performance of the totemic rites.

In the rites that have been described, each group takes care (if we may so express it) of only a small part of nature, of those few species for which it owns totem centres. The preservation of the natural order as a whole therefore depends on the actions of many different groups.

The social structure of the Australian natives is based on two

Kinship

things: a system of local groups, and a system of kinship based on the family. Each small local group is a closed patrilineal descent group; that is, a man is born into the group of his father and his sons belong to his group. Each group is independent and autonomous. The stability and continuity of the social structure depends on the strong solidarity of the local group.

Where there existed the totemic cult which I have just described (and it existed over a very large part of Australia), each local group was a cult group. The totemic ritual served to express the unity and solidarity of the group and its individuality and separation from other groups by the special relation of the group to its *sacra*: the totem centre or centres, the Dawn Beings associated with them, the myths and songs referring to those Beings, and the totems or species connected with the centres. This aspect of the social function of totemism was emphasised, and I think somewhat over-emphasised, by Durkheim.

Durk

There is, however, another aspect, for while the local totemic groups are separate individual and continuing social entities, they are also part of a wider social structure. This wider structure is provided by the kinship system. For an individual in Australian native society, every person with whom he has any social contact is related to him by some bond of kinship, near or distant, and the regulation of social life consists essentially of rules concerning behaviour towards different kinds of kin. For example, a man stands in very close relation to his mother's local group and, in many tribes, in a very close relation to its *sacra*: its totems, totem centres and totemic rites.

RB expands on Durk

social group unity × Kinship

While Australian totemism separates the local groups and gives each an individuality of its own, it also links the groups together. For while each group is specially connected with certain parts of the natural order (e.g. with rain, or with kangaroo) and with certain of the Beings of the World-Dawn, the society as a whole is related through the totemic religion to the whole order of nature and to the World-Dawn as a whole. This is best seen in another kind of totemic cult, part of which consists of sacred dramas in which the performers impersonate various Dawn Beings. Such dramatic dances are only performed at those religious meetings at which a number of local groups come together, and it is on these occasions that young men are initiated into manhood and into the religious life of the society.

Australian society is not merely a collection of separate local groups; it is also a body of persons linked together in the kinship system. Australian totemism is a cosmological system by which the phenomena of nature are incorporated in the kinship organisation. When I was beginning my work in Australia in 1910, a native said to me, '*Bungurdi* (kangaroo) [is] my *kadja* (elder brother).' This simple sentence of three words gives the clue to an understanding of Australian totemism. The speaker did not mean that individuals of the kangaroo species are his brothers. He meant that to the kangaroo species, conceived as an entity, he stood in a social relation analogous to that in which a man stands to his elder brother in the kinship system. I am sorry that there is not time on this occasion to expound this thesis more fully.

The account I have just given of Australian totemism differs considerably from that given by Durkheim. But far from contradicting, it confirms Durkheim's fundamental general theory as to the social function of the totemic religion of Australia and its rites. The two kinds of totemic cult are the demonstration, in symbolic action, of the structure of Australian society and its foundations in a mythical and sacred past. In maintaining the social cohesion and equilibrium, the religion plays a most important part. The religion is an intrinsic part of the constitution of society.

I have dwelt, if only cursorily, with two types of religion: ancestor-worship and Australian totemism. In both of them it is possible to demonstrate the close correspondence of the form of religion and the form of the social structure. In both it is possible to see how the religious rites reaffirm and strengthen the sentiments on which the social order depends. Here then are results of some significance for our problem. They point to a certain line of investigation. We can and should examine other religions in the light of the results already reached. But to do this we must study religions *in action*; we must try to discover the effects of active participation in a particular cult, first the direct effects on the individual and then the further effects on the society of which these individuals are members. When we have a sufficient number of such studies, it will be possible to establish a general theory of the nature of religions and their rôle in social development.

In elaborating such a general theory it will be necessary to determine by means of comparative studies the relations between religion and morality. There is only time to refer very briefly here to the question of religion and morality. As representing a theory that seems to be widely held, I quote the following passages from Tylor:

> One great element of religion, that moral element which among the higher nations forms its most vital part, is indeed little represented in the religion of the lower races.[1]
>
> The comparison of savage and civilised religions brings into view, by the side of a deep-lying resemblance in their philosophy, a deep-lying contrast in their practical action on human life. So far as savage religion can stand as representing natural religion, the popular idea that the moral government of the universe is an essential tenet of natural religion simply falls to the ground. Savage animism is almost devoid of that ethical element which to the educated modern mind is the very mainspring of practical religion. Not, as I have said, that morality is absent from the life of the lower races. Without a code of morals, the very existence of the rudest tribe would be impossible; and indeed the moral standards of even savage races are to no small extent well-defined and praiseworthy. But these ethical laws stand on their own ground of tradition and public opinion, comparatively independent of the animistic beliefs and rites which exist beside them. The lower animism is not immoral, it is unmoral. . . . The general problem of the relation of morality to religion is difficult, intricate, and requiring immense array of evidence.[2]

I agree with Tylor that the problem of the relation of morality to religion is difficult and intricate. But I wish to question the validity of the distinction he makes between the religions of savage sand those of civilised peoples, and of his statement that the moral element 'is little represented in the religion of the lower races'. I suspect that when this view is held it often means only that in the 'lower races' the religion is not associated with the kind of morality which exists in contemporary Western societies. But societies differ in their systems of morals as in other aspects of the social system, and what we have to examine in any given society is the relation of the religion or religions of that society to their particular system of morality.

Dr. R. F. Fortune, in his book on Manus religion, has challenged the dictum of Tylor.[3] The religion of Manus is what may be called a kind of spiritualism, but it is not ancestor-worship in

[1] Tylor, *Primitive Culture*, 3rd ed., 1891, Vol. I, p. 427.
[2] op cit., Vol. II, p. 360.
[3] R. F. Fortune, *Manus Religion*, Philadelphia, 1935, pp. 5 and 356. Dr. Fortune's book is a useful contribution to the study of the social function of religion and deals with a religion of a very unusual type.

the sense in which I have used the term in this lecture. The Manus code of morals rigidly forbids sexual intercourse except between husband and wife, condemns dishonesty and insists on the conscientious fulfilment of obligations, including economic obligations, towards one's relatives and others. Offences against the moral code bring down on the offender, or on his household, punishment from the spirits, and the remedy is to be found in confession and reparation for wrong.

Let us now reconsider the case of ancestor-worship. In the societies which practise it, the most important part of the moral code is that which concerns the conduct of the individual in relation to his lineage and clan and the individual members thereof. In the more usual form of ancestor-worship, infractions of this code fall under religious or supernatural sanctions, for they are offences against the ancestors, who are believed to send punishment.

Again we may take as an example of the lower races the aborigines of Australia. Since the fundamental social structure is a complex system of widely extended recognition of relations of kinship, the most important part of the moral code consists of the rules of behaviour towards kin of different categories. One of the most immoral actions of which a man can be guilty is having sexual relations with any woman who does not belong to that category of his kinsfolk into which he may legally marry.

The moral law of the tribe is taught to young men in the very sacred ceremonies known as initiation ceremonies. I will deal only with the Bora ceremonies, as they are called, of some of the tribes of New South Wales. These ceremonies were instituted in the time of the World-Dawn by Baiame, who killed his own son Daramulun (sometimes identified with the sacred bull-roarer) and on the third day brought him back to life. As the ceremony is conducted, the initiates all 'die' and are brought back to life on the third day.[1]

On the sacred ceremonial ground where these initiations take place there is usually an image of Baiame made of earth, and sometimes one of Baiame's wife. Beside these images sacred rites

[1] The suggestion has been made that we have here the influence of Christianity, but that opinion can be dismissed. The idea of ritual death and rebirth is very widespread in religion, and the three-day period is exemplified every month in every part of the world by the death and resurrection of the moon.

are shown to the initiates, and sacred myths about Baiame are recounted.

Now Baiame instituted not only the initiation ceremonies, which are, amongst other things, schools of morals for young men, but also the kinship system with its rules about marriage and behaviour towards different categories of kin. To the question, 'Why do you observe these complex rules about marriage?' the usual answer is, 'Because Baiame established them'. Thus Baiame is the divine law-giver, or, by an alternative mode of expression, he is the personification of the tribal laws of morality.

I agree with Andrew Lang and Father Schmidt that Baiame thus closely resembles one aspect of the God of the Hebrews. But Baiame gives no assistance in war as Jehovah did for the children of Israel, nor is Baiame the ruler or controller of nature, of storms and seasons. That position is held by another deity, the Rainbow-Serpent, whose image in earth also appears on the sacred ceremonial ground. The position held by Baiame is that of the Divine Being who established the most important rules of morality and the sacred ceremonies of initiation.

These few examples will perhaps suffice to show that the idea that it is only the higher religions that are specially concerned with morality, and that the moral element is little represented in the religions of the lower races, is decidedly open to question. If there were time I could provide instances from other parts of the world.

What makes these problems complex is the fact that law, morality and religion are three ways of controlling human conduct which in different types of society supplement one another, and are combined, in different ways. For the law there are legal sanctions, for morality there are the sanctions of public opinion and of conscience, for religion there are religious sanctions. A single wrongful deed may fall under two or three sanctions. Blasphemy and sacrilege are sins and so subject to religious sanctions; but they may also sometimes be punished by law as crimes. In our own society murder is immoral; it is also a crime punishable by death ; and it is also a sin against God, so that the murderer, after his sudden exit from this life at the hands of the executioner, must face an eternity of torment in the fires of Hell.

Legal sanctions may be brought into action in instances where there is no question of morality or immorality, and the same is true of religious sanctions. It is held by some of the Fathers or doctors of the Christian churches that an upright and virtuous life devoted to good works will not save a man from Hell unless he has attained grace by accepting as true the specific doctrines taught by a church.

There are different kinds of religious sanctions. The penalty for sin may be conceived simply as alienation from God. Or there may be a belief in rewards and punishments in an after-life. But the most widespread form of the religious sanction is the belief that certain actions produce in an individual or in a community a condition of ritual pollution, or uncleanness, from which it is necessary to be purified. Pollution may result from things done unintentionally and unwittingly, as you may see from the fifth chapter of the Book of Leviticus. One who unwittingly has touched any unclean thing, such as the carcase of an unclean beast, is guilty and has sinned and must bear his iniquity. He must make a sacrifice, a trespass offering, by which he may be cleansed from his sin.

Ritual uncleanness does not in itself involve moral condemnation. We read in the twelfth chapter of the same Book of Leviticus that the Lord instructed Moses that a woman who has borne a male child shall be unclean for seven days and her purification must continue for a further three and thirty days, during which she shall touch no hallowed thing, nor come into the sanctuary. If the child she bears is female, the first period of uncleanness is to be two weeks and the period of purification threescore-and-six days. Thus, it is polluting, but no one can suppose that it is immoral, to bear a child, and more polluting if the child is female than if it is male.

The opposite of pollution or sinfulness is holiness. But holiness comes not from leading an honest and upright life, but from religious exercises, prayer and fasting, the performance of penance, meditation and the reading of sacred books. In Hinduism the son of a Brahmin is born holy; the son of a leather-worker is born unclean.

The field covered by morality and that covered by religion are different; but either in primitive or in civilised societies there may be a region in which they overlap.

To return to our main topic, a writer who has dealt with the social function of religions on the basis of a comparative study is Loisy, who devotes to the subject a few pages of the concluding chapter of his valuable *Essai historique sur le Sacrifice*.[1] Although he differs from Durkheim in some matters, his fundamental theory is, if not identical, at any rate very similar to that of the earlier writer. Speaking of what he calls the sacred action (*l'action sacrée*), of which the most characteristic form is the rite of sacrifice, he writes:

> We have seen its rôle in human societies, of which it has maintained and strengthened the social bonds, if indeed it has not contributed in a large measure to creating them. It was, in certain respects, the expression of them; but man is so made that he becomes more firmly fixed in his sentiments by expressing them. The sacred action was the expression of social life, of social aspirations, it has necessarily been a factor of society. . . .
> Before we condemn out of hand the mirage of religion and the apparatus of sacrifice as a simple waste of social resources and forces, it is proper to observe that, religion having been the form of social conscience, and sacrifice the expression of this conscience, the loss was compensated by a gain, and that, so far as purely material losses are concerned, there is really no occasion to dwell on them. Moreover the kind of sacred contribution that was required, without real utility as to the effect that was expected from it, was an intrinsic part of the system of renunciations, of contributions which, in every human society, are the condition of its equilibrium and its conservation.[2]

But besides this definition of the social function in terms of social cohesion and continuity, Loisy seeks for what he calls a general formula (*formule générale*) in which to sum up the part that religion has played in human life. Such a formula is useful so long as we remember that it is only a formula. The one that Loisy offers is that magic and religion have served to give men confidence.

In the most primitive societies it is magic that gives man confidence in face of the difficulties and uncertainties, the real and imaginary dangers with which he is surrounded.

> A la merci des éléments, des saisons, de ce que la terre lui donne ou lui refuse, des bonnes ou des mauvaises chances de sa chasse ou de sa pêche, aussi du hasard de ses combats avec ses semblables, il croit trouver le moyen de régulariser par des simulacres d'action ces chances plus ou

---

[1] 1920, pp. 531–40.   [2] op cit., pp. 535–7.

moins incertaines. Ce qu'il fait ne sert à rien par rapport au but qu'il se propose, mais il prend confiance en ses entreprises et en lui-même, il ose, et c'est en osant que réellement il obtient plus ou moins ce qu'il veut. Confiance rudimentaire, et pour une humble vie; mais c'est le commencement du courage moral.[1]

This is the same theory that was later developed by Malinowski in reference to the magical practices of the Trobriand Islanders.

At a somewhat higher stage of development, 'when the social organism has been perfected, when the tribe has become a people, and this people has its gods, its religion, it is by this religion itself that the strength of the national conscience is measured, and it is in the service of national gods that men find a pledge of security in the present, of prosperity in the future. The gods are as it were the expression of the confidence that the people has in itself; but it is in the cult of the gods that this confidence is nourished.'[2]

At a still higher stage of social development, the religions which give men a promise of immortality give him thereby an assurance which permits him to bear courageously the burdens of his present life and face the most onerous obligations. 'It is a higher and more moral form of confidence in life.'[3]

To me this formula seems unsatisfactory in that it lays stress on what is only one side of the religious (or magical) attitude. I offer as an alternative the formula that religion develops in mankind what may be called a sense of dependence. What I mean by this can best be explained by an example. In an ancestor-worshipping tribe of South Africa, a man feels that he is dependent on his ancestors. From them he has received his life and the cattle that are his inheritance. To them he looks to send him children and to multiply his cattle and in other ways to care for his well-being. This is one side of the matter; on his ancestors he *can* depend. The other side is the belief that the ancestors watch over his conduct, and that if he fails in his duties they will not only cease to send him blessings, but will visit him with sickness or some other misfortune. He cannot stand alone and depend only on his own efforts; on his ancestors he *must* depend.

We may say that the beliefs of the African ancestor-worshipper are illusory and his offerings to his gods really useless; that the dead of his lineage do not really send him either blessings or

[1] op cit., p. 533.　　　　[2] loc cit.　　　　[3] op cit., p. 534.

punishments. But the Confucians have shown us that a religion like ancestor-worship can be rationalised and freed from those illusory beliefs that we call superstition. For in the rites of commemoration of the ancestors it is sufficient that the participants should express their reverential gratitude to those from whom they have received their life, and their sense of duty towards those not yet born, to whom they in due course will stand in the position of revered ancestors. There still remains the sense of dependence. The living depend on those of the past; they have duties to those living in the present and to those of the future who will depend on them.

I suggest to you that what makes and keeps a man a social animal is not some herd instinct, but the sense of dependence in the innumerable forms that it takes. The process of socialisation begins on the first day of an infant's life and it has to learn that it both *can* and *must* depend on its parents. From them it has comfort and succour; but it must submit also to their control. What I am calling the sense of dependence always has these two sides. We can face life and its chances and difficulties with confidence when we know that there are powers, forces and events on which we can rely, but we must submit to the control of our conduct by rules which are imposed. The entirely asocial individual would be one who thought that he could be completely independent, relying only on himself, asking for no help and recognising no duties.

I have tried to present to you a theory of the social function of religion. This theory has been developed by the work of such men as Robertson Smith, Fustel de Coulanges, Durkheim, Loisy. It is the theory that has guided my own studies for nearly forty years. I have thought it worth while to indicate that it existed in embryo in the writings of Chinese philosophers more than twenty centuries ago.

Like any other scientific theory it is provisional, subject to revision and modification in the light of future research. It is offered as providing what seems likely to be a profitable method of investigation. What is needed to test and further elaborate the theory is a number of systematic studies of various types of religion in relation to social systems in which they occur.

I will summarise the suggestions I have made:

1. To understand a particular religion we must study its effects. The religion must therefore be studied *in action*.

2. Since human conduct is in large part controlled or directed by what have been called sentiments, conceived as mental dispositions, it is necessary to discover as far as possible what are the sentiments that are developed in the individual as the result of his participation in a particular religious cult. *Durk*

3. In the study of any religion we must first of all examine the specifically religious actions, the ceremonies and the collective or individual rites.

4. The emphasis on belief in specific doctrines which characterises some modern religions seems to be the result of certain social developments in societies of complex structure.

5. In some societies there is a direct and immediate relation between the religion and the social structure. This has been illustrated by ancestor-worship and Australian totemism. It is also true of what we may call national religions, such as that of the Hebrews or those of the city states of Greece and Rome.[1] But where there comes into existence a separate independent religious structure by the formation of different churches or sects or cult-groups within a people, the relation of religion to the total social structure is in many respects indirect and not always easy to trace.

6. As a general formula (for whatever such a formula may be worth) it is suggested that what is expressed in all religions is what I have called the sense of dependence in its double aspect, and that it is by constantly maintaining this sense of dependence that religions perform their social function.

[1] ' . . . among the ancients what formed the bond of every society was a worship. Just as a domestic altar held the members of a family grouped about it, so the city was the collective group of those who had the same protecting deities, and who performed the religious ceremony at the same altar.' Fustel de Coulanges, op cit., p. 193.

CHAPTER IX

ON THE CONCEPT OF FUNCTION IN SOCIAL SCIENCE[1]

THE concept of function applied to human societies is
based on an analogy between social life and organic life.
The recognition of the analogy and of some of its implications is not new. In the nineteenth century the analogy, the concept
of function, and the word itself appear frequently in social philosophy and sociology. So far as I know the first systematic
formulation of the concept as applying to the strictly scientific
study of society was that of Emile Durkheim in 1895. (*Règles de la
Méthode Sociologique.*)

Durkheim's definition is that the 'function' of a social institution is the correspondence between it and the needs (*besoins*
in French) of the social organism. This definition requires some
elaboration. In the first place, to avoid possible ambiguity and
in particular the possibility of a teleological interpretation, I
would like to substitute for the term 'needs' the term 'necessary
conditions of existence', or, if the term 'need' is used, it is to be
understood only in this sense. It may be here noted, as a point
to be returned to, that any attempt to apply this concept of function
in social science involves the assumption that there *are* necessary
conditions of existence for human societies just as there are for
animal organisms, and that they can be discovered by the proper
kind of scientific enquiry.

For the further elucidation of the concept it is convenient to
use the analogy between social life and organic life. Like all
analogies it has to be used with care. An animal organism is an
agglomeration of cells and interstitial fluids arranged in relation
to one another not as an aggregate but as an integrated living
whole. For the biochemist, it is a complexly integrated system
of complex molecules. The system of relations by which these

---

[1] This paper, which is based on comments that I made on a paper read by
Dr. Lesser to the American Anthropological Association, is reprinted from
the *American Anthropologist*, Vol. XXXVII, p. 3, 1935, where it accompanied
Dr. Lesser's paper.

units are related is the organic structure. As the terms are here used the organism is *not* itself the structure; it is a collection of units (cells or molecules) arranged in a structure, i.e. in a set of relations; the organism *has* a structure. Two mature animals of the same species and sex consist of similar units combined in a similar structure. The structure is thus to be defined as a set of relations between entities. (The structure of a cell is in the same way a set of relations between complex molecules, and the structure of an atom is a set of relations between electrons and protons.) As long as it lives the organism preserves a certain continuity of structure although it does not preserve the complete identity of its constituent parts. It loses some of its constituent molecules by respiration or excretion; it takes in others by respiration and alimentary absorption. Over a period its constituent cells do not remain the same. But the structural arrangement of the constituent units does remain similar. The process by which this structural continuity of the organism is maintained is called life. The life-process consists of the activities and interactions of the constituent units of the organism, the cells, and the organs into which the cells are united.

As the word function is here being used the life of an organism is conceived as the *functioning* of its structure. It is through and by the continuity of the functioning that the continuity of the structure is preserved. If we consider any recurrent part of the life-process, such as respiration, digestion, etc., its *function* is the part it plays in, the contribution it makes to, the life of the organism as a whole. As the terms are here being used a cell or an organ has an *activity* and that activity has a *function.* It is true that we commonly speak of the secretion of gastric fluid as a 'function' of the stomach. As the words are here used we should say that this is an 'activity' of the stomach, the 'function' of which is to change the proteins of food into a form in which these are absorbed and distributed by the blood to the tissues.[1] We may note that the function of a recurrent physiological process is thus a correspondence between it and the needs (i.e. necessary conditions of existence) of the organism.

---

[1] The insistence on this precise form of terminology is only for the sake of the analogy that is to be drawn. I have no objection to the use of the term function in physiology to denote both the activity of an organ and the results of that activity in maintaining life.

If we set out upon a systematic investigation of the nature of organisms and organic life there are three sets of problems presented to us. (There are, in addition, certain other sets of problems concerning aspects or characteristics of organic life with which we are not here concerned.) One is that of morphology—what kinds of organic structures are there, what similarities and variations do they show, and how can they be classified? Second are the problems of physiology—how, in general, do organic structures function, what, therefore, is the nature of the life-process? Third are the problems of evolution or development—how do new types of organisms come into existence?

To turn from organic life to social life, if we examine such a community as an African or Australian tribe we can recognise the existence of a social structure. Individual human beings, the essential units in this instance, are connected by a definite set of social relations into an integrated whole. The continuity of the social structure, like that of an organic structure, is not destroyed by changes in the units. Individuals may leave the society, by death or otherwise; others may enter it. The continuity of structure is maintained by the process of social life, which consists of the activities and interactions of the individual human beings and of the organised groups into which they are united. The social life of the community is here defined as the *functioning* of the social structure. The *function* of any recurrent activity, such as the punishment of a crime, or a funeral ceremony, is the part it plays in the social life as a whole and therefore the contribution it makes to the maintenance of the structural continuity.

The concept of function as here defined thus involves the notion of a *structure* consisting of a *set of relations* amongst *unit entities*, the *continuity* of the structure being maintained by a *life-process* made up of the *activities* of the constituent units.

If, with these concepts in mind, we set out on a systematic investigation of the nature of human society and of social life, we find presented to us three sets of problems. First, the problems of social morphology—what kinds of social structures are there, what are their similarities and differences, how are they to be classified? Second, the problems of social physiology—how do social structures function? Third, the problems of development—how do new types of social structure come into existence?

Two important points where the analogy between organism and

society breaks down must be noted. In an animal organism it is possible to observe the organic structure to some extent independently of its functioning. It is therefore possible to make a morphology which is independent of physiology. But in human society the social structure as a whole can only be *observed* in its functioning. Some of the features of social structure, such as the geographical distribution of individuals and groups can be directly observed, but most of the social relations which in their totality constitute the structure, such as relations of father and son, buyer and seller, ruler and subject, cannot be observed except in the social activities in which the relations are functioning. It follows that a social morphology cannot be established independently of a social physiology.

The second point is that an animal organism does not, in the course of its life, change its structural type. A pig does not become a hippopotamus. (The development of the animal from germination to maturity is not a change of type since the process in all its stages is typical for the species.) On the other hand a society in the course of its history can and does change its structural type without any breach of continuity.

By the definition here offered 'function' is the contribution which a partial activity makes to the total activity of which it is a part. The function of a particular social usage is the contribution it makes to the total social life as the functioning of the total social system. Such a view implies that a social system (the total social structure of a society together with the totality of social usages in which that structure appears and on which it depends for its continued existence) has a certain kind of unity, which we may speak of as a functional unity. We may define it as a condition in which all parts of the social system work together with a sufficient degree of harmony or internal consistency, i.e. without producing persistent conflicts which can neither be resolved nor regulated.[1]

This idea of the functional unity of a social system is, of course, a hypothesis. But it is one which, to the functionalist, it seems worth while to test by systematic examination of the facts.

There is another aspect of functional theory that should be briefly mentioned. To return to the analogy of social life and

[1] Opposition, i.e. organised and regulated antagonism, is, of course, an essential feature of every social system.

organic life, we recognise that an organism may function more or less efficiently and so we set up a special science of pathology to deal with all phenomena of disfunction. We distinguish in an organism what we call health and disease. The Greeks of the fifth century B.C. thought that one might apply the same notion to society, to the city-state, distinguishing conditions of *eunomia*, good order, social health, from *dysnomia*, disorder, social ill-health. In the nineteenth century Durkheim, in his application of the notion of function, sought to lay the basis for a scientific social pathology, based on a morphology and a physiology.[1] In his works, particularly those on suicide and the division of labour, he attempted to find objective criteria by which to judge whether a given society at a given time is normal or pathological, eunomic or dysnomic. For example, he tried to show that the increase of the rate of suicide in many countries during part of the nineteenth century is symptomatic of a dysnomic or, in his terminology, anomic, social condition. Probably there is no sociologist who would hold that Durkheim really succeeded in establishing an objective basis for a science of social pathology.[2]

In relation to organic structures we can find strictly objective criteria by which to distinguish disease from health, pathological from normal, for disease is that which either threatens the organism with death (the dissolution of its structure) or interferes with the activities which are characteristic of the organic type. Societies do not die in the same sense that animals die and therefore we cannot define dysnomia as that which leads, if unchecked, to the death of a society. Further, a society differs from an organism in that it can change its structural type, or can be absorbed as an integral part of a larger society. Therefore we cannot define dysnomia as a disturbance of the usual activities of a social type (as Durkheim tried to do).

Let us return for a moment to the Greeks. They conceived the health of an organism and the eunomia of a society as being in each instance a condition of the harmonious working together

---

[1] For what is here called dysnomia Durkheim used the term anomia (*anomie* in French). This is to my mind inappropriate. Health and disease, eunomia and dysnomia, are essentially relative terms.

[2] I would personally agree in the main with the criticisms of Roger Lacombe (*La Méthode Sociologique de Durkheim*, 1926, ch. IV) on Durkheim's general theory of social pathology, and with the criticisms of Durkheim's treatment of suicide presented by Halbwachs, *Les Causes du Suicide*.

of its parts.[1] Now this, where society is concerned, is the same thing as what was considered above as the functional unity or inner consistency of a social system, and it is suggested that for the degree of functional unity of a particular society it may be possible to establish a purely objective criterion. Admittedly this cannot be done at present; but the science of human society is as yet in its extreme infancy. So that it may be that we should say that, while an organism that is attacked by a virulent disease will react thereto, and, if its reaction fails, will die, a society that is thrown into a condition of functional disunity or inconsistency (for this we now provisionally identify with dysnomia) will not die, except in such comparatively rare instances as an Australian tribe overwhelmed by the white man's destructive force, but will continue to struggle toward some sort of eunomia, some kind of social health, and may, in the course of this, change its structural type. This process, it seems, the 'functionalist' has ample opportunities of observing at the present day, in native peoples subjected to the domination of the civilised nations, and in those nations themselves.[2]

Space will not allow a discussion here of another aspect of functional theory, viz. the question whether change of social type is or is not dependent on function, i.e. on the laws of social physiology. My own view is that there is such a dependence and that its nature can be studied in the development of the legal and political institutions, the economic systems and the religions of Europe through the last twenty-five centuries. For the preliterate societies with which anthropology is concerned, it is not possible to study the details of long processes of change of type. The one kind of change which the anthropologist can observe is the disintegration of social structures. Yet even here we can observe and compare spontaneous movements towards reintegration. We have, for instance, in Africa, in Oceania, and in America the appearance of new religions which can be interpreted on a functional hypothesis

[1] See, for example, the Fourth Book of Plato's *Republic*.

[2] To avoid misunderstanding it is perhaps necessary to observe that this distinction of eunomic and dysnomic social conditions does not give us any evaluation of these societies as 'good' or 'bad'. A savage tribe practising polygamy, cannibalism, and sorcery can possibly show a higher degree of functional unity or consistency than the United States of 1935. This objective judgment, for such it must be if it is to be scientific, is something very different from any judgment as to which of the two social systems is the better, the more to be desired or approved.

as attempts to relieve a condition of social dysnomia produced by the rapid modification of the social life through contact with white civilisation.

The concept of function as defined above constitutes a 'working hypothesis' by which a number of problems are formulated for investigation. No scientific enquiry is possible without some such formulation of working hypotheses. Two remarks are necessary here. One is that the hypothesis does not require the dogmatic assertion that everything in the life of every community has a function. It only requires the assumption that it *may* have one, and that we are justified in seeking to discover it. The second is that what appears to be the same social usage in two societies may have different functions in the two. Thus the practice of celibacy in the Roman Catholic Church of today has very different functions from those of celibacy in the early Christian Church. In other words, in order to define a social usage, and therefore in order to make valid comparisons between the usages of different peoples or periods, it is necessary to consider not merely the form of the usage but also its function. On this basis, for example, belief in a Supreme Being in a simple society is something different from such a belief in a modern civilised community.

The acceptance of the functional hypothesis or point of view outlined above results in the recognition of a vast number of problems for the solution of which there are required wide comparative studies of societies of many diverse types and also intensive studies of as many single societies as possible. In field studies of the simpler peoples it leads, first of all, to a direct study of the social life of the community as the functioning of a social structure, and of this there are several examples in recent literature. Since the function of a social activity is to be found by examining its effects upon individuals, these are studied, either in the average individual or in both average and exceptional individuals. Further, the hypothesis leads to attempts to investigate directly the functional consistency or unity of a social system and to determine as far as possible in each instance the nature of that unity. Such field studies will obviously be different in many ways from studies carried out from other points of view, e.g. the ethnological point of view that lays emphasis on diffusion. We do not have to say that one point of view is better than another, but only that they are different, and any particular piece of work should be judged in reference to what it aims to do.

If the view here outlined is taken as one form of 'functionalism', a few remarks on Dr. Lesser's paper become permissible. He makes reference to a difference of 'content' in functional and non-functional anthropology. From the point of view here presented the 'content' or subject-matter of social anthropology is the whole social life of a people in all its aspects. For convenience of handling it is often necessary to devote special attention to some particular part or aspect of the social life, but if functionalism means anything at all it does mean the attempt to see the social life of a people as a whole, as a functional unity.

Dr. Lesser speaks of the functionalist as stressing 'the psychological aspects of culture', I presume that he here refers to the functionalist's recognition that the usages of a society work or 'function' only through their effects in the life, i.e. in the thoughts, sentiments and actions of individuals.

The 'functionalist' point of view here presented does therefore imply that we have to investigate as thoroughly as possible all aspects of social life, considering them in relation to one another, and that an essential part of the task is the investigation of the individual and of the way in which he is moulded by or adjusted to the social life.

Turning from content to method Dr. Lesser seems to find some conflict between the functional point of view and the historical. This is reminiscent of the attempts formerly made to see a conflict between sociology and history. There need be no conflict, but there is a difference.

There is not, and cannot be, any conflict between the functional hypothesis and the view that any culture, any social system, is the end-result of a unique series of historical accidents. The process of development of the race-horse from its five-toed ancestor was a unique series of historical accidents. This does not conflict with the view of the physiologist that the horse of today and all the antecedent forms conform or conformed to physiological laws, i.e. to the necessary conditions of organic existence. Palaeontology and physiology are not in conflict. One 'explanation' of the race-horse is to be found in its history—how it came to be just what it is and where it is. Another and entirely independent 'explanation' is to show how the horse is a special exemplification of physiological laws. Similarly one 'explanation' of a social system will be its history, where we know it—the detailed account of how it came to be what it is and where it is. Another 'explanation' of the same system is obtained by showing (as the functionalist attempts to do) that it is a special exemplification of laws of social physiology or social functioning. The two kinds of explanation do not conflict, but supplement one another.[1]

The functional hypothesis is in conflict with two views that are held by some ethnologists, and it is probably these, held as they often are without precise formulation, that are the cause of the antagonism to that approach. One is the ' shreds and patches' theory of culture, the designation being taken from a phrase of Professor Lowie[2] when he speaks of 'that planless hodge-podge, that thing of shreds and patches called civilisation'. The concentration of attention on what is called the diffusion of culture-traits tends to produce a conception of culture as a collection of disparate entities (the so-called traits) brought together by pure historical accident and having only accidental relations to one another. The conception is rarely formulated and maintained with any precision, but as a half-unconscious point of view it does seem to control the thinking of many ethnologists. It is, of course, in direct conflict with the hypothesis of the functional unity of social systems.

The second view which is in direct conflict with the functional hypothesis is the view that there are no discoverable significant sociological laws such as the functionalist is seeking. I know that

[1] I see no reason at all why the two kinds of study—the historical and the functional—should not be carried on side by side in perfect harmony. In fact, for fourteen years I have been teaching both the historical and geographical study of peoples under the name of ethnology in close association with archaeology, and the functional study of social systems under the name of social anthropology. I do think that there are many disadvantages in mixing the two subjects together and confusing them. See 'The Methods of Ethnology and Social Anthropology' (*South African Journal of Science*, 1923, pp. 124–47).

[2] *Primitive Society*, p. 441. A concise statement of this point of view is the following passage from Dr. Ruth Benedict's 'The Concept of the Guardian Spirit in North America' (*Memoirs*, American Anthropological Association, 29, 1923), p. 84: 'It is, so far as we can see, an ultimate fact of human nature that man builds up his culture out of disparate elements, combining and re-combining them; and until we have abandoned the superstition that the result is an organism functionally interrelated, we shall be unable to see our cultural life objectively, or to control its manifestations.' I think that probably neither Professor Lowie nor Dr. Benedict would, at the present time, maintain this view of the nature of culture.

some two or three ethnologists say that they hold this view, but I have found it impossible to know what they mean, or on what sort of evidence (rational or empirical) they would base their contention. Generalisations about any sort of subject matter are of two kinds: the generalisations of common opinion, and generalisations that have been verified or demonstrated by a systematic examination of evidence afforded by precise observations systematically made. Generalisations of the latter kind are called scientific laws. Those who hold that there are no laws of human society cannot hold that there are no generalisations about human society because they themselves hold such generalisations and even make new ones of their own. They must therefore hold that in the field of social phenomena, in contradistinction to physical and biological phenomena, any attempt at the systematic testing of existing generalisations or towards the discovery and verification of new ones, is, for some unexplained reason, futile, or, as Dr. Radin puts it, 'crying for the moon'. Argument against such a contention is unprofitable or indeed impossible.

CHAPTER X

ON SOCIAL STRUCTURE[1]

IT has been suggested to me by some of my friends that I should use this occasion to offer some remarks about my own point of view in social anthropology; and since in my teaching, beginning at Cambridge and at the London School of Economics thirty years ago, I have consistently emphasised the importance of the study of social structure, the suggestion made to me was that I should say something on that subject.

I hope you will pardon me if I begin with a note of personal explanation. I have been described on more than one occasion as belonging to something called the 'Functional School of Social Anthropology' and even as being its leader, or one of its leaders. This Functional School does not really exist; it is a myth invented by Professor Malinowski. He has explained how, to quote his own words, 'the magnificent title of the Functional School of Anthropology has been bestowed by myself, in a way on myself, and to a large extent out of my own sense of irresponsibility'. Professor Malinowski's irresponsibility has had unfortunate results, since it has spread over anthropology a dense fog of discussion about 'functionalism'. Professor Lowie has announced that the leading, though not the only, exponent of functionalism in the nineteenth century was Professor Franz Boas. I do not think that there is any sense, other than the purely chronological one, in which I can be said to be either the follower of Professor Boas or the predecessor of Professor Malinowski. The statement that I am a 'functionalist' would seem to me to convey no definite meaning.

There is no place in natural science for 'schools' in this sense, and I regard social anthropology as a branch of natural science. Each scientist starts from the work of his predecessors, finds problems which he believes to be significant, and by observation and reasoning endeavours to make some contribution to a growing body of theory. Co-operation amongst scientists results from the

[1] Presidential Address to the Royal Anthropological Institute. Reprinted from the *Journal of the Royal Anthropological Institute*, Vol. LXX, 1940.

fact that they are working on the same or related problems. Such co-operation does not result in the formation of schools, in the sense in which there are schools of philosophy or of painting. There is no place for orthodoxies and heterodoxies in science. Nothing is more pernicious in science than attempts to establish adherence to doctrines. All that a teacher can do is to assist the student in learning to understand and use the scientific method. It is not his business to make disciples.

I conceive of social anthropology as the theoretical natural science of human society, that is, the investigation of social phenomena by methods essentially similar to those used in the physical and biological sciences. I am quite willing to call the subject 'comparative sociology', if anyone so wishes. It is the subject itself, and not the name, that is important. As you know, there are some ethnologists or anthropologists who hold that it is not possible, or at least not profitable, to apply to social phenomena the theoretical methods of natural science. For these persons social anthropology, as I have defined it, is something that does not, and never will, exist. For them, of course, my remarks will have no meaning, or at least not the meaning I intend them to have.

While I have defined social anthropology as the study of human society, there are some who define it as the study of culture. It might perhaps be thought that this difference of definition is of minor importance. Actually it leads to two different kinds of study, between which it is hardly possible to obtain agreement in the formulation of problems.

For a preliminary definition of social phenomena it seems sufficiently clear that what we have to deal with are relations of association between individual organisms. In a hive of bees there are the relations of association of the queen, the workers and the drones. There is the association of animals in a herd, of a mother-cat and her kittens. These are social phenomena; I do not suppose that anyone will call them cultural phenomena. In anthropology, of course, we are only concerned with human beings, and in social anthropology, as I define it, what we have to investigate are the forms of association to be found amongst human beings.

Let us consider what are the concrete, observable facts with which the social anthropologist is concerned. If we set out to study, for example, the aboriginal inhabitants of a part of Australia, we find a certain number of individual human beings in a certain natural environment. We can observe the acts of behaviour of these individuals, including, of course, their acts of speech, and the material products of past actions. We do not observe a 'culture', since that word denotes, not any concrete reality, but an abstraction, and as it is commonly used a vague abstraction. But direct observation does reveal to us that these human beings are connected by a complex network of social relations. I use the term 'social structure' to denote this network of actually existing relations. It is this that I regard it as my business to study if I am working, not as an ethnologist or psychologist, but as a social anthropologist. I do not mean that the study of social structure is the whole of social anthropology, but I do regard it as being in a very important sense the most fundamental part of the science.

My view of natural science is that it is the systematic investigation of the structure of the universe as it is revealed to us through our senses. There are certain important separate branches of science, each of which deals with a certain class or kind of structures, the aim being to discover the characteristics of all structures of that kind. So atomic physics deals with the structure of atoms, chemistry with the structure of molecules, crystallography and colloidal chemistry with the structure of crystals and colloids, and anatomy and physiology with the structures of organisms. There is, therefore, I suggest, place for a branch of natural science which will have for its task the discovery of the general characteristics of those social structures of which the component units are human beings.

Social phenomena constitute a distinct class of natural phenomena. They are all, in one way or another, connected with the existence of social structures, either being implied in or resulting from them. Social structures are just as real as are individual organisms. A complex organism is a collection of living cells and interstitial fluids arranged in a certain structure; and a living cell is similarly a structural arrangement of complex molecules. The physiological and psychological phenomena that we observe in the lives of organisms are not simply the result of the nature of the constituent molecules or atoms of which the organism is built up, but are the result of the structure in which they are united. So also the social phenomena which we observe in any human society are not the immediate result of the nature of individual human beings, but are the result of the social structure by which they are united.

It should be noted that to say we are studying social structures is not exactly the same thing as saying that we study social relations, which is how some sociologists define their subject. A particular social relation between two persons (unless they be Adam and Eve in the Garden of Eden) exists only as part of a wide network of social relations, involving many other persons, and it is this network which I regard as the object of our investigations.

I am aware, of course, that the term 'social structure' is used in a number of different senses, some of them very vague. This is unfortunately true of many other terms commonly used by anthropologists. The choice of terms and their definitions is a matter of scientific convenience, but one of the characteristics of a science as soon as it has passed the first formative period is the existence of technical terms which are used in the same precise meaning by all the students of that science. By this test, I regret to say, social anthropology reveals itself as not yet a formed science. One has therefore to select for oneself, for certain terms, definitions which seem to be the most convenient for the purpose of scientific analysis.

There are some anthropologists who use the term social structure to refer only to persistent social groups, such as nations, tribes and clans, which retain their continuity, their identity as individual groups, in spite of changes in their membership. Dr. Evans-Pritchard, in his recent admirable book on the Nuer, prefers to use the term social structure in this sense. Certainly the existence of such persistent social groups is an exceedingly important aspect of structure. But I find it more useful to include under the term social structure a good deal more than this.

In the first place, I regard as a part of the social structure all social relations of person to person. For example, the kinship structure of any society consists of a number of such dyadic relations, as between a father and son, or a mother's brother and his sister's son. In an Australian tribe the whole social structure is based on a network of such relations of person to person, established through genealogical connections.

Secondly, I include under social structure the differentiation of individuals and of classes by their social role. The differential social positions of men and women, of chiefs and commoners,

of social structure

of employers and employees, are just as much determinants of social relations as belonging to different clans or different nations.

In the study of social structure the concrete reality with which we are concerned is the set of actually existing relations, at a given moment of time, which link together certain human beings. It is on this that we can make direct observations. But it is not this that we attempt to describe in its particularity. Science (as distinguished from history or biography) is not concerned with the particular, the unique, but only with the general, with kinds, with events which recur. The actual relations of Tom, Dick and Harry or the behaviour of Jack and Jill may go down in our field note-books and may provide illustrations for a general description. But what we need for scientific purposes is an account of the form of the structure. For example, if in an Australian tribe I observe in a number of instances the behaviour towards one another of persons who stand in the relation of mother's brother and sister's son, it is in order that I may be able to record as precisely as possible the general or normal form of this relationship, abstracted from the variations of particular instances, though taking account of those variations.

This important distinction between structure as an actually existing concrete reality, to be directly observed, and structural form, as what the field-worker describes, may be made clearer perhaps by a consideration of the continuity of social structure through time, a continuity which is not static like that of a building, but a dynamic continuity, like that of the organic structure of a living body. Throughout the life of an organism its structure is being constantly renewed; and similarly the social life constantly renews the social structure. Thus the actual relations of persons and groups of persons change from year to year, or even from day to day. New members come into a community by birth or immigration; others go out of it by death or emigration. There are marriages and divorces. Friends may become enemies, or enemies may make peace and become friends. But while the actual structure changes in this way, the general structural form may remain relatively constant over a longer or shorter period of time. Thus if I visit a relatively stable community and revisit it after an interval of ten years, I shall find that many of its members have died and others have been born; the members who still survive are now ten years older and their relations to one another may have changed in many ways. Yet I may find that the kinds of relations that I can observe are very little different from those observed ten years before. The structural form has changed little.

But, on the other hand, the structural form may change, sometimes gradually, sometimes with relative suddenness, as in revolutions and military conquests. But even in the most revolutionary changes some continuity of structure is maintained.

I must say a few words about the spatial aspect of social structure. It is rarely that we find a community that is absolutely isolated, having no outside contact. At the present moment of history, the network of social relations spreads over the whole world, without any absolute solution of continuity anywhere. This gives rise to a difficulty which I do not think that sociologists have really faced, the difficulty of defining what is meant by the term 'a society'. They do commonly talk of societies as if they were distinguishable, discrete entities, as, for example, when we are told that a society is an organism. Is the British Empire a society or a collection of societies? Is a Chinese village a society, or is it merely a fragment of the Republic of China?

If we say that our subject is the study and comparison of human societies, we ought to be able to say what are the unit entities with which we are concerned.

If we take any convenient locality of a suitable size, we can study the structural system as it appears in and from that region, i.e. the network of relations connecting the inhabitants amongst themselves and with the people of other regions. We can thus observe, describe, and compare the systems of social structure of as many localities as we wish. To illustrate what I mean, I may refer to two recent studies from the University of Chicago, one of a Japanese village, Suye Mura, by Dr. John Embree, and the other of a French Canadian community, St. Denis, by Dr. Horace Miner.

Closely connected with this conception of social structure is the conception of 'social personality' as the position occupied by a human being in a social structure, the complex formed by *indiv* all his social relations with others. Every human being living in society is two things: he is an individual and also a person. As an individual, he is a biological organism, a collection of a vast number of molecules organised in a complex structure, within which, as long as it persists, there occur physiological and psychological actions and reactions, processes and changes. Human beings as individuals are objects of study for physiologists and psychologists. The human being as a person is a complex of social relationships. He is a citizen of England, a husband and a father, a bricklayer, a member of a particular Methodist congregation, a voter in a certain constituency, a member of his trade union, an adherent of the Labour Party, and so on. Note that each of these descriptions refers to a social relationship, or to a place in a social structure. Note also that a social personality is something that changes during the course of the life of the person. As a person, the human being is the object of study for the social anthropologist. We cannot study persons except in terms of social structure, nor can we study social structure except in terms of the persons who are the units of which it is composed.

If you tell me that an individual and a person are after all really the same thing, I would remind you of the Christian creed. God is three persons, but to say that He is three individuals is to be guilty of a heresy for which men have been put to death. Yet the failure to distinguish individual and person is not merely a heresy in religion; it is worse than that; it is a source of confusion in science.

I have now sufficiently defined, I hope, the subject-matter of what I regard as an extremely important branch of social anthropology. The method to be adopted follows immediately from this definition. It must combine with the intensive study of single societies (i.e. of the structural systems observable in particular communities) the systematic comparison of many societies (or structural systems of different types). The use of comparison is indispensable. The study of a single society may provide materials for comparative study, or it may afford occasion for hypotheses, which then need to be tested by reference to other societies; it cannot give demonstrated results.

Our first task, of course, is to learn as much as we can about the varieties, or diversities, of structural systems. This requires field research. Many writers of ethnographical descriptions do not attempt to give us any systematic account of the social structure. But a few social anthropologists, here and in America, do recognise the importance of such data and their work is providing us with a steadily growing body of material for our study. Moreover, their researches are no longer confined to what are called 'primitive' societies, but extend to communities in such regions as Sicily, Ireland, Japan, Canada and the United States.

If we are to have a real comparative morphology of societies, however, we must aim at building up some sort of classification of types of structural systems. That is a complex and difficult task, to which I have myself devoted attention for thirty years. It is the kind of task that needs the co-operation of a number of students and I think I can number on my fingers those who are actively interested in it at the present time. Nevertheless, I believe some progress is being made. Such work, however, does not produce spectacular results and a book on the subject would certainly not be an anthropological best-seller.

We should remember that chemistry and biology did not become fully formed sciences until considerable progress had been made with the systematic classification of the things they were dealing with, substances in the one instance and plants and animals in the other.

Besides this morphological study, consisting in the definition, comparison and classification of diverse structural systems, there is a physiological study. The problem here is: How do structural systems persist? What are the mechanisms which maintain a network of social relations in existence, and how do they work? In using the terms morphology and physiology, I may seem to be returning to the analogy between society and organism which was so popular with medieval philosophers, was taken over and often misused by nineteenth century sociologists, and is completely rejected by many modern writers. But analogies, properly used, are important aids to scientific thinking and there is a real and significant analogy between organic structure and social structure.

In what I am thus calling social physiology we are concerned not only with social structure, but with every kind of social phenomenon. Morals, law, etiquette, religion, government, and education are all parts of the complex mechanism by which a social structure exists and persists. If we take up the structural point of view, we study these things, not in abstraction or isolation, but in their direct and indirect relations to social structure, i.e. with reference to the way in which they depend upon, or affect, the social relations between persons and groups of persons. I cannot do more here than offer a few brief illustrations of what this means.

Let us first consider the study of language. A language is a connected set of speech usages observed within a defined speech-community. The existence of speech-communities and their sizes are features of social structure. There is, therefore, a certain very general relation between social structure and language. But if we consider the special characteristics of a particular language—its phonology, its morphology and even to a great extent its vocabulary—there is no direct connection of either one-sided or mutual determination between these and the special characteristics of the social structure of the community within which the language is spoken. We can easily conceive that two societies might have very similar forms of social structure and very different kinds of language, or vice versa. The coincidence of a particular form of social structure and a particular language in a given community is always the result of historical accident. There may, of course, be certain indirect, remote interactions between social structure and language, but these would seem to be of minor importance. Thus the general comparative study of languages can be profitably carried out as a relatively independent branch of science, in which the language is considered in abstraction from the social structure of the community in which it is spoken.

But, on the other hand, there are certain features of linguistic history which are specifically connected with social structure. As structural phenomena may be instanced the process by which Latin, from being the language of the small region of Latium, became the language of a considerable part of Europe, displacing the other Italic languages, Etruscan, and many Celtic languages; and the subsequent reverse process by which Latin split up into a number of diverse local forms of speech, which ultimately became the various Romance languages of today.

Thus the spread of language, the unification of a number of separate communities into a single speech-community, and the reverse process of subdivision into different speech-communities, are phenomena of social structure. So also are those instances in which, in societies having a class structure, there are differences of speech usage in different classes.

I have considered language first, because linguistics is, I think, the branch of social anthropology which can be most profitably studied without reference to social structure. There is a reason for this. The set of speech usages which constitute a language does form a system, and systems of this kind can be compared in order to discover their common general, or abstract, characters, the determination of which can give us laws, which will be specifically laws of linguistics.

Let us consider very briefly certain other branches of social anthropology and their relation to the study of social structure. If we take the social life of a local community over a period, let us say a year, we can observe a certain sum total of activities carried out by the persons who compose it. We can also observe a certain apportionment of these activities, one person doing certain things, another doing others. This apportionment of activities, equivalent to what is sometimes called the social division of labour, is an important feature of the social structure. Now activities are carried out because they provide some sort of ' gratification ', as I propose to call it, and the characteristic feature of social life is that activities of certain persons provide gratifications for other persons. In a simple instance, when an Australian blackfellow goes hunting, he provides meat, not only for himself, but for his wife and children and also for other relatives to whom it is his duty to give meat when he has it. Thus in any society there is not only an apportionment of activities, but also an apportionment of the gratifications resulting therefrom, and some sort of social machinery, relatively simple or, sometimes, highly complex, by which the system works.

It is this machinery, or certain aspects of it, that constitutes the special subject-matter studied by the economists. They concern themselves with what kinds and quantities of goods are produced, how they are distributed (i.e. their flow from person to person, or region to region), and the way in which they are disposed of. Thus what are called economic institutions are extensively studied in more or less complete abstraction from the rest of the social system. This method does undoubtedly provide useful results, particularly in the study of complex modern societies. Its weaknesses become apparent as soon as we attempt to apply it to the exchange of goods in what are called primitive societies.

The economic machinery of a society appears in quite a new light if it is studied in relation to the social structure. The exchange of goods and services is dependent upon, is the result of, and at the same time is a means of maintaining a certain structure, a *holistic*

network of relations between persons and collections of persons. For the economists and politicians of Canada the potlatch of the Indians of the north-west of America was simply wasteful foolishness and it was therefore forbidden. For the anthropologist it was the machinery for maintaining a social structure of lineages, clans and moieties, with which was combined an arrangement of rank defined by privileges.

Any full understanding of the economic institutions of human societies requires that they should be studied from two angles. From one of these the economic system is viewed as the mechanism by which goods of various kinds and in various quantities are produced, transported and transferred, and utilised. From the other the economic system is a set of relations between persons and groups which maintains, and is maintained by, this exchange or circulation of goods and services. From the latter point of view, the study of the economic life of societies takes its place as part of the general study of social structure.

Social relations are only observed, and can only be described, by reference to the reciprocal behaviour of the persons related. The form of a social structure has therefore to be described by the patterns of behaviour to which individuals and groups conform in their dealings with one another. These patterns are partially formulated in rules which, in our own society, we distinguish as rules of etiquette, of morals and of law. Rules, of course, only exist in their recognition by the members of the society; either in their verbal recognition, when they are stated as rules, or in their observance in behaviour. These two modes of recognition, as every field-worker knows, are not the same thing and both have to be taken into account.

If I say that in any society the rules of etiquette, morals and law are part of the mechanism by which a certain set of social relations is maintained in existence, this statement will, I suppose, be greeted as a truism. But it is one of those truisms which many writers on human society verbally accept and yet ignore in theoretical discussions, or in their descriptive analyses. The point is not that rules exist in every society, but that what we need to know for a scientific understanding is just how these things work in general and in particular instances.

Let us consider, for example, the study of law. If you examine the literature on jurisprudence you will find that legal institutions

social relations defined

are studied for the most part in more or less complete abstraction
from the rest of the social system of which they are a part. This
is doubtless the most convenient method for lawyers in their
professional studies. But for any scientific investigation of the
nature of law it is insufficient. The data with which a scientist
must deal are events which occur and can be observed. In the
field of law, the events which the social scientist can observe and
thus take as his data are the proceedings that take place in courts
of justice. These are the reality, and for the social anthropologist
they are the mechanism or process by which certain definable
social relations between persons and groups are restored, maintained or modified. Law is a part of the machinery by which a
certain social structure is maintained. The system of laws of a
particular society can only be fully understood if it is studied
in relation to the social structure, and inversely the understanding
of the social structure requires, amongst other things, a systematic
study of the legal institutions.

I have talked about social relations, but I have not so far
offered you a precise definition. A social relation exists between
two or more individual organisms when there is some adjustment
of their respective interests, by convergence of interest, or by
limitation of conflicts that might arise from divergence of interests.
I use the term 'interest' here in the widest possible sense, to
refer to all behaviour that we regard as purposive. To speak of an
interest implies a subject and an object and a relation between
them. Whenever we say that a subject has a certain interest in an
object we can state the same thing by saying that the object has
a certain value for the subject. Interest and value are correlative
terms, which refer to the two sides of an asymmetrical relation.

Thus the study of social structure leads immediately to the
study of interests or values as the determinants of social relations.
A social relation does not result from similarity of interests, but
rests either on the mutual interest of persons in one another, or
on one or more common interests, or on a combination of both
of these. The simplest form of social solidarity is where two
persons are both interested in bringing about a certain result and
co-operate to that end. When two or more persons have a *common
interest* in an object, that object can be said to have a *social value*
for the persons thus associated. If, then, practically all the
members of a society have an interest in the observance of the

social value

laws, we can say that the law has a social value. The study of social values in this sense is therefore a part of the study of social structure.

It was from this point of view that in an early work I approached the study of what can conveniently be called ritual values, i.e. the values expressed in rites and myths. It is perhaps again a truism to say that religion is the cement which holds society together. But for a scientific understanding we need to know just how it does this, and that is a subject for lengthy investigations in many different forms of society.

As a last example let me mention the study of magic and witchcraft, on which there is an extensive anthropological literature. I would point to Dr. Evans-Pritchard's work on the Zande as an illuminating example of what can be done when these things are systematically investigated in terms of the part they play in the social relations of the members of a community.

From the point of view that I have attempted briefly to describe, social institutions, in the sense of standardised modes of behaviour, constitute the machinery by which a social structure, a network of social relations, maintains its existence and its continuity. I hesitate to use the term 'function', which in recent years has been so much used and misused in a multitude of meanings, many of them very vague. Instead of being used, as scientific terms ought to be, to assist in making distinctions, it is now used to confuse things that ought to be distinguished. For it is often employed in place of the more ordinary words 'use' 'purpose', and 'meaning'. It seems to me more convenient and sensible, as well as more scholarly, to speak of the use or uses of an axe or digging stick, the meaning of a word or symbol, the purpose of an act of legislation, rather than to use the word function for these various things. 'Function' has been a very useful technical term in physiology and by analogy with its use in that science it would be a very convenient means of expressing an important concept in social science. As I have been accustomed to use the word, following Durkheim and others, I would define the social function of a socially standardised mode of activity, or mode of thought, as its relation to the social structure to the existence and continuity of which it makes some contribution. Analogously, in a living organism, the physiological function of the beating of the heart, or the secretion of gastric juices, is its relation to the organic structure to the existence or continuity of which it makes its contribution. It is in this sense that I am interested in such things as the social function of the punishment of crime, or the social function of the totemic rites of Australian tribes, or of the funeral rites of the Andaman Islanders. But this is not what either Professor Malinowski or Professor Lowie means by functional anthropology.

Besides these two divisions of the study of social structure, which I have called social morphology and social physiology, there is a third, the investigation of the processes by which social structures change, of how new forms of structures come into existence. Studies of social change in the non-literate societies have necessarily been almost entirely confined to one special kind of process of change, the modification of the social life under the influence or domination of European invaders or conquerors.

It has recently become the fashion amongst some anthropologists to treat changes of this kind in terms of what is called 'culture contact'. By that term we can understand the one-sided or two-sided effects of interaction between two societies, groups, classes or regions having different forms of social life, different institutions, usages and ideas. Thus in the eighteenth century there was an important exchange of ideas between France and Great Britain, and in the nineteenth century there was a marked influence of German thought on both France and England. Such interactions are, of course, a constant feature of social life, but they need not necessarily involve any marked change of social structure.

The changes that are taking place in the non-literate peoples of Africa are of a very different kind. Let us consider an African colony or possession of a European nation. There is a region that was formerly inhabited by Africans with their own social structure. Europeans, by peaceful or forceful means, establish control over the region, under what we call a 'colonial' régime. A new social structure comes into existence and then undergoes development. The population now includes a certain number of Europeans —government officials, missionaries, traders and in some instances settlers. The social life of the region is no longer simply a process depending on the relations and interactions of the native peoples. There grows up a new political and economic structure in which the Europeans, even though few in numbers, exercise dominating influence. Europeans and Africans constitute different classes within the new structure, with different languages, different customs and modes of life, and different sets of ideas and values. A convenient term for societies of this kind would be 'composite' societies; the term 'plural' societies has also been suggested. A complex example of a composite society is provided by the Union of South Africa with its single political and economic structure and a population including English-speaking and Afrikaans-speaking peoples of European descent, the so-called 'coloured people' of the Cape Province, progeny of Dutch and Hottentots, the remaining Hottentots, the 'Malays' of Cape Town, descendants of persons from the Malay Archipelago, Hindus and Mohammedans from India and their descendants, and a number of Bantu tribes who constitute the majority of the population of the Union taken as a whole.

The study of composite societies, the description and analysis of the processes of change in them, is a complex and difficult task. The attempt to simplify it by considering the process as being one in which two or more 'cultures' interact, which is the method suggested by Malinowski in his Introduction to Memorandum XV of the International Institute of African Language and Culture on 'Methods of Study of Culture Contact in Africa' (1938), is simply a way of avoiding the reality. For what is happening in South Africa, for example, is not the interaction of British culture, Afrikander (or Boer) culture, Hottentot culture, various Bantu cultures and Indian culture, but the interaction of individuals and groups within an established social structure which is itself in process of change. What is happening in a Transkeian tribe, for example, can only be described by recognising that the tribe has been incorporated into a wide political and economic structural system.

For the scientific study of primitive societies in conditions in which they are free from the domination by more advanced societies which result in these composite societies, we have unfortunately an almost complete lack of authentic historical data. We cannot study, but can only speculate about, the processes of change that took place in the past of which we have no record. Anthropologists speculate about former changes in the societies of the Australian aborigines, or the inhabitants of Melanesia, but such speculations are not history and can be of no use in science. For the study of social change in societies other than the composite societies to which reference has been made we have to rely on the work of historians dealing with authentic records.

You are aware that in certain anthropological circles the term 'evolutionary anthropologist' is almost a term of abuse. It is applied, however, without much discrimination. Thus Lewis Morgan is called an evolutionist, although he rejected the theory of organic evolution and in relation to society believed, not in evolution, but in progress, which he conceived as the steady material and moral improvement of mankind from crude stone implements and sexual promiscuity to the steam engines and monogamous marriage of Rochester, N.Y. But even such anti-evolutionists as Boas believe in progress.

It is convenient, I think, to use the term 'progress' for the process by which human beings attain to greater control over the physical environment through the increase of knowledge and improvement of technique by inventions and discoveries. The way in which we are now able to destroy considerable portions of cities from the air is one of the latest striking results of progress. Progress is not the same thing as social evolution, but it is very closely connected with it.

Evolution, as I understand the term, refers specifically to a process of emergence of new forms of structure. Organic evolution has two important features: (1) in the course of it a small number of kinds of organisms have given rise to a very much larger number of kinds; (2) more complex forms of organic structure have come into existence by development out of simpler forms. While I am unable to attach any definite meaning to such phrases as the evolution of culture or the evolution of language, I think that social evolution is a reality which the social anthropologist should recognise and study. Like organic evolution, it can be defined by two features. There has been a process by which, from a small number of forms of social structure, many different forms have arisen in the course of history; that is, there has been a process of diversification. Secondly, throughout this process more complex forms of social structures have developed out of, or replaced, simpler forms.

Just how structural systems are to be classified with reference to their greater or less complexity is a problem requiring investigation. But there is evidence of a fairly close correlation *'he was doing ok up to here!*

it pretty much colapses right here. Modern is better. Bummer.

between complexity and another feature of structural systems, namely, the extent of the field of social relations. In a structural system with a narrow total social field, an average or typical person is brought into direct and indirect social relations with only a small number of other persons. In systems of this type we may find that the linguistic community—the body of persons who speak one language—numbers from 250 to 500, while the political community is even smaller, and economic relations by the exchange of goods and services extend only over a very narrow range. Apart from the differentiation by sex and age, there is very little differentiation of social role between persons or classes. We can contrast with this the systems of social structure that we observe today in England or the United States. Thus the process of human history to which I think the term social evolution may be appropriately applied might be defined as the process by which wide-range systems of social structure have grown out of, or replaced, narrow-range systems. Whether this view is acceptable or not, I suggest that the concept of social evolution is one which requires to be defined in terms of social structure.

There is no time on this occasion to discuss the relation of the study of social structure to the study of culture. For an interesting attempt to bring the two kinds of study together I would refer you to Mr. Gregory Bateson's book *Naven*. I have made no attempt to deal with social anthropology as a whole and with all its various branches and divisions. I have endeavoured only to give you a very general idea of the kind of study to which I have found it scientifically profitable to devote a considerable and steadily increasing proportion of my time and energy. The only reward that I have sought I think I have in some measure found—something of the kind of insight into the nature of the world of which we are part that only the patient pursuit of the method of natural science can afford.

CHAPTER XI

SOCIAL SANCTIONS[1]

I N any community there are certain modes of behaviour which
are usual and which characterise that particular community.
Such modes of behaviour may be called usages. All social
usages have behind them the authority of the society, but among
them some are sanctioned and others are not. A sanction is a
reaction on the part of a society or of a considerable number of its
members to a mode of behaviour which is thereby approved
(positive sanctions) or disapproved (negative sanctions). Sanctions
may further be distinguished according to whether they are
diffuse or organised; the former are spontaneous expressions of
approval or disapproval by members of the community acting
as individuals, while the latter are social actions carried out
according to some traditional and recognised procedure. It is a
significant fact that in all human societies the negative sanctions
are more definite than the positive. Social obligations may be
defined as rules of behaviour the failure to observe which entails
a negative sanction of some sort. These are thus distinguished
from non-obligatory social usages, as, for example, customary
technical procedures.

The sanctions existing in a community constitute motives in
the individual for the regulation of his conduct in conformity with
usage. They are effective, first, through the desire of the individual
to obtain the approbation and to avoid the disapprobation of his
fellows, to win such rewards or to avoid such punishment as the
community offers or threatens; and, second, through the fact
that the individual learns to react to particular modes of behaviour
with judgments of approval and disapproval in the same way as do
his fellows, and therefore measures his own behaviour both in
anticipation and in retrospect by standards which conform more
or less closely to those prevalent in the community to which he
belongs. What is called conscience is thus in the widest sense the
reflex in the individual of the sanctions of the society.

[1] Reprinted from the *Encyclopædia of the Social Sciences*, Macmillan Co.,
New York, 1933, Vol. XIII, pp. 531-4.

It is convenient to begin a discussion of sanctions by a consideration of the diffuse negative sanctions, comprising reactions toward the particular or general behaviour of a member of the community which constitute judgments of disapproval. In such reactions there are not only differences of degree—for disapproval is felt and expressed with different degrees of intensity—but also differences of kind. Such differences are difficult to define and classify. In the English language, for example, there are a large number of words which express disapproval of individual behaviour; these vary from discourteous, unmannerly, unseemly and unworthy, through improper, discreditable, dishonourable and disreputable, to outrageous and infamous. Every society or culture has its own ways of judging behaviour, and these might conveniently be studied in the first instance through the vocabulary. But until comparative study of societies of different types has proceeded further no systematic classification of the kinds of diffuse negative sanction is possible. Provisionally the negative moral or ethical sanction may be defined as a reaction of reprobation by the community toward a person whose conduct is disapproved; moral obligations may thus be considered as rules of conduct which, if not observed, bring about a reaction of this kind. Another distinguishable sanction is that whereby the behaviour of an individual is met with ridicule on the part of his fellows; this has been called the satirical sanction. The varieties of diffuse positive sanctions, being less definite than negative sanctions, are therefore still more difficult to classify.

From the diffuse sanctions already described there should be distinguished what may be called (by a wide extension of the term) religious sanctions; these have also been named supernatural sanctions and mystic sanctions, but both these terms have unsatisfactory connotations. The religious sanctions are constituted in any community by the existence of certain beliefs which are themselves obligatory; it is therefore only within a religious community that these sanctions exist. They take the form that certain deeds by an individual produce a modification in his religious condition, in either a desirable (good) or an undesirable (evil) direction. Certain acts are regarded as pleasing to gods or spirits or as establishing desirable relations with them, while others displease them or destroy in some way the desirable harmonious relations. The religious condition of the individual is in these instances conceived to be determined by his relation to personal spiritual beings. The change in the religious condition may elsewhere be regarded as the immediate effect of the act itself, not mediated by its effects on some personal god or spirit, a view common not only in many of the simpler societies, but also found in a special form in Buddhism and in other advanced Indian religions. Sin may be defined as any mode of behaviour which falls under a negative religious sanction; there is no convenient term for the opposite of sin, that is an action which produces religious merit or a desirable ritual condition.

The religious sanctions involve the belief that most unsatisfactory ritual or religious conditions (pollution, uncleanness, sinfulness) can be removed or neutralised by socially prescribed or recognised procedures, such as lustration, sacrifice, penance, confession and repentance. These expiatory rites are also considered to act either immediately, or mediately through their effects on gods or spirits, depending upon whether the sin is regarded as acting in the one way or the other.

While in modern western civilisation a sin is usually regarded as necessarily a voluntary action or thought, in many simple societies an involuntary action may fall within the given definition of sin. Sickness—for example, leprosy among the Hebrews—is often regarded as similar to ritual or religious pollution and as therefore requiring expiation or ritual purification. A condition of ritual or religious impurity is normally considered as one of immediate or ultimate danger to the individual; it may be believed that he will fall sick and perhaps die unless he can be purified. In some religions the religious sanction takes the form of a belief that an individual who sins in this life will suffer some form of retribution in an after-life. In many instances an individual who is ritually unclean is looked upon as a source of danger not only to himself but also to those with whom he comes in contact or to the whole community. He may therefore be more or less excluded for a time or even permanently from participation in the social life of the community. Frequently, if not always, an obligation therefore rests upon the sinner, or unclean person, to undertake the necessary process of purification.

Thus the religious sanctions differ from the other diffuse sanctions by reason of the beliefs and conceptions indicated above, which cannot be defined or described in any simple way. Somewhat similar beliefs underlie magical practices and procedure in relation to luck, but whereas religious observances and the beliefs associated with them are obligatory within a given religious community, the former are comparable with technical procedures, customary but not obligatory.

Organised sanctions are to be regarded as special developments of the diffuse sanctions, frequently under the influence of the beliefs belonging to religion. Organised positive sanctions, or premial sanctions, are rarely developed to any great extent. Honours, decorations, titles and other rewards for merit, including monetary rewards such as special pensions, given to individuals by a community as a whole, are characteristic of modern societies. In preliterate societies a man who has slain an enemy may be given the right to distinguish himself by wearing some special decoration or in other ways.

Organised negative sanctions, important among which are the penal sanctions of criminal law, are definite recognised procedures directed against persons whose behaviour is subject to social disapproval. There are many varieties of such procedures, the most important and widespread being the following: subjection to open expression of reprobation or derision, as, for example, through forcible public exposure by confinement in stocks; partial exclusion, permanent or temporary, from full participation in social life and its privileges, including permanent or temporary loss of civil or religious rights; specific loss of social rank, or degradation, the exact contrary of the positive sanction of promotion; infliction of loss of property by imposition of a fine or by forcible seizure or destruction; infliction of bodily pain; mutilation or branding in which pain is incidental to permanent exposure to reprobation; permanent exclusion from the community, as by exile; imprisonment; and punishment by death. These sanctions are legal sanctions˙ when they are imposed by a constituted authority, political, military or ecclesiastic.

In any given society the various primary sanctions form a more or less systematic whole which constitutes the machinery of social control. There is an intimate relation between the religious sanctions and the moral sanctions, which varies, however, in different societies, and cannot be stated in any brief formula. The primary legal sanctions of criminal law, in all societies except the highly secularised modern states, show a close connection with religious beliefs.

Besides these primary social sanctions and resting upon them there are certain sanctions which may be termed secondary; these are concerned with the actions of persons or groups in their effects upon other persons or groups. In modern civil law, for example, when an individual is ordered by a court to pay damages, the primary sanction behind the order is the power of the court to make forcible seizure of his property or to imprison or otherwise punish him for contempt of court if he fails to obey. Thus secondary sanctions consist of procedures carried out by a community, generally through its representatives, or by individuals with the approval of the community, when recognised rights have been infringed. They are based upon the general principle that any person who has suffered injury is entitled to satisfaction and that such satisfaction should be in some way proportioned to the extent of the injury.

One class of such procedures consists of acts of retaliation, by which is meant socially approved, controlled and limited acts of revenge. Thus in an Australian tribe when one man has committed an offence against another, the latter is permitted by public opinion, often definitely expressed by the older men, to throw a certain number of spears or boomerangs at the former or in some instances to spear him in the thigh. After he has been given such satisfaction he may no longer harbour ill feelings against the offender. In many preliterate societies the killing of an individual entitles the group to which he belongs to obtain satisfaction by killing the offender or some member of his group. In regulated vengeance the offending group must submit to this as an act of justice and must not attempt further retaliation. Those who have received such satisfaction are felt to have no further grounds for ill feeling.

Satisfaction for injury may be obtained also through the duel, a recognised and controlled combat between individuals, or through similar combats between two groups. Among Australian tribes duelling with spears, boomerangs, clubs and shields or stone knives, with the bystanders ready to interfere if they think things are going too far, is a frequently adopted alternative to one-sided retaliation. In these same tribes there are similar regulated combats between two groups, sometimes in the presence of other groups who see that there is fair play. It is often difficult to draw a dividing line between such group combats and warfare; in fact they may possibly be regarded as a special kind of warfare characteristic of primitive rather than of civilised societies. Frequently, therefore, war may be regarded as a secondary social sanction similar to the duel. A political group maintains recognition of its rights by the threat of war if those rights should be infringed. Even in the simplest societies it is recognised that certain acts are right in war and others are wrong and that a declaration of war may be just in certain circumstances and in others unjust, so that the conduct of warfare is to some extent controlled by diffuse sanctions.

Indemnification is often found as an alternative to retaliation as a means of giving and receiving satisfaction. An indemnity is something of value given by a person or group to another person or group in order to remove or neutralise the effects of an infringement of rights. It may be distinguished from a propitiatory gift by the fact that it is obligatory (i.e. subject to a negative sanction, diffuse or organised) in the particular circumstances. A payment made in anticipation of an invasion of rights with the consent of the person or persons receiving it may be regarded as an indemnity. Thus in many societies taking a woman in marriage is regarded as an invasion of the rights of her family and kin, so that before they consent to part with her they must receive an indemnity or the promise of such. In these cases the process of indemnification bears some similarity to that of purchase, which is a transfer of rights of property for a consideration.

In many preliterate societies procedures of indemnification are carried out under the diffuse sanction of public opinion, which compels an individual to indemnify one whose rights he has infringed. In some societies there is a recognised right of an injured person to indemnify himself by forcible seizure of the property of the offender. When society becomes politically organised, procedures of retaliation and indemnification, backed by diffuse sanctions, give place to legal sanctions backed by the power of judicial authorities to inflict punishment. Thus arises civil law, by which a person who has suffered an infringement of rights may obtain reparation or restitution from the person responsible.

In a consideration of the functions of social sanctions it is not the effects of the sanction upon the person to whom they are applied that are most important but rather the general effects within the community applying the sanctions. For the application of any sanction is a direct affirmation of social sentiments by the community and thereby constitutes an important, possibly essential, mechanism for maintaining these sentiments. Organised negative sanctions in particular, and to a great extent the secondary sanctions, are expressions of a condition of social dysphoria brought about by some deed. The function of the sanction is to restore the social euphoria by giving definite collective expression to the sentiments which have been affected by the deed, as in the primary sanctions and to some extent in the secondary sanctions, or by removing a conflict within the community itself. The sanctions are thus of primary significance to sociology in that they are reactions on the part of a community to events affecting its integration.

CHAPTER XII

PRIMITIVE LAW[1]

MANY historical·jurists in contrast with the analytical school have used the term law to include most if not all processes of social control. The term is, however, usually confined to 'social control through the systematic application of the force of politically organised society' (Pound). The limited application, more convenient for purposes of sociological analysis and classification, will be adopted in this article; the field of law will therefore be regarded as coterminous with that of organised legal sanctions. The obligations imposed on individuals in societies where there are no legal sanctions will be regarded as matters of custom and convention but not of law; in this sense some simple societies have no law, although all have customs which are supported by sanctions.

The confusion which has resulted in the attempt to apply to preliterate societies the modern distinction between criminal law and civil law can be avoided by making instead the distinction between the law of public delicts and the law of private delicts. In any society a deed is a public delict if its occurrence normally leads to an organised and regular procedure by the whole community or by the constituted representatives of social authority, which results in the fixing of responsibility upon some person within the community and the infliction by the community or by its representatives of some hurt or punishment upon the responsible person. This procedure, which may be called the penal sanction, is in its basic form a reaction by the community against an action of one of its own members which offends some strong and definite moral sentiment and thus produces a condition of social dysphoria. The immediate function of the reaction is to give expression to a collective feeling of moral indignation and so to restore the social euphoria. Its ultimate function is to maintain the moral sentiment in question at the requisite degree of strength in the individuals who constitute the community.

[1] Reprinted from the *Encyclopædia of the Social Sciences*, Macmillan Co., New York, 1933, Vol. IX, pp. 202–6.

Comparatively little precise information is available concerning penal sanctions in preliterate societies. Among the actions which are known to be treated as public delicts in the simpler societies are incest, i.e. marriage or sexual congress with persons with whom such relations are forbidden; sorcery, or evil magic, by one person against another within the community; repeated breaches of tribal custom; and various forms of sacrilege. In many preliterate societies the penal sanction is applied principally if not solely to actions which infringe upon customs regarded by the community as sacred, so that the sanction itself may almost be regarded as a special form of ritual sanction. Ritual sanctions are derived from the belief that certain actions or events render an individual or a group ritually unclean, or polluted, so that some specific action is required to remove the pollution. In many examples of penal sanction it may plausibly be held that a deed such as incest produces a pollution of the whole community within which it occurs and that the punishment, which may mean the killing of the guilty persons, is a means of cleansing the community. Upon the establishment of a political or executive authority even of the simplest kind disobedience of that authority's commands may be subject to penal sanctions and treated as a public delict; moreover, direct offences against the constituted authority or against the persons in whom that authority rests may be subject to penal sanctions. Thus when the social authority rests in chiefs, an offence which would be a private delict if committed against a commoner may be treated as a public delict when committed against a chief.

In the procedure of a law of private delicts a person or a body of persons that has suffered some injury, loss or damage by infringement of recognised rights appeals to a constituted judicial authority, who declares some other person or body of persons within the community to be responsible and rules that the defendant shall give satisfaction to the plaintiff, such satisfaction frequently taking the form of the payment of an indemnity or damages. A private delict is thus an action which is subject to what may be called a restitutive sanction. The law of private delicts in preliterate societies corresponds to the civil law of modern times. There are, however, certain important differences. In general in modern law actions which fall simply under civil law are those which cause damage but are not subject to reprobation.

Consequently, although the civil sanction expressed through the payment of damages causes loss to the defendant, it is not specifically punitive. Even in modern civil law, however, a magistrate may in special instances award 'punitive damages', thereby expressing the view that the injury committed is of such a kind as to be properly subject to reprobation and therefore to punishment. In modern law when a deed is an offence against morality and at the same time inflicts injury it may become actionable under both criminal and civil law. The emphasis in the punishment for homicide or theft is on its aspect as an offence against the community rather than on the principle that restitution should be made to those who have suffered by the deed.

In preliterate societies private delicts are for the most part killing, wounding, theft, adultery and failure to pay debts; and while they are primarily regarded as constituting an injury to some member of the community they are subject also to moral reprobation as anti-social actions. The sanction is frequently both restitutive and repressive, giving satisfaction to the injured person and inflicting punishment upon the person responsible for the injury; for example, in some African tribes a thief is required to restore to the person whom he has robbed double the value of what he has taken. In its basic form the law of private delicts is a procedure for avoiding or relieving the social dysphoria which results from conflicts within a community. An offence committed against another member or group of the same community, by inflicting a sense of injury upon the victim, creates a disturbance of the social life which ceases only when satisfaction is rendered to the injured person or persons. Thus in African native law a judge is not regarded as having properly settled a case until all parties concerned are satisfied with the settlement.

The distinction between public delicts and private delicts illustrates the fact that the law has no single origin. A deed committed by a member of the community which offends the moral sense of the community may be subject to three sanctions, the general or diffuse moral sanction, which makes the guilty person subject to the reprobation of his fellows; the ritual sanction, which produces in the guilty person a condition of ritual uncleanness that constitutes a danger to himself and to those with whom he is in contact—in such cases custom may require him to undergo ritual purification or expiation or it may be believed that as a result of his sin he will fall ill and die; the penal sanction, whereby the community through certain persons acting as its constituted judicial authorities inflicts punishment on the guilty person, which may be regarded either as a collective expression of the moral indignation aroused by the deed or as a means of removing the ritual pollution resulting from the deed by imposing an expiation upon the guilty person, or as both.

On the other hand, an action which constitutes an infringement of the rights of a person or group of persons may lead to retaliation on the part of the injured against the person or group responsible for the injury. When such acts of retaliation are recognised by custom as justifiable and are subject to a customary regulation of procedure, various forms of retaliatory sanctions may be said to prevail. In preliterate society generally warfare has such a sanction; the waging of war is in some communities, as among the Australian hordes, normally an act of retaliation carried out by one group against another that is held responsible for an injury suffered, and the procedure is regulated by a recognised body of customs which is equivalent to the international law of modern nations. The institution of organised and regulated vengeance is another example of a retaliatory sanction. The killing of a man, whether intentional or accidental, constitutes an injury to his clan, local community or kindred, for which satisfaction is required. The injured group is regarded as justified in seeking vengeance and there is frequently an obligation on the members of the group to avenge the death. The retaliatory action is regulated by custom; the *lex talionis* requires that the damage inflicted shall be equivalent to the damage suffered and the principle of collective solidarity permits the avengers to kill a person other than the actual murderer, for example his brother, or in some instances any member of his clan. When the institution is completely organised, custom requires the group responsible for the first death to accept the killing of one of their number as an act of justice and to make no further retaliation. Retaliatory sanctions may also appear in relation to injuries of one person by another; for example, the recognised right in certain circumstances of one person to challenge another to fight a duel. Among Australian tribes an individual who has suffered injury from another may by agreement of the elders be given the right to obtain satisfaction by throwing spears or boomerangs at him or by spearing him in a non-vital part of the body, such as the thigh. In all instances of retaliatory sanction there is a customary procedure for satisfying the injured person or group whereby resentment may be expressed, frequently by inflicting hurt upon the person or group responsible for the injury. Where it works effectively the result is to provide an expiation for the offence and to remove the feeling of injury or resentment in the injured person or persons. In many societies retaliation is replaced more or less by a system of indemnities; persons or groups having injured other persons or groups provide satisfaction to the latter by handing over certain valuables. The procedure of providing satisfaction by indemnity is widespread in preliterate societies which have not yet developed a legal system in the narrow sense.

Among the Yurok, who are food gatherers and hunters living in northern California in small villages with no political organisation, there is no regular procedure for dealing with offences against the community and therefore no law of public delicts. Injuries and offences of one person against another are subject to indemnities regulated by custom; every invasion of privilege or property must be exactly compensated; for the killing of an individual an indemnity or blood money must be paid to the near kin. After a feud or war each side must pay for those who have been killed on the other side. Only the fact and amount of damage are considered; never the question of intent, malice, negligence or accident. Once an indemnity for an injury has been accepted it is improper for the injured person to harbour any further resentment. As the payment of indemnities is arranged by negotiation between the persons concerned and not by appeal to any judicial authority, the law of private delicts in the strict sense is not present. Among the Ifugao, who cultivate rice on terraced hillsides of northern Luzon in the Philippines and who have no political organisation and no system of clans, 'society does not punish injuries to itself except as the censure of public opinion is a punishment'; that is, there is no law of public delicts, no actual penal sanction. Nevertheless, a person who practises sorcery against one of his own kin is put to death by his kin; on the other hand, incest between brother and sister, parricide and fratricide are said to go unpunished. It is probable, however, that there are powerful and effective ritual sanctions against these acts. An offence committed by one person against another person or an infringement of the rights of one person by another is the occasion of a conflict between the kindred of the two parties, including relatives through btoh father and mother to the third or fourth degree. Retaliation by the killing of the offender or sometimes of one of his kin is the regular method of obtaining satisfaction in cases of murder, sorcery, adultery discovered *in flagrante*, refusal to pay an indemnity assessed for injury suffered, and persistent and wilful refusal to pay a debt when there is ability to pay. Satisfaction is provided in other cases by the payment of indemnities. There are no judicial authorities before whom disputes may be brought; the negotiations are carried out by a go-between who belongs to neither of the two opposed groups of kindred. Certain persons obtain renown for themselves as successful go-betweens, but such persons have no authority and are not in any sense representatives of the community as a whole. During the controversy the two parties are in a condition of ritual enmity or opposition and when a settlement is reached they join in a peacemaking ceremony. A scale of settlement is recognised by custom and in certain circumstances the payments vary according to the class—wealthy, middle class or poor—to which the group receiving or making payment belongs. The Ifugao thus have an organised system of justice, which, however, does not constitute a system of law in the narrow sense of the term since there is no judicial authority.

An important step is taken towards the formation of a legal system where there are recognised arbitrators or judges who hear evidence, decide upon responsibility and assess damages; only the existence of some authority with power to enforce the judgments delivered by the judges is then lacking. It has been argued plausibly that in some societies a legal system for dealing with private delicts has grown up in this manner; disputes are brought before arbitrators who declare the custom and apply it to the case before them; such courts of arbitration become established as regular tribunals; and finally there is developed in the society some procedure for enforcing judgments.

A development similar to this is illustrated by the practices of the A-Kamba, A-Kikuyu and A-Theraka, Bantu peoples to the south and south-east of Mount Kenya in East Africa who live in scattered household communities, keep cattle, sheep and goats and grow grain in hand-tilled fields. They have no chiefs and are

divided into well-defined age grades, one of which consists of
elders who exercise both priestly and judicial functions. If there is
a dispute in which one person believes his rights have been infringed by another, the disputants call together a number of elders
of the district or districts in which they live and these constitute
a court to hear the case. The court acts primarily as a court of
arbitration and as a means of deciding upon the customary
principles of justice by which the dispute should be settled; it
usually takes no steps to enforce the judgment on the losing party
but leaves this task to the claimant. In serious cases, however,
when an offence affects the whole community or when the accused
is regarded as an habitual and dangerous offender so that public
indignation makes the affair one of public concern, the elders
can exercise authority to enforce judgment. The usual procedure
rests on the ritual powers of the elders; they can pronounce a
curse, which is feared as inevitably bringing down supernatural
punishment, on a person who refuses to obey a judgment. The
killing of a member of one clan by a member of another, whether
intentional or accidental, is treated by the court of elders as a
private delict and is settled by the payment of an indemnity to the
relatives of the victim by the killer and his relatives. The elders
also possess limited powers of dealing with public delicts by a
procedure known as kingolle, or mwinge. If a person is held
guilty of witchcraft or is regarded as an habitual offender and
thus as a public danger, the elders may inflict the punishment of
death or may destroy the offender's homestead and expel him from
the district. Before such action may be taken elders from remote
regions must be called in for consultation and the consent of near
relatives of the offender must be obtained.

The Ashanti afford a contrast to the system of the A-Kamba in
that they have a well organised law of public delicts, which are
designated by a native term which means 'things hateful to the
gods'. These include murder, suicide, certain sexual offences
including incestuous relations with certain relatives by descent
and by marriage, certain forms of abuse, assault and stealing, the
invocation of a curse upon a chief, treason, cowardice, witchcraft,
the violation of recognised tribal tabus and the breaking of a command of the central authority issued and qualified with an oath.
The Ashanti conception of the law is that all such actions are
offences against the sacred or supernatural powers on which the

wellbeing of the whole community depends and that unless these offences are expiated by the punishment of the guilty persons the whole tribe will suffer. The judicial functions belong to the king or chief (the occupant of a sacred stool), before whom the offender is tried. The punishment for the more serious offences is decapitation, although in certain circumstances the condemned man and his relatives may 'buy his head'; that is, pay a redemption price by which his life may be saved. The courts of the chiefs do not concern themselves with private delicts, which are denoted 'household cases' and settled by the authority of heads of kinship groups or by negotiations. A dispute concerning a private delict may be brought before the chief indirectly if one of the parties involved swears an oath, which thus makes the dispute a public matter.

While the A-Kamba elders are concerned mainly with private delicts and the Ashanti chiefs with public delicts, there are tribes and nations in Africa and elsewhere in which the central authorities —the chiefs or the king and his representatives—administer both kinds of law, which may always be differentiated by reference to procedure. In the law of private delicts a dispute between persons or groups of persons is brought before the judicial tribunal for settlement; in the law of public delicts the central authority itself and on its own initiative takes action against an offender. Modern criminal law and civil law are directly derived respectively from the law of public delicts and the law of private delicts; but acts which are now regarded as characteristically public delicts, such as murder and theft, are in many preliterate societies treated as private delicts, while the acts which in such societies are most frequently regarded as public delicts are witchcraft, incest and sacrilege.

In its most elementary developments law is intimately bound up with magic and religion; legal sanctions are closely related to ritual sanctions. A full understanding of the beginnings of law in simpler societies can therefore be reached only by a comparative study of whole systems of social sanctions.